Becoming an Anti-Racist Church

OTHER TITLES IN

PRISMS

The Church Enslaved
Michael Battle and Tony Campolo

Disrupting Homelessness
Laura Stivers

Ethical Leadership
Walter Earl Fluker

Lives Entrusted
Barbara J. Blodgett

Open-Hearted Ministry
Michael S. Koppel

Shalom Church
Craig L. Nessan

A Servant's Manual
Michael W. Foss

Spiritual Maturity
Frank A. Thomas

Transforming Leadership
Norma Cook Everist and Craig L. Nessan

Becoming an Anti-Racist Church

Journeying toward Wholeness

Joseph Barndt

Fortress Press

Minneapolis

BECOMING AN ANTI-RACIST CHURCH
Journeying toward Wholeness

Unless otherwise noted, Scripture quotations are taken from the *New Revised Standard Bible*, copyright © 1989 by the Division of Christian Education of the National Council of Churches of Christ in the USA. Used by permission. All rights reserved.

Cover art: Réunion des Musées Nationaux / Art Resource, NY
Cover design: Ivy Palmer Skrade
Interior design: PerfecType, Nashville, TN

Library of Congress Cataloging-in-Publication Data
Barndt, Joseph R.
  Becoming an anti-racist church : journeying toward wholeness / Joseph Barndt.
    p. cm.
  Includes bibliographical references (p. 207) and index.
  ISBN 978-0-8006-6460-2 (alk. paper)
  1. Racism—Religious aspects—Christianity. 2. Race relations—Religious aspects—Christianity. 3. Racism—United States. 4. Race relations—United States. 5. United States—Church history. I. Title.
  BT734.2.B33 2011
  277.3'083089—dc22
                              2010044842

The paper used in this publication meets the minimum requirements of American National Standard for Information Sciences—Permanence of Paper for Printed Library Materials, ANSI Z329.48-1984.

Manufactured in the U.S.A.

15   14   13   12   11   1   2   3   4   5   6   7   8   9   10

To the life and memory of
Wolfram Kistner
and
Lucius Walker Jr.
Theologians, Mentors, Beloved Friends
Who, in the anti-racism struggles in their respective countries
of South Africa and the United States, demonstrated what it means
to stand against principalities and powers

CONTENTS

PREFACE

In 2007, Fortress Press published my previous book, *Understanding and Dismantling Racism: The Twenty-First Century Challenge to White America.* For me, that book represents the culmination of four decades of learning, analyzing, organizing, teaching, and writing about racism. It presents an updated analysis of how systemic and institutionalized racism continues to be embedded in the social fabric of our society, and how the struggle to dismantle racism and shape an anti-racist society must remain our highest national priority. Although I am a Christian and most of my anti-racism teaching and organizing has been focused on the church, I wrote that book for a general audience.

By contrast, this book, *Becoming an Anti-Racist Church: Journeying toward Wholeness,* is written very specifically from a Christian perspective and for a Christian audience. It seeks to apply the analysis of racism delineated in the previous book to the specific context of the church. Its goal is to focus a spotlight on how racism continues to be embedded in the church and how the commitment to shape an anti-racist church needs to be among the highest priorities for every Christian.

There are two primary assumptions upon which this book is based. The first is that the Christian faith stands absolutely and unconditionally in opposition to racism wherever it may be found, whether inside or outside the church. Second, it is my conviction that before the church can effectively participate in efforts to address racism outside the church it needs to be effective in addressing racism within the church.

This book is focused on a particular segment of the church: mainline Protestant and Roman Catholic churches in the United States, all of which are predominantly white. The tragic reality is that the churches of our nation are not only divided and disfigured by denominationalism, but they are just as severely divided and disfigured by racism. Over the course of history, this "white branch" of churches that trace their origins back to Europe has remained separate from all other churches, even while maintaining power over them. The purpose of this book is to help equip Christians to address racism within these predominantly white churches and religious institutions.

Of course, most of these churches are not strangers to the task of addressing their racial separation and racism. The past four or five decades have been replete with programs of integration, diversity, and even anti-racism. Despite all that has been done, however, there has been no serious impact on racism either around us or within. I hope this book will make some small contribution to our next assault on the demonic evil of racism within the church.

As is true for most writers, I feel an overwhelming indebtedness and gratefulness to a host of people in the creation of this book. I have received irreplaceable assistance from many people in its writing. Even more importantly, over the past more than forty years, I have been taught, supported, and carried over the mountainous paths of learning about and struggling for racial justice. I have been privileged to learn at the feet of moral and intellectual giants, to walk with a courageous multitude on paths of justice, and to be welcomed into a community of indefatigable friends and colleagues. I thank you all. Above all, I praise God for a world and a universe with justice and righteousness at its center.

Eleven O'Clock Sunday Morning

"We must face the sad fact that at eleven o'clock on Sunday morning when we stand to sing 'In Christ there is no East or West,' we stand in the most segregated hour of America."

— REV. DR. MARTIN LUTHER KING JR.

Martin Luther King Jr. preached these words in a sermon at the National Cathedral in Washington, D.C., on March 31, 1968, just days before his assassination. He had repeated them on many other occasions as well, referring again and again to the shameful reality of America's racially divided churches. Although Dr. King faced racism and challenged segregation in every part of society, it was the "sad fact" of a segregated church that disturbed him the most.

Fast forward to the present time, and picture yourself attending a church at eleven o'clock on a Sunday morning in a large city, suburb, or small town anywhere in the United States. Look around. What do you see? Whether seated in a jam-packed mega church or a dwindling congregation with far too many empty pews, you will probably see that little has changed. More than four decades after the passage of the Civil Rights Act, when racial segregation is supposed to have become a thing of the past, more than likely the congregation where you are worshipping is composed of all or almost all one racial group, whether white, African American, Latino/Hispanic, Asian American, or Native American. The simple fact is that regardless of the racial or cultural identity of United States churches, eleven o'clock Sunday morning remains today the most segregated hour of the week.

Why has so little changed in nearly half a century? Actually some things have changed. The lines of separation in United States churches are not nearly as strict as they were forty years ago. Many congregations can point to at least some racial and cultural diversity among their members. And a few congregations have achieved significant multiracial diversity. In addition, leadership in historically white denominations often includes some bishops, presiding officers, and pastors who are persons of color. And in the larger society beyond the church, more persons of color hold powerful elected and appointed positions in government and in society. Some of the changes we have seen are very dramatic, including the election of an African American president.

We need to lift up and celebrate these changes. But we must be honest too in recognizing that these achievements are largely remarkable exceptions to the norm, and as such they must not be construed as representative of a changed racial climate. Even though barriers are falling, United States society is still fundamentally defined by race. Racial division is very real in our government, in our commercial life, in our schools, in our residential communities, and, yes, even in our churches.

In our churches! It is very important to begin this book by recalling and agreeing with Dr. King that of all the racial segregation still remaining in our society, it is the segregation of Sunday morning that is the hardest to deal with. For many of us our Monday through Saturday lives are increasingly multiracial, but when the workweek ends and we head for worship on Sunday morning, we pass through doors of churches that are still defined by race. Christian churches in the United States are still mostly separated and color-coded as red, brown, yellow, black, and white, with very little intermingling or interaction taking place among them. Even in the few churches that have managed to achieve a degree of multiracial diversity, cross-racial relationships tend to be characterized by politeness and a superficial paternalism rather than deep conversation and interaction between Christians of different colors. More often than not a "colorblind" approach to race relations is taken, where everyone is said to be the same under their skin, and therefore, issues of race and race relations can be ignored. It is very unusual to find a multiracial church that is actually dealing with multiracial issues and where people are actually talking about and working for racial justice.

> Jesus loves the little children,
> All the children of the world;
> Red and yellow, black and white,
> All are precious in his sight.
> Jesus loves the little children of the world.[1]

Do you remember this song from Sunday school? It is meant to create an image of togetherness. But we are not together yet. Red children, yellow children, brown children, black children, and white children are still being raised in racially segregated churches. Jesus still needs to schedule separate appearances in red, yellow, brown, black, and white churches in order to bring his precious children into his sight.

The Terrible Dilemma of Segregated Sanctuaries

The subject of this book is racism, not racism just anywhere in society, but racism within the church, and particularly within the predominantly white mainline Christian churches in the United States. It is, of course, important for us as Christians to work everywhere, not just in the church, to overcome racial divisions and build racial unity. But we cannot be satisfied with diagnosing and treating the sickness of racism elsewhere in the world if we are not doing the same work in our segregated sanctuaries. It is especially important to ask why the church has such a difficult time facing its own racial divisions and dealing with them.

It is not that the church has no comprehension or understanding of racism; in fact, the opposite is true. Especially during the past forty or fifty years, scholars and other leaders in our churches have contributed a great deal to our society's understanding of racism. The church's biblical and theological perspective has contributed a sharply clarifying lens to other analyses of racism that are based on political, sociological, and psychological points of view. The church has helped us understand that racism is a spiritual problem above all—a sickness of the soul and of the human community. Christianity is uniquely able to diagnose the brokenness of humanity that produces a broken community, as well as to prescribe the medicine required for healing.

But there is a terrible dilemma that we who call ourselves Christian must face: to put it bluntly, the church has a hard time hearing its own message. We are all too comfortable with our segregated congregations. As this book will closely examine, the church throughout history and even today is clearly implicated in promulgating racism, preserving systems and structures of white power, and avoiding and evading our responsibility to deal with it.

This is our terrible dilemma; we—the church—suffer tremendously because of our incapacity to act on our own beliefs, to treat our own sickness. This is the issue that I believe must be given a much higher priority on both congregational and denominational levels. It is not enough to diagnose the sickness of racism in society from a Christian perspective; it is also critically important to diagnose and confront directly this same sickness within the church and to investigate directions for effectively addressing and correcting it.

The Need for Open and Honest Conversation

It is simply impossible to overcome racial divisions and build racial unity—in the church or in any other part of society—without dealing directly and straightforwardly with the subject of racism. To begin with, we must name the problem of racism and acknowledge that dealing with it cannot be avoided. To some people it may sound quite obvious that we have to face openly the subjects of race and racism in order to get past them, but other people will disagree with this and fight very desperately against it. In almost every place in the United States that I visit and have discussions about racism, someone will argue that raising the subjects of race and racism is a negative approach to the problem. The underlying assumption is that we should talk about the "good stuff," the "feel good" things that help us get along. Instead of talking about differences, we should emphasize our sameness and not "see" color.

Readers may recall the United States presidential campaign in 2008, how difficult it was to talk publicly about the significance of having an African American, Barack Obama, as a candidate for the presidency. One side said that talking about race was "using the race card." The other side was afraid that Obama's race would be used against him. The result was a deadly silence about the most visible issue in the campaign. When Obama finally did break the silence, his speech on race in Philadelphia was very helpful in cutting through the fear of discussing this subject.

In the same way, when the issue of racism in the church is raised, often the first reaction is to become defensive. It is difficult to admit that the sins of the world also afflict the church. We fear that exposing the church's defects and imperfections will diminish its sacred identity and function, and negate its claims to moral authority. Perhaps above all we desire to shield the church from attack by outsiders.

Instead of being defensive, however, we would do well to recognize that dealing with racism in the church can be done most effectively from within by people who are part of and who love the church. It is a high priority of this book to encourage open discussion of racism inside the church, to look honestly at our history, no matter how hurtful and embarrassing, and at our current helplessness before racism's awful power over us. My aim is to help lift up the potential strength and power of the church itself to confront and deal with racism.

I want to speak most directly to all who share a deep love for the church, to those who are pained by the continuing power and presence of racism and by the hurtful wounds it leaves. I extend to you an invitation to join me in undertaking two tasks. The first task is to help Christians come together to examine the historical context of racism in the church, to understand the barriers of racism that infiltrate and influence the present mission and structures of the church, and to critically evaluate current programs of multiracial and multicultural diversity in the church. The second task is to help Christians become better equipped with effective strategies to dismantle racism and shape an anti-racist multiracial/multicultural identity in our churches, as well as to become more effective instruments of God in helping to shape an anti-racist society.

Two Central Ideas about Racism

Since the subject of racism is confusing to many people, I present here two central ideas that will guide us throughout this book. The first is that racism is not simply the result of individual prejudice and bigotry, but is more significantly the product of historic institutional power structures. Of course, prejudice and bigotry are a problem in the church, as they are in society, but systemic racism is far more devastating and destructive than individual attitudes and actions. Incredibly powerful barriers to racial justice that were set up long ago are still present within our institutional structures and culture. It is impossible to overcome racial divisions and build racial unity in the church or in society without facing the *systemic power of racism.*

The second central idea is that racism is not only a sin from which we must repent but also an enslavement from which we need to be liberated. Originally the sinful structures of racism erected by white society were intended to imprison people of color, but the jailers have ended up trapped inside their own jail. We who are white are as much enslaved by racism as are people of color. There is no way we can build a path from racial division to racial unity without dealing with the *imprisoning power of racism.* None of us can be free while others are still confined.

These two fundamental concepts—racism is a systemic issue and racism imprisons all of us—will be front and center in each and every chapter of this book. Immersing ourselves in these ideas can open the doors to wonderful new opportunities to transform our churches into the racially just multiracial and multicultural churches they are intended to be.

Getting Personal

For our work together to be fruitful, each of us needs to bring our own personal identity and experience to the conversation. To that end, let me introduce myself. I am a white Lutheran pastor in the Evangelical Lutheran Church in America (ELCA) who has been studying, teaching, and organizing around the subject of racism for more than forty years. Although I have also done this work in secular settings, including colleges and universities, social service organizations, governmental agencies, community organizations, and the like, the majority of my anti-racism teaching and organizing has been in the context of the historically predominantly white denominations. I have worked in ecumenical, interfaith, and interracial settings in Lutheran, Episcopal, Roman Catholic, Reformed, Presbyterian, Methodist, Christian, and Unitarian Universalist churches on national and regional levels and in individual congregations. I have also been a congregational pastor and community organizer in white, African American, Latino/Hispanic, and multiracial settings and in cities including Tucson, Oakland, Chicago, and the South Bronx in New York City.

It is very important for me to be able to trace the path of gradual awareness and understanding of race and racism in my personal life and in society. It is especially necessary for me to acknowledge that most of what I now know to be true about racism has been taught to me by people of color. The most accurate understandings of racism come from people of color and not from white people. In fact, over the years I have had to unlearn most of what I was taught by white people as it became clear to me that what we believe about race relations and racism is at best a confusing distortion of the truth. While growing up, I was taught in conscious and unconscious ways that I should not listen to, trust, believe, or follow the leadership of people of color. I have discovered since that people of color are the experts on racism, while the white community tends to discount, distort, or deny the reality of racism. To understand racism, the first thing we who are white need to do is overcome this negative socialization and learn to listen to people of color and to trust and follow their leadership.

Journeying Together against Racism

In joining me on this journey to understand and dismantle racism in the church, it is important to think about your own identity and the experience you bring. Some readers have been on this path for a long time; others, for a lesser period of time. We are all at different places on the path and we are moving at different paces. White people are usually newer to this path than are people of color. Although most people of color have been aware of their experience of racism all their lives, their experiences of talking about it and analyzing it are different. We who are on this path now have something to teach others, but all of us need to learn more than we already know. For some, this will be your first book on racism and your first opportunity to think and learn intentionally about the subject. For others, this will be one among many books you have read and experiences you have known on a journey that started some time ago. Perhaps you have read my previous book, *Understanding and Dismantling Racism*.[2] Throughout this book, I will make occasional references to that earlier analysis of racism.

On the path toward understanding race and racism, we need to affirm and respect one another's circumstances. And we need to be honest in admitting that no one, including me, is fully clear about how to accomplish our goals, though we trust that lessons learned in past struggles equip us better for what lies ahead. However, we should not be surprised that along the way there are major barriers that challenge us, including the divisions caused by culture, history, and language, and the difficulties of building trust across the lines of racial division.

The path we are on is not unlike that of the Hebrew people in the wilderness heading toward the Promised Land. There were many stops and starts; sometimes they had a clear picture of where they were going, and sometimes they were hopelessly lost. We too are heading together on a path toward a holy land called Racial Justice. And we too have often lost our way. But as a result of our common efforts, that path will one day be a clear and open highway on which anyone can travel.

Perhaps the most important lesson I have learned over the years is that the struggle to overcome racism is a long-term, multigenerational effort that began long ago and will continue for a long time to come. The structures of racism in the United States have been in place for 500 years, and it is crucial to realize that the resistance against racism has been going on just as long. Yet it was less than fifty years ago, during the civil rights movement, that the most important decisions toward changing racist structures were made. Since then, there have been many great advances and successes in this struggle and there have also been enormous failures and setbacks. The task of completing this transformation of our society and its structures will still take generations to accomplish. When I made my first decision to resist racism, I joined millions of resisters who came before me; and when I have taken my last anti-racist action, I know that there will be millions more resisters of racism who will follow after me, until the job is finally done and we have become a racism-free society. It is in fact true, not just a truism, that we have come a long way and we still have a long way to go.

In discerning our path forward in understanding and dismantling racism in the church, it is also highly important to point out the leading role being played by denominations whose membership is primarily people of color, Native Americans, African Americans, Latinos/Hispanics, Asian Americans, and Arab Americans. They have resisted racism in the past in very powerful ways and continue to do so today. Likewise, people from religions other than Christianity, such as Jews and Muslims, have been and still are deeply engaged in working for racial justice in the United States. Above all, we need to recognize the extraordinary role of the African American church throughout our country's history, as the principal leader of all churches in struggles against racism.

As we join this long history of resisting racism, we must realize that the terrible dilemma of the church—the gap between what we teach and what we practice—will not disappear easily, but I deeply believe it can be and will be overcome. Our path needs to lead us to the day when eleven o'clock Sunday morning will be a celebration of an anti-racist multicultural people of God.

Beginning the Journey

I have structured this book to include a chapter, following this introduction, that explores the biblical and theological underpinnings of an anti-racist gospel. This will help us find a common starting place for our journey, a foundation upon which we can build. It is here, too, that we will find the guidance and strength we need to undertake the journey before us.

The rest of the book is divided into three parts, addressing the past, the present, and the future of the church in its struggle with racism. Part 1 is an examination of the history of the church's support of racism, as well as the powerful history of resistance against racism within the church, led especially by the African American church. Part 2 explores the current reality of the imprisoning power of individual, institutionalized, and cultural racism in predominantly white churches. In the third and final part, we turn our attention to creating a vision for a liberated anti-racist church and to an organizing process to tear down the imprisoning barriers of institutionalized racism and create a new identity and structures for an anti-racist multiracial church.

In shaded boxes and call-outs throughout the book I provide suggestions and directions for working together on our journey toward an anti-racist church. In each instance I ask you to think about your own experiences with race and racism both in church and society and then to talk with others about your experiences and your perceptions. I also make suggestions about researching your particular congregation's or denomination's experience with issues of race. I ask you to evaluate your church's current beliefs and activities and to explore ways in which you can personally be part of a process helping your church to work toward freeing itself from the bounds of racism.

Perhaps you are part of a congregational study group or are a student, teacher, or administrator in a church college, university, or seminary that meets regularly to discuss this book. Or maybe you are part of a social service agency or involved in a church-based community organization that is concerned about issues of race. Although my suggestions are addressed to a congregational setting, they are easily adaptable to your particular situation. You will find the first of these suggested activities on the following page.

May God bless us on our journey together.

Your Congregation's Identity

Question 1: Which of the Following Best Describes Your Congregation?

Separate and Segregated?

The vast majority of congregations or Christian communities in the United States fall into this category. While such congregations may have a small percentage of persons from another race, the dominant reality is that of a single race, language, and cultural expression. Some of these "single race" and "single culture" congregations may have made efforts to seek cross-racial and cross-cultural experiences by reaching out and building relationships with neighboring churches or by participating in multicultural programs provided through their denomination.

It is tempting for separate and segregated congregations to have the misguided perception that only multiracial congregations need to be concerned about racism and so to dismiss the importance of dealing with issues of race in their setting. In fact, the more segregated one's life is, the more imprisoned it is in the church's "terrible dilemma" of not being able to hear its own message. It is here in the emptiness and isolation of racial segregation that racism is doing its greatest damage to the body of Christ.

Multiracial and/or Multicultural?

Numerically, congregations that are significantly multiracial and/or multicultural represent a very small minority of the churches in the United States, but such congregations tend to have a greater interest in issues of race. It is important to note that *multiracial* is not the same as *multicultural*, even though the terms are often used interchangeably. A congregation can be multiracial and still have a single culture. There are, for example, a number of formerly white congregations that have successfully attracted significant numbers of people of color, but have not substantially changed the cultural expression of their congregational life. These are still culturally white congregations, even if they have a membership from many races. However, a multiracial congregation can also become multicultural. There are many multiracial congregations that are working very hard and very intentionally to also be multicultural—in other words, to develop their worship, spiritual, educational and organizational life as an expression of the culture of all the racial groups that are represented in their membership.

There are increasing numbers of congregations making intentional efforts to provide ministry in multiracial neighborhoods and communities, and to build congregations that are multiracial and/or multicultural. The decision to become a multiracial congregation is a response to a holy and sacred calling. It is a decision to counter the forces of segregation and to try to bring together under one church roof the reunited family of God. It is also an unusual decision that relatively few congregations have made. This is a highly important "frontier ministry" from which all churches will ultimately benefit. Congregations on this multiracial frontier are learning lessons and developing models of ministry that have the potential of leading many others toward change. This sacred calling is not only important and exciting, it is also a very difficult ministry, in which participants work against serious odds and are challenged by many very difficult barriers.

Question 2: Where Is Your Congregation on the Journey toward Anti-Racism?

Whether in a separate and segregated or a multiracial/multicultural congregation, it is possible to avoid facing the questions of race and racism. In fact, in multiracial/multicultural congregations, the subject of racism is sometimes avoided with even greater tenacity. So much emphasis is placed on "just getting along" with people of other races that the "R-word" is seen as off-limits. *Is your congregation dealing with the subject of racism? If so, how?*

Question 3: Where Is Your Denomination on the Path?

Although some congregations are independent of denominational affiliation, most are part of a larger church, and are very much affected by the directions that are taken by their denomination, either on a national or regional (diocesan, synodical, district) level. Every denomination in the United States has been deeply affected by its history around the subject of race and racism. Especially as a result of the civil rights movement in the 1960s, every denomination has had to make new decisions regarding this subject. The position and programs of a denomination on the subjects of race and racism have a major effect on local congregations. The race and culture of a congregation are very likely a reflection of the race, culture, and history of the denomination. If a congregation is attempting to become multiracial and multicultural, it will make a major difference if it is supported, encouraged, and equipped by denominational programs. Moreover, if a congregation decides to deal with racism and is not supported by its denomination, the task will be made much more difficult. Conversely, a denominational program to deal with racism on a national or regional level cannot be effective if it does not reach into its congregations. *What is your denomination doing about this subject of race and racism, both on a regional and national level?*

Many white denominations were divided into separate churches in previous centuries, usually along north/south geographical lines, because of positions on slavery or racial segregation. Some of these same divided churches have also fairly recently been reunited. Some other denominations that were historically separated along black and white racial lines have also been recently united as a single church.[3] *Has your denomination been part of a merger that reflects an effort to overcome past racial divisions?*

chapter one

Setting the Biblical Context:
Reclaiming an Anti-Racist Gospel

*"Heaven and earth will pass away, but my words
will not pass away."*

—MATTHEW 24:35

Starting with Scripture

It should be clear by now that the aim of this book is to address the church with hard and critical questions about an extremely difficult subject. It is understandable if readers might feel a bit anxious about this at first and worry that someone might ask, "Who do you think you are? Who gave you the right to do this?" In response, I believe it is important to affirm that we *do* have the authority to undertake this bold venture. In fact, we have a mandate to do so—a mandate that comes directly from God.

We do not need to devise new holy words or invent new teachings in order to claim religious authority to work against racism or any other form of injustice. Centrally placed within the Holy Scriptures is an indelible foundational message of God's intention for justice and peace for all humanity. The Bible and the historic Christian faith call the church and all Christians to take a stand uncompromisingly against the evil of racism and for the equality and unity of all humankind. We need to place our efforts to understand and eliminate racism in church and society squarely in the context of these teachings, allowing them to become our essential tools and primary guides in understanding racism and how it can be brought to an end. If we do not do this, but attempt instead to reflect on racism and work to end racism without the support of our beliefs and our faith, we risk making our faith irrelevant to matters most central to our lives. On the other hand, if we do take our faith with us on this journey, we will not only have authority and guidance, but we will be affirmed and strengthened to go places where we otherwise may not have the courage to go.

To help us begin thinking theologically and biblically about racism, I offer four principles concerning how the Bible and our faith can guide us. These are foundation stones upon which to build a biblically supported analysis of racism. Throughout the book, I will expand on these and invite you to add your own examples, images, and insights:

1. We are the family of God.
2. The inseparability of Jesus and justice.
3. Taking back stolen sacred stories.
4. We are called and carried on the shoulders of witnesses who struggled before us.

These four foundation stones represent the clear understanding of the Bible and the Christian faith that the whole human family is created by God to exist in unity and equality, and they represent a clear judgment that any violation of God's intentions, including racism, is a sin against both God and humanity. The scriptural message of God's intervention and redemption is an invitation and a command to us today to repent of our divisions, to be forgiven, restored, and empowered to rebuild God's human family on the basis of unity, love, and justice. Let's look at each of these foundation stones more closely.

Foundation Stone 1:
We are the family of God.

God created us to be family, and, by virtue of God's creation, we are all sisters and brothers. This may sound like an obvious statement that everyone agrees with, but, in fact, it is a very radical statement that establishes the primary rationale and motivation for working against racism. This message is central to the Bible, from Genesis, the first book, to Revelation, the last. God is our Creator/Parent, and therefore all human beings are sisters and brothers in a common family. Sisterhood and brotherhood is a God-given relationship every human being shares.[1]

This familial relationship is indelible. Our sisterhood and brotherhood in the family of God is imprinted in our hearts, minds, and souls. It is part of our spiritual DNA. We did not choose it and we cannot choose to undo it. We may love it, we may hate it, we may protest it, or we may ignore it. But the truth is, regardless of our color—red, brown, yellow, black, or white—we are all in the family for good.

The reason it is so important to emphasize this first theological principle is that racism and all forms of injustice seek to deny this familial relationship and to exclude groups of people from the family. The entire story of human injustice is a history of people attempting to kick each other out of the family. We are constantly faced by one group of humans saying to another:

I don't like you because of your race. I don't want you in my family. I don't like you because of your gender, your class, your tribe, your religion, your nationality, your sexual orientation, your looks, your size, your behavior. *Get out of my family!* You and everyone like you are no longer my brothers or my sisters.

It is even more frightening and horrifying that when one group thinks they have successfully removed these "others" from their family, they then assume the right to hurt, torture, and slaughter those people whom they have made into "aliens and strangers," those whom they have cast out of the human family. This is the history of the broken family of God. Each of us has stories to tell about being part of a group that was cast out or that cast out others—or both. Our acts have done terrible damage to our sisters and brothers and to ourselves. The consequences are brokenness and division in the human family, God's family. Like Humpty Dumpty, it is seemingly impossible to put us back together again.

Nevertheless, the basic scriptural message is that no matter how hard we try to end this relationship, we cannot stop being sisters and brothers. The ones we hurt, torture, and kill are never strangers and aliens outside the family, but rather our sisters and our brothers within the family. God has created this family, and this relationship between us is indelible. The central purpose of the Christian faith is to put the family of God back together again. The incarnation, crucifixion, and resurrection of Jesus are God's actions to overcome brokenness and division, to restore our relationships as sisters and brothers. To participate in the restoration of the family is the central mission and calling of the church. Whenever and wherever we work for justice and peace, we are working to restore the family. Our affirmation that we are the family of God and our work to end racism are part of God's highest priority to restore God's family and make it whole again.

Foundation Stone 2:
The inseparability of Jesus and justice.

Justice is at the heart of the biblical message. God's opposition to all forms of societal inequality and the call for a radically inclusive community are at the center of the gospel of Jesus Christ. Jesus made it abundantly clear throughout his ministry that God is on the side of the broken people—the poor, the imprisoned, the blind, and the oppressed. In his first sermon, he quoted from the prophet Isaiah in announcing the central purpose of his ministry:

> "The Spirit of the Lord is upon me,
> because he has anointed me
>   to bring good news to the poor.
> He has sent me to proclaim release to the captives

> and recovery of sight to the blind,
>   to let the oppressed go free,
> to proclaim the year of the Lord's favor." (Luke 4:18-19)

In recent decades, a "theology of liberation" has emerged as an exciting new artic-ulation of theology by churches living in the context of poverty and oppression. With its central focus on justice, liberation theology has become increasingly popular and influential in many churches, particularly in communities of color in the United States and in developing nations around the world.

Liberation theology emphasizes that the actions of God recorded in the Old and New Testaments are almost always described in terms of liberating broken and oppressed people. Moses was sent to free the Hebrew people from enslave-ment in Egypt. Isaiah proclaimed comfort and release to the captives of Babylon. The prophets were sent to demand justice for the poor who were being oppressed by rich countrymen. The psalmist prayed for rescue from those who do injustice. Jesus came proclaiming good news for the downtrodden and oppressed.

The central themes of liberation theology are that God takes sides where issues of justice are concerned, that God's first option is for the broken and the oppressed of the world, and that justice and liberation should be the central focus of the ministry of the Christian church. This theological perspective insists that the gospel of Jesus Christ has always been and is still today a message of free-dom intended first and foremost to reach people suffering from the injustices of poverty, racism, and other forms of oppression. Jesus himself is understood as a victim of oppression who lived and died for the sake of those who are downtrod-den, poverty-stricken, suffering, sick, and dying.

Liberation theology insists that this central Christian message is unchanging and unchanged. The gospel of Jesus Christ is a gospel of freedom for oppressed people in the twenty-first century as it was for those in the first century. It is good news to those who are poverty-stricken in the ghettos of our land and throughout the world. It is the proclamation of liberty to the captives in our prisons and on our reservations. It is sight for those who cannot see, strength for those who can-not walk, community for those who are lonely, and freedom for the oppressed people of the United States and the world.[2]

A Radically Inclusive Gospel

Liberation theology's understanding of the priority of Jesus for justice and his identification with poor and oppressed people does not, however, leave out the rich and the oppressor. Quite the opposite. Jesus is very explicit in his teaching that *everyone* is broken and in need of liberation, the oppressor perhaps even more so than the oppressed, the rich even more so than the poor.

When this becomes clear, the "exclusiveness" for the broken and oppressed that is the distinctive mark of liberation theology quickly turns around to reveal itself as a mark of radical "inclusiveness." From the biblical point of view, "broken and oppressed" defines the reality of all humanity. We are all in need of liberation, and we are all offered the gift of unconditional acceptance, and this unconditional acceptance is seen as the true heart of the gospel of justice.

In terms of racial justice, this means that liberation in not only needed by people of color, but by everyone on all sides of the racial divide. God's liberation is for people of all colors. For the sake of all of us, the pursuit of racial justice becomes central to the gospel of Jesus Christ.

Tension about Justice in the Church

Not everyone in the church agrees with the premise that justice belongs at the center of the biblical message. Throughout history, there have been great tensions about the place of justice in the gospel and in the mission of the church. Many Christians allow issues of social justice only at the far edges of the gospel's implementation. Some even believe that such "earthly matters" are totally unrelated to and irrelevant to the gospel.

Tragically, in predominantly white and middle-class churches of European descent, the centrality of justice in Scripture is not usually given much prominence and is not proclaimed to be a central purpose of the churches' ministry. In fact, in the United States the most serious theological tensions and divisions in many churches revolve around whether "social gospel" has a legitimate place in the church at all. The theological subjects of sin, salvation, and eternal life are all too often dealt with as purely spiritual matters and are kept separated and segregated from the secondary concerns of social issues and charity.

Even when there is general agreement on the importance of justice, groups within the church often stand on opposite sides of specific issues of justice. While such differences of opinion are understandable, they can have disastrous consequences. There is no clearer example of this than the tragic reality that the church has stood just as often on the side of those who endorse racism as it has been on the side of those who struggle against it

In this book there is no place for debating the question of the biblical priority of justice, including racial justice. The underlying assumption is that anyone who names the name of Jesus is called to participate in the ministry of justice in the world as a central part of the mission of the church. Moreover, no justice task is more important in the Christian church than to stand against racism and to work for the dismantling of racism in the church and in society. I am completely convinced that the weight of the biblical message and the historical theology of the church lead incontrovertibly toward this belief. In fact, I believe deeply that the temptation to maintain a church where justice, especially racial justice, can be placed on the periphery of our mission is comparable to the temptation of early Christians to place a pinch of incense on the emperor's altar as a sign of their allegiance to the emperor. In doing so they sought to keep themselves safe from the consequences of choosing Christ above all else.

I was not taught this always, nor did I always believe it. Over the years, I have gained theological understanding that I did not get when I went to seminary more than forty years ago. I have learned to believe that God's call to work for earthly justice, especially to end racism, is not a marginal or unimportant social teaching of the church, but is a central part of the Christian message of redemption, transformation, and reconciliation. Racism needs to be understood as a devastating expression of the sinfulness and brokenness of humanity. The struggle to overcome racism is part of the completion of God's redemptive plan to restore justice and wholeness in our world and to all of creation.

Foundation Stone 3:
Taking back stolen sacred stories.

In every era of history, those who have sought to exclude sisters and brothers from the family have used the word of God—the Holy Scriptures and the teachings of the Christian church—to support their aims. The Bible and other sacred stories have been twisted and distorted to make it seem that God is in favor of racism and supports other forms of oppression. Opposing racism and other forms of injustice is deemed to be political, and, consequently, not something Christians are supposed to get involved in. When this happens, the truth is being stolen and made into a lie; the Bible is being turned upside down. If we are going to be equipped to work for the elimination of racism, we need to turn the Bible right side up again. We need to take back stolen stories and reclaim an anti-racist gospel.

One of the most pervasive misinterpretations of the Bible that has been taught and believed throughout United States history—both in the church and society in general—is that God endorses the superiority of white people; that God actually approved of the enslavement of Africans and mass killing of American Indians. This is just one example of the perversion of truth. Sexism, classism, nationalism, warfare, and racism have all been defended as religious causes backed by God and supported by the church. Time and again, preachers have stood in pulpits, waving a Bible over their heads, to justify an evil action by one group against another by claiming God's approval.

Throughout much of United States history, the blatant lies of white supremacy were believed by most of society, not just by the Ku Klux Klan and other hate groups. They were even taught and believed within most of our own churches. Though most of us no longer believe the teachings that claim religious support for overt racism, there still exist many dangerously subtle and sophisticated ways in which the Bible and the Christian faith are misused to defend racism. Many of us are caught up easily in believing these stolen stories, and we pass them along to others without even realizing we are promoting racism and white supremacy. Consider the following examples.

Stolen Story 1: The Defense of Individualism

- "I don't need anyone. I only need to rely on myself."
- "My relationship with God is strictly a private and individual matter."
- "I got what I have by my own personal initiative. It had nothing to do with my gender, my class, or my race."

Individualism and exaggerated private initiative are principal doctrines of American civil religion that are taught everywhere, including within the church. Not only is individualism in direct conflict with the central teachings of Christianity, it is a primary support for racism. We need to recognize and support individual rights as part of all human rights, of course, but not the "I-pulled-myself-up-by-my-bootstraps" mentality that places individual self-reliance and self-achievement above reliance on community. This "super individualism," which brags, "I got what I have because I earned it, and if they had ambition and initiative, they could have it too," is destructive of community. It represents itself and identifies itself as part of the teachings of the Christian faith, and it is used in overt and subtle ways, especially by white people, to take personal credit for what actually are the benefits of racism and to blame people of color for not having what racism has taken from them. To some degree, all of us have been socialized into an individualistic mindset that supports racism and perpetuates this stolen story.

Stolen Story 2: Charity in Place of Justice

- "Please help the poor and needy this Christmas by giving toys and turkeys."
- "You can rescue this child from poverty—or you can turn the page."
- "The Bible says, 'The poor you will always have with you.'"

It feels good to give from our plenty to help someone in crisis or struggling to survive. Churches in the United States, along with private and public agencies, are justifiably proud of their charity, the social services they provide, and their acts of goodwill toward those in need. However, we often are caught on an endless treadmill of contributing to the immediate needs of the poor without also working to bring poverty to an end. It is not enough to work to reduce the effects of poverty, racism, and other forms of oppression, when justice calls us to dismantle the systems that create and perpetuate these evils.

Doing charitable deeds is a clear biblical mandate, but there is something wrong if in feeling good about doing charity we forget about doing justice. "What does the Lord require of you, but to do justice, and to love kindness, and to walk humbly with your God" (Micah 6:8). When charity is a substitute for justice and a means to support racism and other forms of injustice, it is a stolen sacred story.

Stolen Story 3: Justification of Riches

- "You're so rich; God has really blessed you."
- "God just gave me a new car, and you can have one too, if you believe."
- "God has blessed America with riches and strength."

The most blatant of all stolen stories may be the attribution of wealth and other material blessings as gifts of God. On radio and television, from the podium and pulpit, we hear over and over again that we are a blessed nation, a blessed people. We hear it so often that it flows from our lips without thinking: "I feel so blessed." But if the riches of a select people reflect the intentional blessing of God, does it not follow that the poverty of so many others must also be the will of God? If I am rich because of God's blessing, others must be poor because of God's curse.

We would be shocked to hear a purse snatcher describe his booty as a blessing from God, but it is acceptable religious language for us to describe our country as a gift from God, despite the fact that this land we call "our land" is property stolen from America's indigenous peoples. If 2 percent of the world's people own more than 50 percent of the wealth, while the bottom half of the world's adult population owns barely 1 percent of global wealth; and if one billion people in the world suffer from hunger and malnutrition, and 24,000 people die every day from hunger or hunger-related causes, there has to be some reason other than the will of God to explain this inequality.[3]

Taking Back Stolen Stories

Is there any one among us who hasn't been taken in by these distortions? In order to effectively deal with racism in the church and in society, we need to reject these and other stolen sacred stories and reclaim that which the Bible and the Christian faith truly teach us. We need to clearly renounce the way God's name has been used throughout history to support poverty, racism, war, and genocide, and we need to reject every effort to continue that practice in our present-day lives. We must turn the Bible right side up, and rid ourselves of the conscious and unconscious use of sacred stories to uphold injustice.

There is plenty of biblical precedence to help us do this. The righteous anger of the prophets and of Jesus himself at the support given by religious people to the injustices surrounding them should help put words into our mouths.

> I hate, I despise your festivals, and I take no delight in your solemn assemblies. . . . Take away from me the noise of your songs; I will not listen to the melody of your harps. . . . But let justice roll down like waters, and righteousness like an ever-flowing stream. (Amos 5:23-24)

> Then [Jesus] entered the temple and began to drive out those who were selling things there; and he said, "It is written, 'My house shall be a house of prayer'; but you have made it a den of robbers." (Luke 19:45-46)

A surprise awaits us when we take back sacred stories that have been stolen to defend racism, the surprise of an anti-racist gospel. This gospel isn't new, but it has been so distorted and disguised that we didn't recognize it. It is up to us to reclaim this gospel in our efforts to understand and combat racism.

Foundation Stone 4:
We are called and carried on the shoulders of witnesses who struggled before us.

We are not alone in this journey to reclaim an anti-racist gospel and shape an anti-racist church. We are part of an enormously large, centuries-old movement of saints who have been called by God to stand against all forms of injustice. With the birth of the church, this calling became part and parcel of the Christian faith. In our own calling, we are being carried on the shoulders of a great cloud of Christian witnesses who struggled before us.

To understand this in greater depth, we need to go back to the time of the church's beginning, when the early Christians were learning to be Christians and suffering great oppression and injustice at the hand of the emperor for the efforts. The Christian community then faced the same terrible dilemma we face today: they knew that God had called them to carry out an extremely difficult task, but they were having trouble finding the courage to do it. Like the church today, they had trouble hearing and following their own message. It was only as they discovered their collective power in working and praying that they were able to overcome enormous odds and win victories over oppression.

The Company They Kept

One of my favorite examples of standing together against evil is found in the letter to the Hebrews in the New Testament. Hebrews was written at a time when Christians were being forced to choose between allegiance to Christ and allegiance to the Roman emperor. If they remained true to their faith, they faced losing their lives. But if they switched their allegiance from Christ to the emperor, their lives would be spared. All they had to do was acknowledge the emperor's claim to be God by taking a little pinch of incense and placing it on the emperor's altar. Once done, the rewards of Roman citizenship would be restored and they would be permitted to continue to worship Jesus. They only had to acknowledge that the emperor was equal in power and authority to God.

With their lives on the line, the choice was tempting. The writer of Hebrews wrote to motivate Christians to persevere in saying no to the emperor and to recommit themselves to Christ, even if it meant death. The writer reminded them that, in centuries past, thousands upon thousands of God's people were faced with the same choice. The writer named heroes of the past, including Noah and his family, Abraham and Sarah, Moses and the Hebrew people who fled from

Egypt, and many more—a great cloud of witnesses—to inspire the early Christians to remain steadfast in faith and to stand strong in the face of threat of persecution by the government.

> Therefore, since we are surrounded by so great a cloud of witnesses, let us also lay aside every weight and the sin that clings so closely, and let us run with perseverance the race that is set before us. (Hebrews 12:1)

A choice had to be made: either to join the cloud of witnesses or to be cut off from them forever. Saying yes to the emperor's tempting offer would result in cutting themselves off from this great body, a fate far worse than any imaginable form of torture and death. But saying no to the emperor meant maintaining a living connection to these saints of God—a connection that not even the emperor's sword could sever. The choice was theirs. The fate of the church and its connection to God's people throughout the world and throughout the ages was in their hands.

The Company We Keep

The same choice is before us today as we work to restore the family of God. Do we follow the witness of those who went before us by standing faithful to our God of justice and righteousness? Or do we capitulate to the values of the empire and, in doing so, continue to receive the rewards produced by racism, classism, nationalism, and other forms of oppression and injustice? The fate of the church today and its connection to God's people throughout the world is in our hands As we stand with many other sisters and brothers in this early part of the twenty-first century preparing for the next steps in working to end racism and other forms of injustice, we need to be clear that the call of God heard in the past by the saints who struggled before us is now ours to hear. God's call and the company of a cloud of witnesses are invincible weapons for combating racism and for building a multiracial and multicultural society.

The struggle against racism that has been going on in our country for more than five hundred years is one of many campaigns against injustice over the centuries. This courageous and indefatigable movement of resistance began in response to the first act of racism in 1492. Millions of resisters have gone before us; millions more will follow after us until the job is finally done and we have become a racism-free society. As Christians we are called by God to join this movement; this is an essential and fundamental part of what it means to follow Jesus. When we said yes to the invitation to follow Jesus, we were saying yes to being workers for justice, and in particular to being workers to end racism and to construct a racially just church and society. Who from your denomination, either from the distant past or in recent times, has worked for peace and justice in our nation?

Whether sitting alone reading this book or part of a study group in a congregation, university, or seminary, you are part of the much larger community of the family of God, a family to which we all belong. Perhaps you use traditional theological language to describe this community, such as "the communion of saints" or "the body of Christ." Or maybe your experience and orientation has taught you to add new and more contemporary expressions describing your participation in "The Movement" or "The Struggle" for "The Beloved Community." These different expressions are not incompatible with traditional theological language, but are complementary ways of seeing ourselves in the company of others, working for justice in the world. All great efforts to correct injustice in the world, whether they deal with oppression of nation against nation, class against class, gender against gender, or race against race, are interrelated and are part of the sacred task of restoring the family of God. Like the early Christians, the letter to the Hebrews reminds us that we too are surrounded by a great cloud of witnesses, and we too are called to "lay aside every weight and the sin that clings so closely, and run with perseverance the race that is set before us."

> *Who from your denomination, either from the distant past or in recent times, has worked for peace and justice in our nation?*

Looking Racism in the Eye

Make no mistake about the seriousness of the task before us. To confront racism is to confront the diabolical presence of evil. To take on this enemy within the church and society is to take on a threatening killer that will resist elimination until its very dying moment. Yet, only by recognizing the presence of this enemy in ourselves, our churches, and every part of society is there a chance of actually overcoming this monster that will not easily be made to go away.

It takes courage to stare this malicious enemy in its face. We need to pray fervently for the ability to overcome our fear of doing so. As St. Paul has taught us, we cannot take on the power of evil without putting on the armor of God. If we are going to take on the diabolical power of racism, we need a solid rock to stand on.

> For we do not wrestle against flesh and blood, but against principalities, against powers, against the rulers of the darkness of this age, against spiritual hosts of wickedness in the heavenly places. Therefore take up the whole armor of God, that you may be able to withstand in the evil day, and having done all, to stand. (Ephesians 6:12-13)

Part I

The Past:
Racism and Resisting Racism
in Church History

*"The only way out is back through. In order to get well
you have to go back through what made you sick in the
first place."*[1]

—REV. JOHNNY RAY YOUNGBLOOD

The present is a product of the past. In the church's past is a painful history of
racism, resulting in a divided and sick Christianity today. There can be no
understanding of how racism functions today in the church or anywhere else in
society without knowing this history. Nor can we begin to comprehend our task
of eliminating racism in the church or in society without having a clear picture of
efforts to end racism in times before us. In order to move forward to the future,
we must remember the past and deal openly and honestly with it. Following are
two stories that illustrate that remembering history, particularly the long and
complex history of racism and resistance to racism in the church, is critically
important and, in the end, profoundly spiritually healing, even if agonizingly
painful.

The MAAFA Suite

St. Paul's Baptist Church, a large African American congregation in Brooklyn,
New York, has a weeklong observance each year called the MAAFA. Named
after a Kiswahili word describing an unspeakable and inexpressible catastro-
phe, MAAFA is used to represent the African holocaust of enslavement of an

estimated 70 million people and the indescribable horrors it produced. The Rev. Johnny Ray Youngblood, senior pastor of St. Paul's Church, led his congregation in creating a movement to commemorate the MAAFA as an annual passion story. At the center of this annual event is "The MAAFA Suite . . . A Healing Journey," a three-hour dramatic psychodrama portraying the pain of African enslavement and the power of survival. Other churches and community groups around the United States have adopted the MAAFA observance as a means of "healing through remembrance."

The MAAFA observance places strong emphasis on healing the "wounded warrior" from the destructive power of racism. The goal is not only healing, however, but also reclaiming the power to struggle to dismantle racism and to change the society responsible for the wounding. In the end, the restored warrior and the restored faith community become a stronger part of organizing the struggle to change society.[2]

Traces of the Trade: A Story from the Deep North

In 2006, filmmaker Katrina Browne produced a historical documentary called *Traces of the Trade* that even today dramatically affects the lives of many white people, including members the Episcopal Church USA, the denomination within which it originated. *Traces of the Trade* explores the story of white wealth inherited from the slave trade.

Years before making the documentary, Browne discovered that her ancestors, the DeWolf family from New England, were one of the largest slave-trading families in United States history. From 1769 to 1820, three generations of DeWolf men trafficked in human beings. The family owned forty-seven ships that were used to transport thousands of Africans across the Middle Passage into slavery and enabled the DeWolfs to amass an enormous fortune.

In the film, the DeWolf descendants retrace the steps of the Triangle Trade, visiting the DeWolf hometown of Bristol, Rhode Island, slave forts on the coast of Ghana, and the ruins of a family plantation in Cuba. Back home, the family confronts the question of what to do now. In the context of growing calls for reparations for slavery, family members struggle with the question of how to think about and contribute to repairing the damages of racism. In doing so, Browne and her family reach the core of the issue of racism for white people: exaggerated and unwarranted power and privilege. And they come to the realization of the need for healing and transformation not only in the society at large, but inside themselves.[3]

Our Own Healing through Remembering Church History

The healing that participants in the MAAFA Suite and *Traces of the Trade* received through remembering their painful history of racism and resistance to racism is possible for us too, and for the congregations and denominations to which we belong. In fact, it is critical that we seek healing through remembering, for, as philosopher George Santayana warns: "Those who cannot remember the past are condemned to repeat it."[4] But before we can add our chapters to the story of confronting racism in the church in the present and in the future, we must become acquainted with the chapters that precede us.

The goal of part 1 is to help us see how the present reality in which we live is a product of our past. All of us suffer from the pain and sickness of racism that happened before we were even born. And all of us are beneficiaries of the healing and reconciliation made possible by the struggles by people who resisted racism in the recent and distant past. We must know this history in order to understand the present and to face up to the changes that need to be made to assure that the future isn't a repeat of the past. For this reason, the chapters that follow focus on the history of racism and resistance to racism in the church:

2. A Tale of Two Churches
3. Racism in U.S. Church History
4. Anti-Racism in U.S. Church History
5. Racism and Anti-Racism in the Post–Civil Rights Era

The Larger Context of Societal History

Although this book is concerned primarily with the church's story, it is important to emphasize and underscore that the church's story is part of the world's story. Not only do we need to connect the church's present with its past, but it is just as important that we connect the church's history to the history of the world outside the church. It is critically important to have a general knowledge of the history of race and racism in society before developing the contextual history of race and racism in the church. Hopefully, readers will bring some awareness of this wider history to the reading of this book. However, it may be helpful to recall some broad strokes of this history before moving forward.

For starters, it is a surprise to many people to learn how recently the idea of race and the practice of racism appeared in the history of the western world. Race and racism, as we understand them today from a western perspective, are relatively new phenomena. Contrary to the beliefs of many, before the fifteenth century A.D., no one thought in terms of "race" as we do today. Humans have always oppressed other humans—tribes fought tribes, nations overwhelmed nations, aristocracy subjugated peasantry, men dominated women—but practices of oppression by one "race" toward another began only about five hundred years ago.

Contemporary racism began with the European creation of the idea of race in the context of global discovery and colonial expansion in the sixteenth and seventeenth centuries. The idea of race, a social/political construct with no basis in reality and without scientific validity, was joined with its equally violent ideological twin, colonialism, to create a new form of oppression that exceeded all others in cruelty and violence. In the European discovery of the "new world," the idea of superior and inferior races was used to justify the brutal process of colonial occupation and conquest. The primary purpose of race and racism was to establish the superiority of the Caucasoid (European/white) race and to justify European dominance over all other races, as well as the taking of their land and resources. Over the course of the following centuries, the people of the world were divided into separate races, and the white race declared itself superior and supreme to all others. All history since that time has been (and still is today) devastatingly and destructively affected by colonialism and racism.

Although racism and colonialism's effects were global in scope, it was in the Western Hemisphere, and particularly in the shaping of our own nation in the eighteenth century, that racism took on the unique form that we know. White supremacy was formally established within United States political, economic, and social structures, under the principle that the land and its resources exist for the white race, and all other races exist to serve white people. In addition to the "superior" white race, five other "inferior" races were legally created, with extensive laws defining and controlling them: Native Americans, African Americans, Latinos/Hispanics, Asian Americans, and Arab Americans/Middle Eastern people. Each of these racialized groups was aggressively and violently oppressed, and each of them has a long history of determined resistance to their oppression.

The dramatic changes brought about in the civil rights movement in the 1960s and 1970s were the result of centuries of resistance by all people of color and also by many white people. At the same time, contrary to popular belief, the civil rights movement did not resolve the issue of racism in the United States. It did, however, result in the end of legalized apartheid and segregation and established a new foothold for the continuing struggle for racial justice that was to follow.

There is not space in this book for a more detailed description of the birth of race, racism, and colonialism in Europe in the sixteenth century and the evolution of these ideas in the American colonies and the nation of the United States. Since I and others have described such history elsewhere, I will refer, when necessary, to particular resources that readers may find helpful.[5]

Chapter two

A Tale of Two Churches

*"A shoot shall come out from the stump of Jesse,
and a branch shall grow out of his roots."*

—ISAIAH 11:1

A Church with Two Personalities

Throughout its long history, the Christian church has been both shamefully *for* racism and courageously *against* it, standing at least as often on the side of racism as it has stood in opposition to it. This chapter will paint a portrait of a church with two personalities, a racist church and an anti-racist church. Readers need to prepare for a great deal of emotional trauma and to be torn again and again from one side to the other.

There is an indisputable historical record of the Christian church repeatedly taking positions and actions that were wrongly on the side of racism and even claiming divine authority to do so by twisting and distorting the Bible and the teachings of the Christian faith. It is very important to be open and honest about this. Only as we shine the light of truth on these shameful and disgraceful actions can we seek guidance on how to follow a path toward forgiveness and reconciliation.

At the same time, from another perspective, it is possible to see a marvelously contrasting picture of the church proclaiming a powerful message against racism, a message that has given millions of exploited and oppressed people the hope and strength to struggle for survival and to participate boldly in the struggle for racism's elimination. Some of the most courageous and effective leaders in struggles for racial justice over the course of history have come from within the church.

The strength, leadership, and determination of these prophets are witness to the power of the Christian faith.

To explain this dual vision of the church being both for and against racism, it is necessary to realize that the Christian church is not a single entity with only one history. Rather, it is a complex arrangement of separate churches and different denominational bodies that often have been at odds with each other over many issues, including those of race and racism. Moreover, there are often diverging and conflicting layers intertwined within the same denomination, with each layer having its own life and history. These dynamics play a key role in our response to racism today.

The Church before Racism

The Christian church has had two personalities almost from the very beginning, often resulting in separate and conflicting paths. Especially with regard to issues of injustice and oppression, the church has been divided, sometimes taking sides in adamant support of oppressors, and at other times standing courageously and compassionately on the side of the oppressed.

During its first few centuries, two contrasting theological, political, and cultural constructs developed in the church that determined how it would respond to many issues throughout its history. One construct, often referred to as a theology of glory, emphasizes God's strength and God's ultimate power and victory over evil. The other, a theology of the cross, emphasizes God's vulnerability and God's willingness to identify with the pain and suffering in the world.[1]

Although these contrasting theologies help define the split personality of the Christian church, another contributing factor is differing constituencies. The church that espouses a theology of glory, or triumphal theology, tends to be comfortable identifying with the ruling political power and the influential leaders of the nation in which it resides. The church that embraces a theology of the cross identifies more with people on the lower end of the economic spectrum, with people whose lives are given over to serving society with little choice or reward. The names I will use to describe these two churches with their contrasting personalities are the "Ruler's Church" and the "People's Church."

The Ruler's Church appears strong, powerful, and confident, even to the point of arrogance. It is characterized by a philosophy of success. Its triumphal theology emphasizes God's power and glory, the resurrection, and victory over suffering and death. The Ruler's Church takes up residence in magnificent cathedrals. It identifies comfortably with the rich and powerful and sits at table with rulers and generals. It is less at ease in the presence of the poor and rejected of the world, but it often places a high priority on works of charity and social services.

The People's Church seems weak and unsuccessful in comparison to the Ruler's Church. It seems to be somewhat antisocial in that it maintains a careful distance from the rich and powerful Ruler's Church and even occasionally speaks to it with a sense of prophetic anger and judgment. The People's Church, with its theology of the cross, emphasizes God's identification with the poor and suffering and the brokenness reflected in the crucifixion.

Before going any further, I need to clarify that in these depictions I am *not* contrasting the Roman Catholic Church and the Protestant Church. Readers who are aware of the long history of conflict between the Roman Catholic and Protestant churches may be tempted to see a repetition of those old and worn-out categories. In fact, the Ruler's Church with its triumphal theology is as present in Protestantism as it is Roman Catholicism, and the People's Church with its theology of the cross is as present in Roman Catholicism as it is in Protestantism.

A further clarification: while I am making a sharp distinction between these two personalities, in fact, as we will see, they often overlap each other in ways that at times make them indistinguishable. Many characteristics of the People's Church are present in the Ruler's Church, and many characteristics of the Ruler's Church are present in the People's Church. Nevertheless, there are times when separated by the forces of history that these two personalities are clearly distinguishable.

The characterization of these two personalities will be especially helpful in understanding the story of racism and resisting racism within churches in the United States. In the history of racism in the United States, the Ruler's Church has been more often than not identified with middle- and upper-class people, most of whom are white. The People's Church has been closely identified with the poor and working class and with people of color. Uncomfortable though it may be, as we explore more deeply in succeeding chapters, we will see a long history of support for racism in the United States by predominantly white mainline Protestant and Roman Catholic churches who identify with the ruling powers and defend themselves with a triumphal theology of success and glory. And we will see that resistance to racism has been largely an activity of churches of color, which have a clear understanding of the theology of the cross, especially the African American church.

Split Personalities: Saints and Sinners

Although tempting, it is important not to be overly judgmental of the Ruler's Church nor to overly romanticize and idealize the People's Church. Both churches have their legitimacy and their limitations. As with any split personality, the problem is the separation and exaggeration of two disintegrated identities and their isolation from each other.

There is a legitimate place in the church for glory, power, and triumph. The message of the resurrection—God's victory over death and the promise of a triumphal second coming of Christ—give the church and individual Christians a sense of hope and confidence that the future belongs to God. The problem is that the Ruler's Church, with its triumphal theology, all too quickly becomes the "triumphalistic church," placing its confidence in humans (especially governments and rulers), rather than in God, and turning its back on those who, like Christ, are acquainted intimately with suffering and rejection.

And there is clearly a legitimate place in the church for a theology of the cross, with its identification with suffering and oppression. But it is particularly important not to put the People's Church on a pedestal by portraying it as a perfect church with faultless and humble saints who were consistently good and courageous. Even as we celebrate its heroic history and its incredible survival against all odds, the People's Church is also characterized by the weakness and shortcomings of all human organizations. In the historical setting where we will be exploring its resistance to racism, the People's Church was composed of imperfect, often self-righteous people who fought with each other, made many mistakes, were often very afraid, and were tempted to quit. Nevertheless, despite all its frailties and in the midst of its weaknesses, the achievements of the People's Church are evidence of the power and inspiration of the anti-racist gospel.

The Birth of the Two Churches

There is an important and very interesting story about how these two churches—Ruler's Church and the People's Church—came into being. Fairly early in the church's history, in A.D. 313, one of the most amazing political events of all time took place. The Emperor Constantine, ruler of the most powerful nation on earth, declared Christianity, which at the time was a very minor, unpopular, and illegal religion, to be an officially sanctioned religion of the Roman Empire. Until that moment, Christianity had been a small Middle Eastern religious movement that existed largely underground because of persecution, but was gradually expanding eastward and southward into parts of Asia and Africa. When Constantine received a vision of a sign of the cross in the sky and heard the words, "In this sign, conquer," all that changed. He gave Christianity his official seal of approval, essentially tearing the church from its Middle Eastern roots and transplanting it to Rome.

Most importantly, when these changes took place, the cross, the church's most important symbol, was transformed from a sign of suffering into an emblem of military conquest. The Christian church became nationalized with its center in Rome, and then eventually spread to the rest of Europe in what some have described as the "European captivity of the church."[2] Thus the Ruler's Church was born and over time it determined much of the rest of the triumphal history of European Christianity, including shaping the dominant personality of the yet-to-be-born Church of the Reformation.

However, a significant part of the church did not conform to the new order of things. The wrenching transformation into a nationalized religion split the church in two, leaving behind, nearly unnoticed, part of the original church we have identified as the People's Church. For a long time, this "remnant" maintained a quiet, less visible life following a path that identified with the poor and the way of the cross. Many religious orders of monks and nuns followed this path, helping to keep the image and work of the People's Church alive.

Caught between the Ruler's Church and the People's Church were millions of adherents to Christianity, mostly peasants who may have resembled monks and nuns in their lifestyle of poverty, but did not choose it voluntarily. They had scarce awareness of their identification as a separate People's Church, for they gave their loyalty to the triumphal church and state, which in return gave them work, paid their meager salaries, and forgave their sins on Sunday morning.

More than a millennium passed as the two personalities of the church continued on separate, yet often overlapping, paths, being pulled and pushed in conflicting directions. The strongest and most visible path of the Ruler's Church created a growing bond between church and state. The crusades and other "holy wars" fought in Jesus' name and, ostensibly, for his sake expanded the dominion of the church and culminated in the solidification of the Holy Roman Empire. The triumphal church and the triumphal state became inseparable and almost indistinguishable, while the People's Church suffered mostly in silence beneath the crushing foot of the state and the Ruler's Church.[3]

The Reformation Changes Little

Tragically, the Reformation movement in the sixteenth century did not heal the church's split personality. As new denominations—Lutheran, Reformed, Church of England, and others—came into being, the split intensified. The personalities of the Ruler's Church and the People's Church took on separate lives within each denomination and, over time, in the sects, factions, and offshoots of each that inevitably followed. In fact, due to the Reformation the Ruler's Church became more evident than ever as Protestant state churches were formed, providing the blessings of God upon children of enlightenment, the industrial revolution, and the capitalist economic system. With appalling tirades against Jews and Turks and persecution of non-conforming religious minorities, including the Anabaptists, the Reformation inadvertently built into the foundations of the newly formed Protestant church an ideological basis for the most violent nationalist religious and racist excesses in Europe and in the United States yet to come. The Reformation had many positive achievements, but this last was arguably among the most disastrous contributions to contemporary history.

Following the Reformation, an inseparable bond was forged between powerful European nations and state churches. Increasingly European culture became indistinguishable from the Christian faith. This perpetuated the Ruler's Church, which gave Christians even greater permission to identify with political oppressors and still claim to represent the gospel. Charles Villa-Vicencio, a South African theologian, describes a bourgeois church with little relationship to the peasant majority:

Whatever the fundamental cause of these reform processes (economic, the rise of nationalism and/or the spiritual renewal), the consequence was the emergence of a bourgeois church. The control of the church, and more particularly the Protestant church, had shifted from the imperial aristocracy to the bourgeois princes, but the peasants continued to be marginalized and excluded from the socio-political identity of the church.[4]

This same bond between church and state was replicated in the United States. In time historians recognized the Ruler's Church as the official representative of Christianity in United States history.

The Birth of Racism and Colonialism

About a century before the Reformation, the nations of Europe began to discover the existence of the rest of the world, marking the beginning of the colonial conquest of Africa, the Americas, and Asia. By the end of the long history of colonialism, virtually every piece of land on earth would experience occupation and control by one or more European nations. Europeans claimed ownership of the entire world, its lands, its peoples, and its resources.

Along with colonialism came its evil twin, racism. The European, or Caucasian, race declared itself superior to all other races and assumed the role of dominance over them. With pseudo-scientific inaccuracy, the world was divided by colonizing nations into superior and inferior races for the sole purpose of justifying global dominance. With the new tool of white supremacy in hand, European colonial powers were enabled to validate and defend their acquisition of the world's lands as their legal possession, and the property of their white descendents. The consequences are still with us. The world today is defined and divided by the fruits of colonialism and racism, and we are faced with the gigantic task of resolving race-based systemic inequity and political, economic, and social dominance of others by the white race.

The Role of the Church as Midwife

Where was the church during the birth of colonialism and racism? Tragically, it was very much in the middle, playing the role of midwife. The colonialization and racialization of the world happened in the name of God, with the official endorsement of the Ruler's Church. At this dramatic moment in history, representatives of the Ruler's Church enthusiastically climbed on board colonial ships and joined the exploration and appropriation of new worlds. They traveled as chaplains on the high seas of discovery, representing the official church of their particular colonizing nation: the Roman Catholic Church of Spain and Portugal, the Reformed Church of the Netherlands, the Lutheran Church of Germany, and the Church of England.

These dignitaries of the Ruler's Church took the high road to which they were accustomed, riding in first-class cabins with royal representatives and military leaders. Upon landing on foreign shores, while spokespersons for the government laid claim to the newly discovered land in the name of their Queen or King, spokespersons for the church provided their blessing on the transaction in the name of the Father and of the Son and of the Holy Spirit.

In each new place the cross represented God's endorsement of the conquerors as they laid claim to ownership of its land, its resources, and its people. Once again, the cross, originally a symbol of the suffering of the oppressed, became a sign of triumphal conquest, sanctioning the invasion and subjugation of virtually every place and person on earth outside of Europe.

For the record, it is important to note that there was not unanimity within the church about participation in this global confiscation. The dual personalities of the church were clearly evident in the debate over the rightness and wrongness of colonialism and racism. For example, although there were papal bulls issued in the Roman Catholic Church endorsing the colonial enterprise, there were also papal bulls that attempted to curb or condemn the cruel practices of slavery.[5] Likewise, despite participation by Protestant churches with governmental colonial enterprises and slavery, there were also protests about the excesses by pastors and missionaries.[6] For the most part, however, dissenting voices were ignored. As the colonial enterprise advanced into the eighteenth and nineteenth centuries, the Ruler's Church became more and more identified with the racism and colonialism of oppressor nations. Although there is danger of overgeneralization, European churches in colonial territories throughout the world carried out the ecclesiastical function of thanking God for blessing colonial enterprises with success, security, and material possessions. Dealing with poverty and other expressions of human suffering had little to do with defining their religious role. These problems, if addressed at all, were viewed either as temporary conditions that could be overcome by individual effort, or responded to with charitable assistance.

The People's Church Rides in Steerage

The Ruler's Church was not the only ecclesiastical passenger on board the colonial ships in the age of discovery. The People's Church was also a passenger on the same ships as they sailed toward their global conquests. It was not riding in first class, however, but in steerage, along with servants, vassals, and slaves of the ruling aristocracy. Then, upon arrival in new lands, the People's Church shared a home with indentured servants, imported slaves, and colonized peasants.

The role played by the People's Church in the new land is not popularly known, since in describing the age of discovery and colonization, history books usually portray only the accomplishments of the Ruler's Church. Nevertheless, the People's Church quietly provided the spiritual strength that the oppressed and suffering needed to survive. And it helped to maintain their vision of freedom. Above all, it nurtured a spirit of resistance and rebellion among the victims of the early years of colonial conquest and racism. It not only helped keep hope alive; it also planted seeds that would later emerge as struggles for liberation throughout the world, struggles that would determine the path of history for centuries to come.

These same struggles, however, would even further divide the Ruler's Church from the People's Church. Villa-Vicencio gives examples of the conflicting activities of these two churches on a global scale during the last half of the twentieth century:

> Since those heady days of missionary triumphalism this distinction between two different kinds of political involvement has left an indelible mark on the church. Confessing Christians in Nazi Germany were condemned by church and state alike for resisting Hitler, while the involvement of the Deutsche Christen on the side of Hitler was regarded as theologically legitimate. In Smith's Rhodesia the church vacillated in its affirmation of social justice, in Latin and Central American dictatorships the institutional churches have in many instances preached an ethereal spirituality that has left the poor to die in the streets, and in the Philippines, South Korea and elsewhere, bishops, priests, nuns, and catechists have been tortured and assassinated by rulers who regard themselves as Christians. In South Africa . . . even the most "liberal" churches question the more radical involvement of Christians against the state.[7]

Today in the twenty-first century, denominations and congregations are still racially defined and racially divided, still suffering from the historic division between the Ruler's Church and People's Church. We are still a church with a "split personality," caught by tensions between a theology of triumph and a theology of the cross and divided by political allegiances and loyalties to a Ruler's Church or a People's Church. Even as we focus specifically on the issues of race and racism in the church and the long-term task of racial healing, we need to keep in mind the context of this deeper reconciliation we seek. In the following chapter, we will explore this reality more deeply in the context of describing the history of racism in the United States churches.

A Church with Two Personalities:
It's in Our Genes

Before you turn to the next chapter, pause for a moment and ask how much of this tale of two churches with two personalities is already part of your consciousness. To what degree are you aware of the impact of this history on your denomination's early history in the United States or in predecessor churches in Europe? Do you sense the presence of a dual personality in the genetic makeup of your church? Have you experienced competition and conflict caused by the predominance of one identity or the other? How have you experienced either a theology of triumph or a theology of the cross in your church?

Readers who are on the topside of society are less likely to be conscious of the contradictory reality of the church's two personalities than those on the underside of society. It should not be surprising that one of the distinguishing factors in how you perceive the role of the church in your life is the degree to which you have experienced human oppression. It makes a great deal of difference if your experience has taught you to understand the gospel and look at the world through the lens of a triumphal theology or a theology of the cross. Each of us has internalized a racial identity and a worldview that helps us see or not see the reality of poverty, race, and racism. Going forward, we will explore ways in which the church has played a very powerful role in helping us form this awareness.

Racism in United States Church History

> *I accuse you, says the Lord, and I accuse your children's children . . .*
> *for my people have committed two evils:*
> *they have forsaken me, the fountain of living water, and dug out*
> *cisterns for themselves, cracked cisterns that can hold no water.*
>
> —JEREMIAH 2:9, 13

The history of racism in the church in the United States is a story of God's beloved New Israel committing the same evils as the Israel of old: making alliances with an idolatrous nation and practicing idolatry and injustice among its own people. The voice of God through Jeremiah reaches through the pages of the Bible, accusing our forebears and ourselves, their children's children, of forsaking God, the source of living water, and depending instead on water from leaky cisterns.

Bartolomé de las Casas: Villain or Hero?

The history we are about to explore is confusing and contradictory. An example can be seen in the following story, which is in its different parts both heartbreaking and heartwarming. It is about Bartolomé de las Casas, a contemporary of Christopher Columbus, who before becoming a Dominican priest, worked alongside Columbus as an enthusiastic participant in colonial adventure. Shocked and appalled, however, by the cruel torture and genocide against the indigenous Taino people carried out by Columbus, de las Casas repented of his involvement and became a critic of colonialism. He became an advocate for the Taino, demanding that they be released from their suffering and from slavery and servitude. Tragically, he proposed that enslaved Africans be substituted in their place, a proposal for which he later repented. Eventually de las Casas was appointed the first resident bishop of Chiapas, Mexico. Even though he became increasing critical of colonialism's policies, he was never able to separate himself from being its official representative. Today he is castigated by some as a symbol of the church's participation in racism and colonial conquest. Others revere him for his resistance to racism and colonialism's cruelties, as well as for his caring and compassionate leadership of the church. His actions both for and against racism, his timidity, courage and vacillation from one to the other has led him to win recognition as both villain and hero of the past.

The Church: Villain or Hero?

As with the life of Bartolomé de las Casas, there are two incongruous and conflicting sides to the long story of the church's involvement with racism in the United States. One side is painful, tragic, and villainous. The other side is amazing, wonderful, even heroic. We need to begin with the painful side, because too often we try to avoid, deny, or forget that the Christian church not only provided sanction and support for racism in American society but tragically allowed racism to thrive in the life of the church.

The stories of the church's involvement in racism will be very difficult for many to read and discuss. Our instincts are to protect the church by countering these stories with positive ones. We must, however, become acquainted with this shameful side of our history, no matter how hard it is to do so. Part of the difficulty is that a significant amount of this history has been forgotten, or deliberately erased. In history books written largely by representatives of predominantly white mainline denominations we seldom read confessions of the church's identification with white supremacy, its sanction of genocide against Indians and enslavement of Africans, its silence during times that called for a prophetic witness to justice. In recent years, attempts have been made to apologize for these actions and non-actions, but they have been mostly weak and ineffective. Yet, if we are to reclaim a place of integrity with an anti-racist gospel and an anti-racist church, it is important to reverse the denials that this sacrilege was committed in God's name. Before we can become effective Christian resisters of racism in the twenty-first century, we need to recognize and keep in our consciousness the blasphemous ways in which our churches and our nation have misused God's name to support racism in centuries past.

The Church in Colonial America

Indian Genocide, in God's Name

Christopher Columbus arrived in 1492, with a sword in one hand and a cross in the other. He was pathetically lost, but he quickly regained his bearings and triumphantly claimed the newly discovered land, its peoples, and its resources for

God and for Queen. While Columbus is recognized and acclaimed as a hero in popular history for his accidental discovery, historians have taken little notice of his cruel and savage treatment toward Native American people.

But it was Columbus's cruel and savage treatment that Native Americans noticed most. In order for the Europeans to take possession of, settle, and prosper in their newly acquired land, Columbus initiated a path of genocide that over the next few centuries took the lives of millions upon millions of indigenous people. Although it is impossible to be completely accurate, at the time of the invasion of Columbus there were approximately twelve million Native Americans occupying the lands that later became the United States (some estimates are as high as twenty million). By the mid-1800s, when the United States had expanded to the Pacific Ocean and "won the west," there were less than one million remaining. The colonial enterprise carried out a genocidal undertaking that resulted in the deaths of more than eleven million Native American people.

God Blesses America

The church joined the colonial enterprise and brought God's blessing upon its goals and accomplishments. The blessing began when representatives of the church arrived with Columbus on America's shores, and gave God's approval to Spain's taking of the land. The blessing continued when other colonial enterprises from England, Holland, France, and elsewhere followed suit, each claiming their own piece of North America in God's name. Over the next two centuries, churches of various denominations—Roman Catholic, Anglican, Reformed, Lutheran, Methodist, Congregational, Quaker, Mennonite, and more—followed on immigrant ships in Columbus's wake. They put down ecclesiastical roots in the new world, helping to establish and settle the colonies. In Jamestown, Plymouth, and New Netherlands, American colonists established structures of religion that became part and parcel of the ruling colonial governments.

About this we must be clear: the churches participated fully in the taking of the land and in the massacres of indigenous peoples, not only as they settled comfortably in eastern cities and rural farmlands but also as they traveled westward with pioneer wagons. The churches provided spiritual strength and courage for early explorers. They also provided theological support for the belief that Native American peoples were not human and that genocide was an acceptable action.

Yes, there was dissent. There were voices of disapproval by representatives of the People's Church who challenged the genocide and ministered to victims. But the protests, which were few and far between, were all too easily dismissed, drowned out by the booming voice of the Ruler's Church, which with near unanimity supported racial domination, land acquisition, and Native American extinction. Bishop Steve Charleston of the Choctaw Nation writes:

The colonization of the Americas by European imperialism, aided and abetted by the Christian church, continues to haunt this hemisphere. Indigenous people, who are the survivors of one of the most systematic efforts at ethnic cleansing in the history of the world, remain in the shadow of what I believe must be named the American apartheid.[1]

Slavery, in God's Name

The story gets worse. Not only were the Bible and the Christian faith used to support and defend Native American genocide, they were also employed to provide a religious ideological foundation for the enslavement of many millions of Africans and for the system of chattel slavery in the American colonies and in the United States following independence from England. Over the course of two and a half centuries when slavery was the law of the land, most slaveholders and their political defenders used their perceptions of the will of God to justify their actions. Following emancipation, slavery was replaced by segregation and apartheid, and white supremacy, represented as the official governmental position, was defended with blatant expressions of religious belief.

> Defenders of slavery noted that in the Bible, Abraham had slaves. They point to the Ten Commandments, noting that "Thou shalt not covet thy neighbor's house . . . nor his manservant, nor his maidservant." In the New Testament, Paul returned a runaway slave, Philemon, to his master, and, although slavery was widespread throughout the Roman world, Jesus never spoke out against it. . . . Defenders of slavery argued that the institution was divine, and that it brought Christianity to the heathen from across the ocean. Slavery was, according to this argument, a good thing for the enslaved. John C. Calhoun said, "Never before has the black race of Central Africa, from the dawn of history to the present day, attained a condition so civilized and so improved, not only physically, but morally and intellectually."[2]

But it was not only governmental appropriation of religious language and beliefs; the church also took full and active part in carving the sinful foundation of slavery into the political and cultural framework of our nation and into the theological framework and practices of church denominations. This activity left enduring and painful wounds in the fabric of our society, as well as persistent scars of race-based denominational division present to this very day. Of course the pro-slavery voice in the churches was not a united voice. From the very beginning, there was division within churches over the issue of slavery. Some Christian leaders sought abolition of slavery; others, compromise. Shamefully, some saw great possibilities for advancing the kingdom of God by converting and baptizing (but not freeing) slaves. A few denominations made weak protests against slavery, but did not seriously confront slaveholding among their own clergy and members. The fact remains that until a decade or two before emancipation, most denominations either openly supported or silently accepted the system of slavery.

Missions to Indians and Slaves: Caring to Death

The same churches that supported oppression against Native Americans and enslaved Africans carried out intensive mission enterprises among these people with the professed purpose of caring for their souls. Missions were organized to convert and educate Indians and slaves. Many such efforts were sincere, well meaning, and deeply caring. There were missionaries who protested the cruelty and mistreatment they witnessed and tried to protect victims from brutality. But, no matter how well meaning they may have been, missionary efforts were instrumental in defeating, pacifying, and controlling Indians and making more obedient slaves. It is important to note that, while efforts were being made to baptize slaves, teach them Christian values, and, in some cases, admit them into church membership, great care was taken to ensure an unbroken sense of partnership between Christian missionaries and slave owners.

The purpose for the churches' missionary work was to save souls, not bodies. For the most part, preaching the gospel to enslaved Africans was not intended to help them fight for their freedom, though inadvertently this turned out to be the most important benefit. In fact, in order to counter any tendency to associate the Christian ideas of "freedom in Christ" with the idea of freedom from slavery, laws were passed in most colonies preventing slaves from using their Christian identity as a legal argument for being released from the bonds of slavery.[3] Thankfully, ultimately slaves found in the Christian faith a foundation for their struggles for freedom.

With few exceptions, Christian missionary enterprises toward Native Americans and enslaved Africans served the purposes of conquerors and enslavers. Since this is quite the opposite conclusion than one finds in most church history books, we may find this conclusion at first somewhat difficult to swallow. Nevertheless, I believe that our ability to confront and eradicate racism in the twenty-first century requires our coming to grips with this reality. Only as we understand and accept this ugly part of our past can we initiate redemptive and reparative strategies for becoming a reconciled anti-racist church in the future.

A Look inside Proslavery Colonial Churches

Harsh as it sounds, if one judges not only by actions but also by inaction, the fact is that there was not a single mainline denomination—Episcopalian, Lutheran, Reformed, Methodist, Baptist, Roman Catholic, Congregationalist, or any other—in colonial America that was not proslavery. Only a few denominations, such as the Mennonites and Quakers, expressed sufficient contrary witness to white supremacist and proslavery positions in ways that shaped an "anti-slavery" denominational identity. Larry E. Tise, in his book *Proslavery: A History of the Defense of Slavery in America, 1701–1840,* documented the ideology, writing and organizing activities of 275 prominent proslavery clergymen. On the importance of clergy leadership in the society at that time, he writes:

> I found quite early in my research that the antebellum clergy provided essen-
> tial social leadership in manners quite distinct from the patterns to which
> we are accustomed in the twentieth century . . . one could find among the
> ranks of the ministry some of the most superbly educated, socially aware,
> and powerfully stationed (both symbolically and actually) leaders America
> could boast. As educators, writers, reformers, orators and spiritual leaders,
> clergymen constituted the largest, most vocal, and most readily accessible
> national elite in American society.[4]

The weighty influence of the white church on society in both the North and South provided sanction and support for slavery and other forms of racism. Most denominations found ways to tolerate or openly permit their clergy and members to own slaves, to take ownership of Indian lands, and to exclude people of color from membership or to segregate them and treat them as second class members. One might have hoped that in the transition from colony to nationhood, all of this might have changed. But that was not the case. The American Revolution's message of freedom and independence, whether it came from the mouths of politicians or preachers, remained exclusively aimed toward reaping benefits for immigrants from Europe.

The Church in the Newly Formed United States of America

A White Supremacist Nation, by Divine Providence

Our founding fathers conveyed a powerful message about God and freedom in our new nation, but it was a message that had to wait for centuries before it would have a positive impact on the issues of race and racism. That message, written forthrightly in the Declaration of Independence, strongly proclaims the authority of the Creator and divine providence in the birth of the United States of America:

> We hold these truths to be self-evident that all men are created equal, that
> they are *endowed by their Creator* with certain inalienable rights, among these
> are life, liberty, and the pursuit of happiness, that to secure these rights gov-
> ernments are instituted among men. We . . . solemnly publish and declare,
> that these colonies are and of right ought to be free and independent states.

> ... And for the support of this declaration, *with a firm reliance on the pro-*
> *tection of divine providence,* we mutually pledge our lives, our fortunes, and
> our sacred honor.[5]

Most leaders of the new nation made very few decisions without appealing to God's authority. Like many leaders today, they repeatedly and publicly cited reliance on God and divine providence to justify their personal beliefs and public actions. This was especially the case in their defense of a number of racist decisions.

Although early national leaders had severe disagreements about slavery's continuation (disagreements based on differences in religious beliefs as well as economic ideology), they eventually came to an uneasy compromise that allowed for slavery to continue. However, the founding fathers were solidly unified in their certainty that the nation was destined by God to have an exclusively white citizenry, and to be led by its male counterparts. It was the will of God, they were sure, for the United States to be a white nation. Even those who argued fervently against slavery could not imagine a multiracial nation, particularly a nation that included indigenous Americans and immigrant Africans among its citizenry. Nor could they imagine a God who would contradict them in these beliefs. In the improbable event of slavery's abolition, they confessed to helplessness in deciding what to do with millions of freed slaves whom they were certain could not be citizens. In fact, they prepared for the unlikely day when slavery end by exploring multiple plans for exporting ex-slaves.

To reinforce national commitment to a white citizenry, the first naturalization law passed in the United States, the Naturalization Law of March 26, 1790, limited naturalization to "free white persons" and excluded indentured servants, slaves, freed slaves, and, later, Asian Americans:

> [A]ny alien, being a free white person, who shall have resided within the
> limits and under the jurisdiction of the United States for the term of two
> years, may be admitted to become a citizen thereof. . . .[6]

Thus, when the United States became a nation, the systematic decimation of Indian nations and the system of slavery begun in the colonial times were permitted to continue. The defining of a white citizenry based on principles of white supremacy became the basis for nearly two centuries more to exclude people of color—Native Americans, African Americans, Latinos/Hispanics, Asian Americans, and Arab Americans—from participating in full citizenship. Most importantly for this story, for the majority of our nation's leaders, such decisions were based on their personal religious conviction that they were following the guidance of divine providence. An example can be seen in the following quote from Stephen Douglas in his debates with Abraham Lincoln in the campaign for presidency in 1858.

> I tell you that this Chicago doctrine of Lincoln's—declaring that the negro
> and the white man are made equal by the Declaration of Independence and

by Divine Providence—is a monstrous heresy. The signers of the Declaration of Independence never dreamed of the negro when they were writing that document. They referred to white men, to men of European birth and European descent, when they declared the equality of all men. . . .[7]

The Churches and White Supremacy

It was not just the personal religious beliefs of our nation's founders that supported these racist decisions. None of this could have been accomplished without the support of the institutional churches. As in colonial times, following American independence the churches went along with the political program. Most denominations and their congregations provided continuing support for much of the government's actions, particularly with regard to racial matters.

Following independence, the churches quickly transformed from European colonial outposts to national ecclesial bodies that reflected, for the most part, the image of national political beliefs. They preached a gospel of divine providence that blessed the creation of the new nation. They compared the crossing of the Atlantic and the founding of the American nation to God's leading the Hebrew people across the Jordan and the establishment of the nation of Israel. There was little doubt in the mind of most church leaders and the membership of most denominations that the strength and power of the United States was a direct product of God's selective national blessing, and that the continuation of these divine blessings required a loyalty to nation that was virtually indistinguishable from loyalty to God.

Thus, the Ruler's Church became an indelible part of the United States. As a self-defined white national church comprised of many denominations, it presented itself as the new American religion. As throughout its history, the Ruler's Church in the United States took on a nationalist fervor and patriotism that identified most strongly with riches and power. From the very beginning of our nation and for the next nearly two centuries, mainline Protestant and Roman Catholic churches perpetuated a white supremacist, proslavery civil religion that approved of multiple expressions of racism. Most denominations came to at least tepid agreement, if not outright and enthusiastic support for the belief in the superiority of the white race and a divinely blessed exclusively white nation. It is very important for Christians in the twenty-first century to have the honesty and courage to remember this even as we are search for heroic exceptions to this history.

Tise quite convincingly demonstrates the significance of clergy leadership, including heads of denominations (bishops, moderators, and the like), college and university presidents and faculty, publishers and authors, in defending and maintaining the system of slavery. He made the interesting discovery that almost half of the published defenses of slavery were written by ministers, more than half of whom also owned slaves.

Nearly all of them saw abolition as an infidel movement at variance with true religion and the Bible. . . . They found slavery to be a natural condition of society. They found in the Bible ample evidence of God's favor on the institution, as well as proof for a widely held Hamitic curse on the Negro race. They battered down all notions that men are created equally and are thereby entitled to equal rights. They further held that the Negro was a degraded being incapable of enjoying the fruits of liberty and was, indeed, a very present threat to the perpetuation of freedom.[8]

Emancipation and the Last-Minute Conversion of Northern Churches

It took almost another hundred years after independence before the system of slavery was finally brought to an end, but the handwriting was on the wall as far back as when the United States was becoming a nation. The question that had not been answered and for which there appeared to be no answer was how to end slavery and still preserve the divinely inspired principles and political program of white supremacy, with all its economic benefits. In the absence of an answer, the nation was driven to an impasse and civil war became inevitable.

Leading up to the war, the nation and the churches became increasingly divided in their search for answers to this question. There was great tension, especially between churches in the North and the South, as they debated these issues. As time progressed and confrontations over slavery increased, the dispute pitted Christian against Christian and split Protestant denominations into Northern and Southern streams, the effects of which are still with us today. The differences solidified and caused institutional separation within denominations, including the Presbyterians, who divided in 1838; the Methodists, in 1844; and the Baptists, in 1848.

As noted earlier, prior to a few decades before emancipation, no denominations other than Quakers and Mennonites took unequivocal stands against slavery. At the last moment, however, in what can be compared to deathbed conversions, one Northern church after another jumped to the other side, identifying themselves as abolitionists in opposition to slavery. These crossings over to the anti-slavery side were very important, of course, and cause for great celebration. But it is unfortunate that most church historians recall only where things ended up and not the hundreds of years of prior support of slavery.

As the Civil War inevitably approached and the line in the sand between proslavery and anti-slavery advocates became more firmly drawn, the number of abolitionist churches in the North increased significantly. Quakers and Mennonites were joined by more and more denominations whose official positions were anti-slavery. When war finally came, almost all Northern-based denominations were prepared to join sides with the Union against the Confederacy. Of course, no matter how late they had come to the struggle, they were welcomed to the growing collaboration of anti-slavery churches.

It is important to understand, however, that regardless of the strength of the abolitionist position held by these churches, they generally continued to promulgate the God-inspired belief in the superiority and supremacy of the white race and the inferiority of African Americans and other people of color. Most did not accept the idea of side-by-side co-citizenry with African Americans in the nation of the United States or in the kingdom of God. We need to realize this distinction in order to comprehend what happened after the Civil War, when the institution of slavery officially ended only to be replaced by a new form of slavery called segregation.

The Church after Emancipation

Neither emancipation nor the passage of the Thirteenth, Fourteenth, and Fifteenth Amendments to the Constitution altered the dedication of the United States and its churches to the principles of white supremacy, or to the belief that dominance over people of color is destined by divine providence. During the hundred years remaining before the civil rights movement would finally signal deeper changes, the nation hung desperately onto its racist beliefs and practices, and onto the goal of completing the divine mission to own and control all the land and resources "from sea to shining sea"—and beyond. The white churches, for the most part complied, supported, and shared in the pursuit of this mission.

From Slavery to Segregation, in God's Name

In 1877, twelve years after the guns fell silent in the war between the North and South, the United States military withdrew from the south and the period known as Reconstruction crashed to an end. A new form of enslavement of African Americans began, with incredible violence and hostility. Jim Crow laws were formalized on state and regional levels and, in 1896, with the *Plessey* v. *Fergusson* Supreme Court decision, the nation inaugurated the formal structures of apartheid segregation. This system replaced slavery as the means of domination over blacks by the white society. Aggression against African Americans became more severe than ever as it became bitterly clear that the reason for fighting a costly civil war had not been resolved.

In many ways, the situation for African Americans was worse than it had ever been during slavery. The African American community was almost totally abandoned, with no more rights or protection than when they had been enslaved. They lived in terror as they faced domination and oppression by the Ku Klux Klan and White Citizens Counsels, enforced by local and state segregation laws and by a national system of apartheid that completely ignored the Thirteenth, Fourteenth, and Fifteenth Amendments.

To make matters worse, due to a shift in the demand for labor caused by economic conditions and industrial development, black workers migrated from the

South to the North at the turn of the century, bringing millions of black families to Northern metropolitan areas. It quickly became clear that post–Civil War racism was not just a southern phenomenon, as racial segregation and other forms of racial oppression became a way of life for many in the North. During this time and well into the early years of the civil rights movement, white denominations willingly conformed and stridently obeyed the laws of apartheid segregation in the United States, joining the rest of the white nation in promoting intentional and official institutional arrangements of separate and unequal development. Nearly all Northern and Southern churches pronounced God's blessing upon the national policies of segregation and followed similar rules themselves. Most official records establishing these rules on denominational and congregational levels have been lost or misplaced, either intentionally or unintentionally. There are many people alive today, however, who remember the practices of segregation that excluded African Americans and other people of color from church membership or participation in worship, and the strict rules that assigned separate seating for blacks and insisted that people of color receive communion only after the white people had received it.

We will explore in the next chapter how black churches responded to segregation by creating increasingly strong and independent black denominations. For now, suffice it to say that during the nearly one hundred years from the end of slavery until the end of segregation, the distance between blacks and whites in the nation and in the churches grew larger and racially defined differences became sharper. It was inevitable that when the white church and the black church met next in the struggle for civil rights it would involve a confrontation between a stubbornly triumphal Ruler's Church and a defiant People's Church, a confrontation from which neither church would emerge the same ever again.

How the West Was Won in God's Name

Meanwhile on the nation's expanding western edge, there was little doubt among national leaders or church leaders about the will of God in the continued destruction of American Indian nations, taking of their land, and placing them on reservations. The removal of entire American Indian nations from the east coast to the Midwest via the deadly "trail of tears" was virtually completed before the Civil War. Continuing down this genocidal path soon became acceptable to almost everyone, including the churches. National policies were shaped dedicated to the annihilation of all Native American peoples or to containing them on reservations. By the turn of the twentieth century, with the support and sanction of United States churches, these policies resulting in the military conquest and virtual extermination of a race and the appropriation and acquisition of their land had been largely achieved. There was an increase of Christian missionary efforts among Native Americans during this period, intended partly to provide protection and care for the native peoples. More often these efforts ended up assisting the conquerors. Repeatedly, the encouragement for Indians to convert to Christianity, accompanied with the promise of better treatment and better reservation land, became instead another weapon for their defeat by the United States military.

Many denominations assisted the United States government in coercing American Indians onto reservations and creating Native American boarding schools in order to "civilize" them. This enterprise was subtler than military annihilation but it was equally destructive of life. Native American children forced to leave their families experienced intentional cultural genocide under the guise of education. The explicitly stated goal of stripping them of home, family, language, customs, and culture was to "get the Indian out of the Indian" in order to create a second-class white person. The tearful apologies of church leaders in Canada and the United States today for these mission schools and the payments of reparations churches have been ordered to pay by the courts does not begin to atone for the misrepresentation of the authority of the gospel in the sinful participation of the church in the systematic destruction and genocidal annihilation of Native American peoples.[9]

Other Races and Manifest Destiny, also in God's Name

There were many other race-based decisions and actions carried out in the name of God in the hundred years from the 1860s to the 1960s, as the United States continued to grow and develop as a nation. New "races"—Latino/Hispanic and Asian American—were created. The purpose of furthering racial categorization was to continue building a hierarchical structure of racial dominance with the white race at the top. It is not within the purview of this book to trace these events in detail, but I cannot stress enough that "divine providence" continued to be used to defend these expressions of racial oppression and the extent to which the churches conformed to them.

In addition, the "divinely inspired" doctrine of Manifest Destiny carried principles of white supremacy into international expansion and dominance, leading to United States acquisition of 55 percent of Mexico, Alaska, Puerto Rico, the Virgin Islands, Cuba, the Philippines, Guam, Panama, and Hawaii, and formalizing the political assumption that every part of North, Central, and South America are legitimate targets of United States economic and military interests. The following quote from Senator H. V. Johnson, a United States senator in 1847, is representative of much of the political and religious thinking of the day.

> I believe we should be recreant to our noble mission, if we refused acquiescence in the high purposes of a wise Providence. War has its evils. In all ages it has been the minister of wholesale death and appalling desolation; but however inscrutable to us, it has also been made, by the Allwise Dispenser of events, the instrumentality of accomplishing the great end of human elevation and human happiness. . . . It is in this view, that I subscribe to the doctrine of "manifest destiny."[10]

The stories could and should go on. They are restricted only by space and time. But I hope I have made the point that until the civil rights movement succeeded in convincing the majority of churches and United States citizens to change their position and affirm the fundamental principles of racial equality, our nation and our churches were not at all embarrassed to claim the status of white superiority and its accompanying rewards. In fact, they were proud to do so. The warning that "those who do not remember history are bound to repeat it" applies especially to the danger we face if we fail to finish the struggle against that which now embarrasses us so much. For, as we shall see, even the accomplishments of the civil rights movement were not enough; in many ways, they created new ways for white dominance to continue with ecclesiastical support.

Uncovering Your Own Church's History

Regardless of whether your denomination came to these shores as an immigrant church or was born and bred in the United States, at some place along the path to the present, your church joined other churches in participating in racism. I encourage you to research your denominational history to see how your denomination fits into the history presented in this chapter. Your contribution will lead to very practical considerations and conclusions when we eventually reach the point of planning present-day action to combat racism. Following are some questions to guide your research.

1. Who were your forefathers and foremothers in your denomination?
2. How did they bring your church into the evolving history of this country?
3. In what ways did your denomination participate in the history of racism and help give birth to the problems of the present day?
4. How did your denomination explain or defend its racist beliefs and actions?
5. How did your denomination deal with those who attempted to resist racism or to correct its shameful consequences?

Chapter four

Resisting Racism
in United States Church History

As they go through the Bitter Valley,
they make it a place of springs.[1]

—PSALM 84:6

It cannot be said often enough or emphasized strongly enough that the evil of racism in our nation and in our churches is only half of the story. There is another story, a far better story to be told. It is the incredibly courageous and powerful story of the struggle to end racism.

Throughout history there have been those with profound courage who were willing to stand up publicly and struggle against racism. From the very beginning, church people have joined together with non-church people in this powerful resistance. The amazing truth is that there was, there is, and there will continue to be an anti-racist church that stands for racial justice. Painfully uncomfortable as it may be, it is important to remember the public stance of white supremacy on the part of the triumphalistic Ruler's Church. But it is at least equally important to celebrate the resistance and struggle of the People's Church that rose again and again to cry out for justice and freedom for all people.

In every period of history, there are stories about heroes and heroines from every walk of life and every race and class; there are electrifying victories that mark the steady beat of strides toward freedom. We have now arrived at the point in this writing where these stories can be told. Instead of encountering the Bible and the Christian faith distorted to serve the purposes of evil, we meet an anti-racist gospel proclaimed by those who throughout history have reclaimed the liberating truth that we are all sisters and brothers in God's family, and who have dedicated their lives to bringing this truth to life. Because of their arduous and painful struggle, we are able today to pick up the mantle and carry the struggle against racism further along the path. This is the amazing story of the anti-racist church. In our learning about this heroic church of the past, we will find models for our becoming an anti-racist church in the twenty-first century.

The Anti-Racist Church

As I described earlier, the People's Church and the Ruler's Church arrived in the new world at the same time, sailing on the same immigrant ships but in very different accommodations; the representatives of the Ruler's Church in first class, members of the People's Church—indentured servants and slaves—in steerage. When they disembarked on America's colonial shores, the two churches maintained their separate and unique identities, with the People's Church evolving, as one might expect, with a less assuming and far more modest presence than the Ruler's Church. From its campfire meetings, its ramshackle churches, and its secret gatherings of slaves came the plaintive cry of spirituals and gospel music: "Swing low, sweet chariot, comin' for to carry me home!" As the songs of the People's Church pleaded for relief from pain, suffering, and powerlessness, so its prayers were cries for protection and release.

There was a great deal of difference between the music of the People's Church and the organ-accompanied hymns sung in the sacred sanctuaries of the Ruler's Church. The sermons preached in these churches were also different. In counterpoint to the triumphal message of the Ruler's Church, the People's Church preached the theology of the cross that gave millions of exploited and oppressed people the strength to survive, to keep hope, and to fight for their liberation.

The People's Church had no formal political power. It did not seek nor seldom received public recognition. Nevertheless, at times its voice, filled with prophetic anger, was powerful and clearly heard demanding justice for the oppressed. Some of the most courageous and brilliant leaders in the struggle for racial justice were raised within the People's Church: Harriet Tubman, Sojourner Truth, W. E. B. Dubois, Dr. Martin Luther King Jr., and many thousands of others. They are the "great cloud of witnesses" who surround us still and call us to join them in shaping an anti-racist church. Their campaigns for freedom were opposed by other Christians, rejected by the Ruler's Church, and attacked by the highest offices of the land. But their strength and determination gave witness to the power of the truth, even while the official Christian message was twisted and confused by others who claimed to be truth's legitimate guardians.

More exactly, where could one find the People's Church in this story of racism and resistance to racism? Where was this body of people who stood with the oppressed and proclaimed their liberation? Where could its voice be heard? The answer is three-fold:

1. *The African American Church.* The most important and most powerful voice against racism came from the oppressed themselves.

2. *The Abolitionist Churches.* The second voice came from the small body of white denominations that stood squarely against slavery.
3. *Dissent within Proslavery Churches.* The third voice emerged from movements of dissent within white mainline Protestant and Roman Catholic churches.

As we take a brief look at these three expressions of the anti-racist church during three particular times in history, I encourage you to continue to search for your predecessors in the churches of your ancestors. For, just as surely as each of us is embarrassed by our inheritance from those who supported the evil of the past, it is certain too that the blood of heroes and heroines who resisted racism is running in our veins.

The Anti-Racist Church Resists Slavery

Stony the road we trod,
Bitter the chast'ning rod,
Felt in the days when hope unborn had died;
Yet with a steady beat,
Have not our weary feet,
Come to the place for which our fathers sighed?[2]

The African American Church

The African American church was once called the Negro church, then the Black church, and more recently the African American church. Now the title Church of African Descent is gaining in popularity. It also has many denominational names, including a number of derivatives of Methodism, among them African Methodist Episcopal (AME and AME Zion) and Christian Methodist Episcopal (CME). There are varieties of Baptists: National Baptists, Progressive Baptists, and just plain Baptists. And there are innumerable forms of Pentecostal and non-denominational churches, contributing to far more than a hundred thousand congregations, large and small, worshipping in cathedral-like buildings and in storefronts on poor ghetto streets. The African American church was born around slave campfires where Christianity met and married African religion and culture, and it arguably bears the truest and clearest expression of undiluted, justice-centered biblical gospel. It shares a common faith with Christians of every race and nation, and yet it has a unique identity and culture that sets it apart from all others. Throughout the history of the United States, the African American church has been the source of spiritual life and the center of community for African American people.

Other denominations of color—Native American churches, Latino/Hispanic churches, Asian American churches, and Arab American churches—have also participated in very powerful ways in resisting racism. And other religious faiths, especially Jews and Muslims, have been and are still deeply engaged in working for racial justice in the United States. A sizable number—albeit almost always in the minority—of white members of historically white denominations have also provided powerful witness to the anti-racist at the center of the Christian message. To understand the history of religious resistance to racism in the United States, we must recognize the contributions of these.

Nonetheless, the primary leadership of church-based resistance to racism has always come from the African American church. It stood opposite the Ruler's Church, strongly challenging its pervasive support of racism. The African American church gave its members solace in suffering and strength to survive the punishing power of slavery's onslaught. And it provided centuries of leadership in the struggle to bring an end to slavery, and following emancipation in the continuing march toward freedom. Above all, the African American church played then, as now, a crucial role in preserving the theological understanding of God's option for the poor and of Christianity's central purpose of redemption and liberation of the broken and oppressed.

The African American church came into being at the very same time the system of slavery was introduced into the American colonies. White slave masters taught slaves a twisted and distorted version of the Bible as part of their strategy of dehumanization and pacification. They misinterpreted and distorted scriptural passages, such as the one from Paul's letter to Titus that says slaves should obey their masters. They supported theological perspectives that encourage submission and obedience as a virtue. And they portrayed the biblical church as a white church with a white God who favors white people as a superior race.

But enslaved Africans were far more intelligent than their masters imagined. They saw through the thinly veiled misrepresentations of Scripture. They read other passages from Paul's letters that spoke of freedom, not slavery. They paged back from Paul to the liberating message of Jesus and further still to the Old Testament story of the Hebrew people being set free from bondage of Egypt. The African American church reclaimed these stolen sacred stories of freedom and transformed the oppressor's religion back into the story of justice and righteousness, of God's identification with the poor and oppressed, and of the liberation of the people of God. The African American church proclaimed hope in an anti-racist gospel, helped create a way for slaves to survive, and, ultimately, contributed significantly to shaping the path to resistance and freedom.

From the very beginning, the African American church produced a powerful movement for survival and liberation. The early church usually met in secret, in gatherings that doubled as enclaves for planning how to survive and plotting how to escape. In the late 1700s and early 1800s, freed slaves in the North began to organize independent black denominations and anti-slavery societies, most often in response to offensive and oppressive behavior of white churches. For example, Absalom Jones and Richard Allen organized the Free African Society after experiencing racist treatment by leaders of a white Methodist congregation in Philadelphia in 1787 and, in 1816, founded the African Methodist Episcopal Church. Other denominations such as the Christian Methodist Episcopal Church, various expressions of the Baptist church, and other historic African American churches came into being in similar ways before and after emancipation.

The African American church had and still has an innate understanding of the gospel of freedom, an understanding that God has always been on the side of slaves, leading them in their struggle for freedom. While there are many complex stages in the historic struggle for emancipation, the People's Church was at the center of this accomplishment, persistently crying out for freedom while the voice of the Ruler's Church provided unyielding support for slavery.

The Abolitionist Churches: Quakers and Mennonites

Although the African American Church was at the center of resistance to slavery, it is impossible to understand the path toward emancipation without being aware of the role played by the many white Christians who helped to shape the abolition movement. For the most part, these were individuals or small groups of white Christians who did not represent the majority or the official position of their white denominations. There were, however, two very important exceptions. The Quakers and Mennonites, historic "peace" churches, stood almost alone during the entire time of slavery as white denominations who professed with near unanimous voice that slavery and slaveholding are incompatible with the Christian faith.

These abolitionist churches were greatly influenced by the oppression they experienced in Europe because of their Anabaptist beliefs. The personal and painful experiences they brought with them to the American colonies quickly translated into a strong and unwavering opposition to slavery. The first formal white protest against slavery in the American colonies was a document signed by Mennonites and Quakers in Germantown Pennsylvania in 1688. A few years later, in the early 1700s, the Quakers officially assumed a strong anti-slavery position.[3]

After the American War of Independence, Quakers and Mennonites founded the first anti-slavery society in the United States: the Pennsylvania Society for Promoting the Abolition of Slavery. Soon other national, regional, and state anti-slavery societies were organized. These attracted Christians from other denominations who were dissatisfied with the stance their churches had on slavery. Quakers and Mennonites were predominate in these societies, but membership also included significant numbers of Methodists, Presbyterians, Congregationalists, and Unitarians, whose own denominations continued to be ambivalent about the slavery question. Until just a few decades before emancipation, no denominations except Quakers and Mennonites were prepared to formally identify and act consistently with such unpopular activities. Although anti-slavery societies were independent organizations and not official churches, they became virtual abolitionist denominations.

Dissent within Proslavery Churches

The third voice of the People's Church speaking in opposition to slavery came from small but powerful minority groups within major proslavery denominations, the very churches whose influence in society provided sanction and support for African slavery and Indian oppression. The theology of triumphalism, characterized by a holy nationalism, was not the only point of view expressed within "proslavery" denominations. The theology of the cross that identified with the weak and powerless was doggedly proclaimed by small but powerful anti-slavery groups who courageously identified with the idea of a People's Church while still remaining loyal to their denominations. These dissenting members brought the voice of anti-slavery societies and other independent anti-racist Christian organizations inside their denominations. This minority presence espousing a People's Church theology continually challenged the denominations' stands on slavery and other forms of racism. It was a sign of their strength that these factions occasionally forced churches to make official statements acknowledging that the nation should work slowly to end slavery or encouraging church members not to own slaves.

As the march toward the Civil War inexorably progressed and the tensions that divided the nation between North and South and between slave states and free states grew, churches also split into pro-slavery and anti-slavery factions, some even splintering into Northern and Southern denominations. The new Northern divisions produced strong anti-slavery positions. As important as these anti-slavery positions were in contributing to the growing sentiments that would bring slavery to an end, for the most part these northern churches did not believe in equality, nor were they willing to adopt internal practices that demonstrated acceptance of African Americans on an equal basis.

> . . . [abolitionist] agitation helped bring about sectional schisms in the Methodist and Baptist churches in the mid-1840s and the New School Presbyterians in 1857. Even after those divisions, however, abolitionists protested that the Northern church branches tolerated thousands of border state slave owners in their fellowship. . . . Despite noteworthy gains during the 1850s, undiluted abolitionism remained a minority viewpoint in the Northern churches, and few blacks received equal treatment in Northern religious bodies.[4]

Anti-Slavery Stories in Every Denomination

Every present-day denomination descended from United States colonial times has a unique anti-slavery story waiting to be discovered or remembered. Hopefully, readers will be inspired to research their own church's history. Some are relatively easy to trace. African American denominations can find in written records as well as oral traditions and music a vivid memory of the blending of African religion and Christian gospel that produced a powerful movement for survival and freedom, resulting later in a variety of African American denominations. Other denominations of color, such as the Native American church and various expressions of Latin/Hispanic and Asian American churches, can follow streams of history in oral and written forms that record their early origins and their survival in the midst of racist oppression.

On the other hand, finding such stories in historically white churches is more difficult. Nonetheless, it is easier to find records of white resistance *to* racism than it is to find records *of* racism, because churches tend to cover up and even destroy such shameful records. It is particularly gratifying to find stories reflecting proud moments, when white women and men courageously stood against an overwhelming majority and confessed a creed of freedom and anti-racism.

To encourage you to research your denomination's pre-Civil War history of resistance to racism, I offer an example from my own Lutheran tradition. On the whole, Lutherans were not strong anti-slavery advocates, nor did they champion the cause of free blacks in the North or the South. So it was rewarding for me to discover the story of the Frankean Synod in upper New York state (*synod* is a Lutheran word for "district" or "diocese"). In 1838, the president of the Frankean Synod, confronting the "apathy of Christians and the silence of ministers of [the] gospel," rallied members to "rebuke the sin of slavery." The synod unanimously passed a resolution stating "that we conceive it to be our imperative duty to speak boldly and plainly against this great national and heinous sin [of slavery]."[5] For congregations to continue membership in the Frankean Synod, they had to agree to this radical abolitionist stance that declared moral war against slavery.

The Anti-Racist Church from Emancipation to the Civil Rights Movement

Free at last! Free at last! Thank God Almighty, we are free at last![6]

It was a shout for joy, a hymn of praise, and a statement of victory. There were grounds for great celebration at the conclusion of the Civil War when slaves were freed, and even more so over the next five years, from 1865 to 1870, when the prohibition of slavery was constitutionalized by the Thirteenth Amendment and further clarified and guaranteed by the Fourteenth and Fifteenth Amendments. Years of resistance by slaves and by their allies had gotten them the victory.

Resurgent Racism and New Resistance

It was a short-lived celebration. Slavery may have ended, but racism in the United States took on new forms and continued stronger than ever. After a brief period of Reconstruction, segregation and economic imprisonment replaced slavery as the means of control over blacks by the white society. The African American community in the north and in the south, with far fewer white allies than during slavery, was left to fend for itself against this new onslaught.

Racist oppression against other peoples of color also intensified. Extermination of Native American peoples and expropriation of their lands continued without interruption as the United States frontier spread to the Pacific Ocean. Survivors were forced onto reservations. During these next decades, America's racism became more deeply entrenched. White supremacy reached its fullest expression, and systems of racist oppression came to include complex legal and cultural controls of Hispanic/Latino and Asian American peoples as well.

With little respite from the years of struggle against genocide and slavery, a new period of resistance was called into being. In the nearly one hundred years that followed emancipation, by force of necessity and by miracle of divine and human spirit, the powerful struggle of peoples of color against racism grew even stronger. In the interest of survival, the need to resist racism was felt increasingly in the north and the south, in rural areas and cities, on Indian reservations, in the southwest on land taken from Mexico, in Puerto Rico, Cuba, and rapidly growing Asian American communities. The more oppressive the system of white racism became, the stronger the resistance and the more powerful the response of various communities of color. The scene was now set for the century-long path leading to the civil rights movement.

On the surface, there didn't seem to be much happening in the resistance against racism in the century from the 1860s to the 1950s. But below the surface, there was an enormous amount of organizing and activity, although for the most part it was visible only to those most deeply involved in the struggle. It is impossible to understand the seemingly sudden explosion of the civil rights movement and the other movements of the 1950s and 1960s, without an awareness of this underground preparation during decades before.

Once Again the African American Church Leads the Way

What was happening in the churches during the century following the Civil War contributed significantly to the advancement toward the civil rights revolution. Just as in the struggle against slavery, the African American church was at the center of new efforts to survive and resist. Responding to segregation and rejection by white churches, African American denominations grew exponentially during this time. The African Methodist Episcopal (AME and AME Zion) expanded into the South, where their presence had not been welcome prior to the end of slavery. Then, in 1870, the southern-based Colored Methodist Episcopal Church (CME, now named Christian Methodist Episcopal) was founded. The National Baptist Convention was established in 1894. As racial segregation became the norm in many states, these churches not only resisted, but provided leadership, encouraged education and economic growth, and were often the primary link between the African American and white communities. During this time, African American church leaders were also deeply involved in the founding of many African American colleges and universities, as well as other institutions and organizations that became the backbone of the African American community and contributed to the infrastructure for survival.

With the Supreme Court decision *Plessey* v. *Fergusson* in 1896 affirming the legality of segregation, an official apartheid system was ushered into the United States. The organizing that followed in African American churches and the wider African American community was truly amazing in its power and accomplishments, carving an ever widening and deepening path that led inexorably to the civil rights movement. As the African American community, with churches leading the way, assumed a larger identity and greater strength, the ability and resolve to challenge white racism also increased. It was only a matter of time before a strong and determined people who would no longer tolerate second-class citizenship would come face to face with the facade of white superiority and the structure of white domination.

Other Churches of Color: Increasing Resistance to Racism

During this era in United States history, new denominations of color other than African American began to be organized. These were identified specifically on the basis of racial and ethnic identity, and included, for example, Korean-American, Japanese-American, and Chinese-American denominations. The number of Latino/Hispanic members in the Roman Catholic Church expanded greatly during this time, and a number of Protestant Latino/Hispanic denominations also came into being.

Economic oppression and other forms of racial discrimination against Asian Americans and Latinos/Hispanics escalated during these years. While the new churches had little public involvement in resisting racism, they increasingly focused on ministries to help members deal with social needs and to provide spiritual strength to help their members to survive the experience of prejudice and discrimination. Through these activities the foundations were laid upon which anti-racist movements within these race-based churches would be built in decades to come.

White Churches after Emancipation

With the end of slavery, most white denominations quickly retreated to old positions, joining the rest of the white society in supporting and practicing segregation. Both in the North and South, they demonstrated clearly in word and deed that despite their belated opposition to slavery, they were not interested in true equality between whites and African Americans. The tragic truth is that the white churches' slowness in coming to support the end of slavery was matched only by the speed of their early departure from the dwindling ranks of those in support of equality for ex-slaves after the Civil War had ended. Segregation was practiced just as strongly in most white churches as in the larger society.

However, there were very important positive developments within white denominations at this time. These did not have an immediate effect or direct relationship to racial matters, but they provided a foundation and a framework for what would later bring about significant changes with regard to race and racism. The first of these was the social gospel movement, and the second was the ecumenical movement.

The Social Gospel Movement

In the late nineteenth and early twentieth centuries in Europe and the United States, a growing awareness and concern emerged in white churches for economically and socially disenfranchised people in their own white communities, especially children. It became known as the "social gospel movement." Many churches began to redefine their mission as not only preparing souls for the next world, but also caring about conditions of people's lives in this world. White Christians became increasingly concerned with social problems such as poverty, inequality, crime, slums, hygiene, and schools. The social gospel movement also profoundly influenced the development of secular institutions focused on social welfare and issues of social concern. Virtually all modern laws and social institutions designed to protect the most vulnerable and defenseless people from the destructive effects of society can trace their beginnings to the time of the social gospel movement.

Initially, the social gospel movement was just another segregated phenomenon in which white denominations focused newfound commitment to charity and justice on the needs of white people. Eventually, however, it had significant, if unintentional, effects on racial issues and on the struggle against racism. First, many of the demands of the civil rights movement, as well as much of its underlying ideology, sought equal application of the benefits of the social gospel to people of color. Second, following the civil rights movement, white churches and other social welfare institutions within the white society began to apply the principles of the social gospel toward communities of color. Third, many other movements for justice during the past fifty years, including anti-war organizing, liberation theology, and liberation movements in other countries were deeply influenced by the social gospel.

The Ecumenical Movement

In the early years of the twentieth century, the ecumenical movement came into being in an effort to reverse the direction of an increasingly divided denominationalism. Christian churches began to re-approach each other with a desire for unity, giving birth to the World Council of Churches and a large number of national councils of churches. The ecumenical movement was greatly influenced by the social gospel movement, and increasingly addressed issues of suffering and need, as well as social injustices in society.

The Federal Council of Churches, organized in 1905, and its successor, the National Council of Churches in the USA, created in 1950, provided the central impetus for the ecumenical movement in the United States. The National Council of Churches played a very important role in the civil rights movement, offering a setting for voices of dissent against segregation to be heard and to organize for action.

In the years following the civil rights movement, the theme of ecumenicity turned slowly toward the reuniting of racially divided churches, and the remerging of denominations that were separated on a North-South divide before the Civil War. Given the continuing reality of our segregated sanctuaries, it is still a task only barely begun.

The Anti-Racist Church and the Civil Rights Movement

The moral arc of the universe is long, but it bends toward justice.
—Theodore Parker, quoted by Dr. Martin Luther King Jr.

When the civil rights movement took place during the decades of the 1950s and 1960s, a long burning fuse reached the point of detonation and nothing could stop the ensuing revolutionary explosion. It is impossible to understate the importance and the effects of what was accomplished within this nation and within its churches as a result of the civil rights movement. Not only were the laws of segregation and apartheid ended, more importantly the American way of life was permanently transformed and changed. Even though we are now viewing these accomplishments from the perspective of nearly half a century later, and realizing how much needs yet to be done, nevertheless it is important to pause for a moment to evaluate the great achievements of that decade. This great step forward was nothing less than the fulfillment of what should have been the original intentions of our nation's founders.

The African American Church Again at the Front

We need to recognize and celebrate how much of the leadership of the civil rights movement came from the church. There have been few times in history when the church provided such strong direction in moving a nation toward justice. Once again, it was the African American Church with its courageous organizers and eloquent leaders unswervingly dedicated to a worldview of justice and equality and to a hope that would not die who provided the movement's impetus and direction. Their church buildings became sanctuaries and organizing centers.

Their ministers became leaders, organizers, and advocates on the frontlines, where they lead marches, went to jail, and even died. While ministers were leading the Southern Christian Leadership Conference (SCLC), their teenage sons and daughters were helping to shape and strengthen the Student Nonviolent Coordinating Committee (SNCC) and the Congress of Racial Equality (CORE). Their young children were going directly from Sunday school to the frontlines of the movement, joining and even leading their elders by modeling their willingness to stand courageously for freedom.

Of course, the church did not act alone. Many groups shared leadership of the complex movement. People from all walks of life joined the mass demonstrations, suffered painful beatings, went to jail, and paid the ultimate price in losing their lives. But the presence of the African American church and its leaders was visible everywhere, and the victories could not have been won without them. Nor could they have been won, Martin Luther King Jr. repeatedly reminded the demonstrators, without the strength and presence of God. "The universe is on the side of justice. It says to those who struggle for justice, 'You do not struggle alone, but God struggles with you.'"[7]

A Presence of Individual White Christians

There were also a large number of white people who participated courageously in the civil rights movement. Many were Christians from predominantly white denominations who, in a pattern not unlike the anti-slavery movement more than a century earlier, stood strongly against the racist convictions and actions of their fellow white Christians. It is important to note that for the most part, they acted as individuals and seldom officially represented their denominations. Especially in the early years of the movement, prior to 1968, most white denominations took particular care not to be identified with the movement. Not only did they join the nation's political leaders in vacillation and indecision, they were also extremely reluctant to confront their own internal policies and practices of segregation.

At least two important exceptions need to be mentioned. The first is the National Council of Churches (NCC), which stood strongly from the very beginning with African American church leaders, organizing and advocating for change. Throughout the years of the movement, the presence of the NCC made a significant spiritual and political contribution. With its leaders visibly present at significant public moments such as the March on Washington, and with a network of advocates and organizers in the cities and countryside of the north and south as the struggles for rights took place, the NCC provided a strong witness in the name of the Christian church, even when the churches they supposedly represented were not prepared to do so.

The second exception is the Unitarian Universalist Association of Congregations (UUA). Already committed to racial justice as part of their foundational beliefs, the UUA national board of trustees was in session in March 1965 when Dr. Martin Luther King Jr. and the leaders of the Selma to Montgomery march issued a call for clergy and other church members from across the country to join them. The Board of Trustees voted as a body to go to Selma and represent their denomination on the march. It was on that march that Rev. James Reeb, a UUA minister, was killed, offering to the world a witness of a white person willing to die in the struggle against racism.[8]

The White Church Comes on Board

It was not until tragedy struck with the assassination of Dr. Martin Luther King Jr. on April 4, 1968, that the rest of the white mainline churches came on board and began to have more than a borderline presence in the movement. The shot that rang out in Memphis on that day still ricochets back and forth across the nation, echoing inside all of us. Fourteen years after the *Brown* v. *Board of Education* decision by the United States Supreme Court that mandated desegregation of schools, white churches were finally willing to follow the leadership of the African American church. Moved by the seismic effects of King's horrendous assassination, the doors of the mainline churches were finally shaken open, and most publicly declared themselves to be committed to the civil rights movement. These actions were too late to have a major effect on the direction of the movement itself (the most important civil rights legislation had already been passed, and the civil rights movement and other movements were already showing signs of involuntarily being forced to end), but the most important effect was on the churches themselves. In grief, guilt, and repentance, white churches became more open and invitational, as they began to use their own theological language of "inclusive community" in ways that had never been done before.

The Churches and the Other Movements

The civil rights movement was not one, but many movements. It represented the aspirations and struggles of all people of color in the United States: African Americans, Native Americans, Latinos/Hispanics, Asian Americans, and Arab Americans. Christian individuals, congregations, and, at times, entire denominations, were involved in these movements, sometimes positively, sometimes negatively. For example:

The Church and the Farm Worker Movement

The United Farmer Workers of America (UFW) was a union organized in 1962 to represent the agricultural laborers of the United States. Cesar Chavez was the UFW's top organizer and inspirational leader. Chavez was a Roman Catholic whose understanding of the difficulties of farm workers and their aspirations for justice was informed directly by the teaching of the Roman Catholic Church. The union publicly adopted the principles of non-violence championed by Mahatma Gandhi and Dr. Martin Luther King Jr. Large numbers of priests, ministers, and laity from Roman Catholic and Protestant churches participated in the strikes, demonstrations, and other aspects of the work of the UFW. Still today, farm worker ministries continue in many denominations, and within most denominations there is a mix of support for and opposition to immigration justice and protection of immigrants' rights.

The Church and the American Indian Movement

The American Indian Movement (AIM), an Indian activist organization in the United States, was founded in 1968. AIM's dramatic actions in the struggle for Native American rights included occupying Alcatraz Island in San Francisco for eighteen months from 1969 to 1971, seizing and occupying the Bureau of Indian Affairs headquarters in Washington, D.C., in 1972, and a standoff at Wounded Knee, South Dakota, on the Pine Ridge Indian Reservation in 1973. During the height of AIM activity in the 1960s and 1970s, there was significant presence and assistance by many individuals from the churches. However, the Christian churches generally did not support the work and aspirations of AIM.

Concluding Comments

In the previous chapter we took a close and painful look at how the Christian church and Christian individuals have supported racism. In this chapter we learned the other side of the story, the history of the church's participation in resisting racism. From the time of Columbus through the civil rights era, the church participated in struggles for racial justice. More often than not, it was the African American church and other churches of color that were the leaders in these efforts. But oftentimes, individual white Christians and white churches followed their lead, even if with reluctance. Clearly, after the conclusion of the civil rights movement, there was still work to be done for the church to move toward becoming a truly anti-racist church. The focus of the chapters ahead is on identifying what has been done, uncovering what remains to be done, and equipping the church today for the task.

Completing the Story: Heroes and Heroines in Your Denomination.

The final step in this summary of 500 years of resistance to racism belongs to the reader. Your task is to research how your denomination participated in struggles for racial justice during the past five hundred years. I especially encourage you to seek out stories of individual heroes and heroines in your denomination. You can learn much about this history from the official positions and actions of your church, but stories about Christian individuals are important in putting flesh on the bones of your historical account. I hope you will find the time and energy to do the research, and to bring to life the role of your church in this history.

If you are from a denomination of color, your research should be aimed not only to reveal the painful experience and effects of racism on the life of your church, but also the contributions it made to the long journey of resistance. Many of your heroes and heroines may be already well-known public figures. But there are also very many who have made enormous contributions to the struggle, and yet whose names have never been lifted up beyond local recognition.

If you are from one of the predominantly white mainline Protestant or Roman Catholic denominations, your research will be more difficult and complex. You will need to dig deep in your history to discover the stories of dissent from within. It is important to lift up the names of white heroes and heroines who resisted the racism of the church and society throughout history. When we dig into the white church's memories, we find examples such as these:

- In 1930, Jessie Daniel Ames, a white Methodist laywoman from Texas, recruited 40,000 Southerners to be part of a movement to end lynching.[9]
- Individuals and congregations from various white denominations in California supported Japanese Americans sent by the United States government to concentration camps. They looked after their homes and property, took care of their legal affairs, sent badly needed supplies, wrote letters of recommendation and encouragement, and defended them as loyal and patriotic Americans.[10]
- In the 1960s, many priests and nuns from the Roman Catholic Church took part in civil rights marches and in organizing farm workers throughout the country.
- Jonathan Daniels, an Episcopal seminarian, sacrificed his life when he was murdered while participating in a voter registration drive in Alabama in 1965.
- Paul Boe, a Lutheran pastor who participated in the American Indian Movement occupation of Wounded Knee in 1971, chose to go to jail rather than testify in federal judicial proceedings against AIM.

Who were the abolitionists in your church during the time of slavery? Can you find the names of persons during the late nineteenth and early twentieth century who said no to segregation, no to discrimination against Native Americans, African Americans, Latinos/Hispanics, Asian Americans, or Arab Americans? Who were the activists from your denomination who defied the authorities of both church and society, and participated in the marches and demonstrations of the 1960s?

And the list of heroes and heroines will go on and on, as within each denomination, readers discover they are "surrounded by a cloud of witnesses" whose lives call us to continue where they left off.

chapter five

Racism and Resisting Racism
in the Post–Civil Rights Church

*So you also must consider yourselves dead to sin
and alive to God in Christ Jesus.*

—ROMANS 6:11

We move now to the final step in this historical recounting of racism and resisting racism within the church, with an exploration of what happened after the civil rights movement, from the early 1970s up to today. The period began with a sense of optimism about the end of racial hatred and division and the beginning of a new future of togetherness. There was hope that churches divided by the history of racism could find together a new sense of oneness and unity. In these next pages, history and present meet and our faces begin to appear in the story as we explore how much still remains to be accomplished for these hopes to be realized. Only as we comprehend the degree to which racism has been overcome and the degree to which racism is still present in our churches today will we be able to devise new ways to continue to oppose and dismantle racism.

Decades of Change and No Change

Progress has been made. There is no question that many dramatic and positive changes have taken place in society as a whole as well as in our churches since the legalized system of segregation in the United States was ended and new civil rights legislation was passed. In the places where we live, shop, play, and pray, walls that segregated people of one race and color from another have fallen. Laws that guarantee civil and human rights for all people have been written. From the schoolhouse to the White House, doors of opportunity have been opened.

Multicultural diversity and inclusiveness have been placed on the top ten priority list in virtually every institution in our country. Step by step and decade by decade, we have advanced on the path toward racial equality. What positive changes do you see in race relations and racial justice in our country since the 1960s? Where do you see the absence of progress, or even setbacks?

> *What positive changes do you see in race relations and racial justice in our country since the 1960s? Where do you see the absence of progress?*

The ugly truth, however, is that racism is still with us and we need to identify where. In our faltering steps, progress has been impeded time and again. Despite our nation's new path toward openness and diversity, regular eruptions of racial crises testify to the fact that rather than an orderly step-by-step path to racial justice and reconciliation, we have traveled a bumpy road of jumps and starts, of one step forward and two steps back. It seems at times that there has been no change at all and that we are moving in the opposite direction of our goal. Every day the news media carries stories of tragedy, violence, pain, and anger caused by issues of race and racism, reminding us that racism has not gone away.

Statistics illuminate this reality even more clearly: in virtually every measurable area of life, the gap between white society and people of color has changed very little. Comparative measurements of employment, education, health care, social services, and housing reveal continuing racial disproportionality and disparity. Residential segregation has increased rather than decreased, despite token integration of many white communities. The intersection of poverty and racism still leaves a far greater percentage of people of color with lower incomes than white people.[1]

While our nation remains severely divided by race, racism has taken on new forms; it is today more disguised and subtle than in earlier times, making the path toward change more difficult. Like climbing Mount Everest, the first part of the journey is easier and more gradual than closer to the top, where the steeper and more difficult slopes make the climb much more dangerous.

How Much Has Changed in Our Churches?

Likewise in our churches, there have been both positive changes and setbacks. Depending on your age, your personal memories may reach back only a few years or more than a few decades, but it is important to realize that in the years since the end of the civil rights movement, much has been happening in our churches to counteract the racism of the past. Most denominations have worked diligently to create a new self-identity, reflecting openness and welcoming for all people. Programs have been developed on national, regional, and local levels to improve race relations. Nearly every denomination has created intentional programs to build multicultural diversity and inclusiveness. All of these programs are aimed toward the hope of ultimately coming to a place of racial reconciliation and equality. What positive changes do you see in race relations and racial justice in our churches since the 1960s? Where do you see the absence of progress, or even setbacks?

However, just as in the rest of society, the question must be asked how much has really changed? To what extent are we reaching these lofty goals? It is not enough to simply have these programs in operation; the critical question is, how effective have they been? Whatever the number of official programs that exist on a denomination-wide level, the bottom line question is to what extent have efforts to deal with the continuing problem of racial division and inequality accomplished what we have set out to do?

> *Since the 1960s, what positive changes do you see in race relations and racial justice in our churches? Where do you see setbacks?*

Not only do we need to ask these questions within the national administrative offices of our denominations, but hard questions need to be asked also within our local parishes and congregations. How many sermons are being preached, how many educational classes are being taught, how many other programs and activities have been put into practice on a congregational level that focus on the continuing task of understanding and dismantling racism? Most importantly, how effective are we in reaching out to serve all the people in our neighborhoods and community?

In this chapter, as we trace the path and measure the progress toward change in our churches over nearly five decades, it will become clear that racism in our churches has not yet gone away. In fact, the most difficult part of the journey remains before us. There have been many accomplishments, but despite efforts extended and lives expended, despite changes in understanding and commitment, despite decades of efforts toward diversity and inclusiveness, the power hold of racism is still in place.

Are We Prepared to Accept the Death of Racism?

We need to be honest. For nearly 500 years mainline Protestant and Roman Catholic churches in the United States existed exclusively to serve the needs of white Christians. Consequently, facing a "new" commandment to serve everyone with equity regardless of racial identity has been difficult and traumatic. We have been asked to make dramatic changes in the way we look at ourselves, our beliefs, and our world. In a very real way, this is akin to an old way of life dying in order for new life to be born. This image is familiar to us from a theological perspective—our faith and our baptism call us to daily death and resurrection—but from a "real life" standpoint, it is startlingly new and shocking to us.

The fact is that racism must die before a new way of life can come into being. There can be no compromise or coexistence with racism. It is not enough to "reduce racism," to make its effects less harmful. In every part of church and society—individually, institutionally, culturally—racism must be ended completely. For some of us the end of racism will be welcomed immediately with great rejoicing. For others the change will seem strange, even frightening, at least initially. Regardless of our personal feelings, the fact is that the promise of new life, a resurrection of the human spirit, and the possibility of a reconciled society await us on the other side of racism. But are we prepared to accept the death of racism?

We must be clear: racism hasn't died yet. And it is a long way from happening. New life is still struggling to be born amidst the wreckage and debris of racism's onslaught. There is still a great struggle ahead. And in order to participate in that struggle we must become an anti-racist church, committed to working step by step toward the death of racism.

Stages of Grief

Ron Chisom, director of the People's Institute for Survival and Beyond, uses a helpful image to comprehend the trauma that a white person experiences in adjusting to the approaching end of racism and the coming of a new way of life. He compares this adjustment to the stages of grief identified by Elisabeth Kübler-Ross that a person goes through in dealing with the death of a loved one: denial, disbelief, guilt, anger, bargaining, depression, and, finally, the transformative process of acceptance.[2] According to Chisom, white people go through these same stages when faced with the reality of our own racism and the task of giving up the benefits that racism gives us.

1. We deny our racism and reject the idea that racism does anything for us.
2. We get mad at anyone who accuses us of racism.
3. We feel guilty when we realize the truth of our racism.
4. We try bargaining; we say that we will admit to racism if others do and we will give up its benefits if others do.
5. We become depressed, feeling an overwhelming sadness in losing that which racism has given us.
6. We finally accept the reality of racism and the necessity that it must die within us.

Stages of Collective Grief

The way in which Chisom uses these stages of grief to describe individual change in white people can also be used to portray an entire community or institution collectively responding to efforts to end racism. During recent decades, our entire society can be seen as going together through these stages of denial, disbelief, guilt, anger, bargaining, and depression, working to eventually reach a collective transformed stage of acceptance. In the next pages I will apply these stages of grief specifically to the church, as a way of comprehending what has changed in the church and what has not changed and to assess where we are today. What stage do you think our nation is in today? Our churches? How close is each to moving to the next stage?

> *What stage do you think our nation is in today? Our churches? How close is each to moving to the next stage?*

While I believe there is value in tracing this history in this way, I want to be clear that while these stages might apply to a group generally, there are always variations and exceptions. For example, although the end of segregation in the 1960s can be seen generally as a time when our nation and churches moved out of denial of the existence of racism, it is obvious that measurable portions of our population are still stuck in denial and seem determined to never move beyond it.

We also need to take into consideration the role that regression plays in how we move through these stages of grief. For instance, an individual, institution, or parts of society may move from denial to another stage, only to revert back to denial because of some traumatic experience. Regression can take place at any stage in the grief process. It is also the case that persons or groups within a larger body can be at different stages in the process. For example, a denomination or portions of all denominations may have moved on to bargaining, while others remain stuck at guilt or anger. Nevertheless, I believe it is possible to see general movement of our churches through these stages of grief that parallels similar movement in the rest of society.

For purposes of our discussion, I am placing the stages in a slightly different order than originally proposed by Kübler-Ross. The stages of depression and bargaining are reversed, because I believe that this order—denial, guilt, anger, depression, bargaining, and acceptance—is more realistic when considering the interactions of a collective group of people.

The End of Denial—April 4, 1968

It is not unusual for a society to collectively refuse to admit the reality of its own injustices. Denial of the Holocaust in Germany is one clear example. The refusal to admit the wrongness of apartheid in South Africa is another. To understand collective denial of racism or other forms of oppression, we need to comprehend how untruths are internalized within a society. The denial of injustice by an entire people is created and perpetuated by machinery of socialization that is designed to shape the opinions and understandings of society. For hundreds of years, white people in the United States were socialized to believe that they were superior to people of color. It was rare to find a white person who did not wear rose-colored glasses that gave a false perception of the reality of racism. In such a bigoted society, it was a very unusual for individuals to experience a pinprick sufficient to burst the bubble of internalized lies that supported the racist beliefs of socialized racism. When we take up this subject more thoroughly in chapter 8, we will see that the amnesia and anesthesia in a people's common consciousness is not simply a matter of individual failure to pay attention, but a virulent societal affliction that can only be likened to a deadly virus.

Our nation and churches entered into the decades of the 1950s and 1960s in virtually complete denial about racial conditions, tensions, and problems. Until that time, machinery designed to create and guide our national racial consciousness was humming along as planned. The common view of the vast majority of people was that all is well, so long as we are "free, white, and twenty-one," and "those people are kept in their place." Dr. King described our nation as having complete amnesia, noting that it took only a few short days for a story of racial travesty to move from front page headlines, to the newspaper's back page, and then completely out of our collective consciousness.

Given this background, the sudden and nearly universal end of the nation's collective denial about racism in the 1960s was an extremely unusual and unexpected event. Like the fall of the Berlin Wall in 1989 and the end of South African apartheid in 1990, the collapse of racism's underpinnings seemed to happen almost overnight, even though the weakening of its foundations had been developing over a long period of time. For those living in collective denial of racism's inhumanity, realizing that this pretense could no longer be maintained came as a jarring jolt, seemingly without warning. In hindsight, the about-face in our national consciousness seems focused on a single terrifying moment: the assassination of Dr. Martin Luther King Jr. on April 4, 1968. For our churches, perhaps more than any other segment of the stunned and horrified nation, it was a moment when one could almost hear the curtains of denial falling from where we were hiding from the reality of racism in our Sunday morning sanctuaries and in our denominational church administration bureaucracies. King's assassination brought nearly all white denominations on board the civil rights movement, essentially moving them collectively from the stage of denial to the stage of guilt. The aftershocks from that moment are still reverberating in our churches today.

A Decade of Guilt and Anger

Guilt is the second stage of grief. In times of grievous human sinfulness, when the protective coating of long-time denial is removed and a soulful sickness is revealed, guilt is an important step in allowing a process of healing to begin to take place. Guilt can move a person or a people forward toward repentance, reconciliation, and wholeness. But, while guilt can provide an initial motivating thrust forward and is an essential element in the early steps of coming to grips with evil, guilt has little sustaining power. The first collective reaction when exposed to the reality of racism might be momentary paralysis caused by embarrassment over the wickedness uncovered. But guilt must also spur a people to ask: "What must we do about this terrible thing that has been done?" And then to act: "We have to make up for it."

An illustration comes to mind from the experience of my own denomination. By coincidence (some might say by divine providence), the bi-annual convention of the Lutheran Church in America (LCA) was scheduled to take place in Atlanta, Georgia, in August 1968, just four months after Dr. King's assassination. Naturally, convention leaders and delegates had a heightened awareness of the significance of the convention's place and time. In the early and mid-1960s, the LCA had already begun slowly and reluctantly to become aware of the need to speak and act in response to racial turmoil in our nation. In convention in August 1968, this Lutheran denomination moved collectively out of the stage of denying the reality of racism and their complicity in it. Motivated by guilt and repentance, the LCA took dramatic steps to raise consciousness about racism and right a terrible wrong. A program called "Justice and Social Change" was developed and given priority one to be implemented over the next several years. The program aimed to have church councils from every one of the more than six thousand LCA congregations participate in racial awareness workshops. These workshops, led by a national cadre of trainers, were designed to develop new understandings of racial conditions in the United States and of the movement toward racial integration. How was the public and collective consciousness of your denomination transformed by the dramatic events of the civil rights movement, and especially by the assassination of Dr. King?

> How was the public and collective consciousness of your denomination transformed by the dramatic events of the civil rights movement, and especially by the assassination of Dr. King?

I want to emphasize that these initial responses of white denominations, such as the LCA, were motivated primarily by guilt rather than by a clear sense of justice or an understanding of the path to racial reconciliation. Guilt may be effective in motivating people to act at the outset, but it does not promote lasting action, because its focus is primarily inward, not outward. Guilt inspires some willingness to make amends, but something else is required for further development. In the early and mid-1970s, guilt was responsible for the churches' timid entry into support of a movement toward racial integration. But the denominations were still a very long way from declaring that racism must come to an end. A first step had been taken, but it was no more than a first step and it was complicated by the presence of anger.

Responding to Anger

Guilt and anger are close companions. In fact, in the grieving process anger is probably best understood not as a separate stage that follows guilt but as simultaneously present alongside it. Anger is a very complex part of grief. It can be anger at self or at God, or anger hurled indiscriminately at anyone who happens to be nearby. In the interplay of guilt and anger, white people directed their anger not only toward people of color, but toward other white people, namely white people who participated in forcing the wrongdoing of racism out of hiding and into the light. Adding to the complexity, people of color who for a very long time had swallowed the anger they felt for having been hurt by racism were now free to vent it publicly.

The early 1970s was a very angry period in the saga of race relations in the United States. When white society began to face its guilt for racism, long pent up feelings of anger and rage were set loose among people of color, particularly African Americans and Native Americans. Sometimes anger was released with punishing force. Not surprisingly, this increased the guilt of the white community, but the attacks also angered them. Nowhere in the church was this simultaneous presence of guilt and anger more powerfully revealed than in the story of the "Black Manifesto."

The "Black Manifesto" was produced at a National Black Economic Development Conference held in Detroit, Michigan, in 1969, sponsored by the newly formed Interreligious Foundation for Community Organization (IFCO). It demanded 500 million dollars from churches and synagogues in reparations for centuries of enslavement and oppression of African American people. Led by James Foreman, organizers disrupted worship services over the next year at churches, including Riverside Church in New York City, and occupied the headquarters of major denominations, including the Episcopal Church, demanding that the churches respond to the manifesto. Although the manifesto was written in revolutionary language, the money was to be used for what generally would be considered normal economic development projects, including a southern land bank, a black university, training projects, and an anti-defamation league. Nevertheless, in the midst of emotional and highly visible public debate, the demands of the manifesto were quite shocking to the general Christian public. They were quickly dismissed with pious platitudes and bureaucratic maneuvering by embarrassed denominational leaders. There were exceptions, however. Several denominations, including the Christian Church (Disciples of Christ) and the Mennonite Church, responded with positive programs in support of black development.

The "Black Manifesto" was one of the earliest attempts to address the central issues involved in correcting the ravages of racism. But because it was presented at such an emotionally charged moment, the manifesto served as a tool for confrontation rather a contribution to rational discussion. It offers a clear illustration of the confusing intersection of guilt and anger as white churches were faced with being unprepared to deal with the possibility of the end of racism. I believe that the demands the manifesto presented still need to be taken with great seriousness, especially in the light of the discussions taking place in churches and society today about apologies and reparations for racism's immeasurably destructive impact on people of color throughout our nation's history.

* * *

Perhaps it is possible in retrospect to find a bit of humor in the attempts of radical groups to take advantage of ecclesiastical guilt and the efforts of church officials either to avoid or to take their own advantage of the demands of the radical groups. Talk show hosts on late night television would have had a field day poking fun at the church in the 1970s. Vine Deloria Jr., an American Indian author, historian, theologian, and activist, offers a pithy analysis of the time in *God Is Red.* Even while seriously seeking to comprehend the interplay of radical activists and guilty religious leaders, Deloria suggests the following, only partially tongue-in-cheek:

> Many Lutherans were ecstatic when informed by Indians that they were guilty of America's sins against the Indians, and they embarked on a massive program of fund-raising to pay for their alleged sins. But they were not the only victims. Because the Presbyterians, Episcopalians, and Congregationalists all gleefully responded to the accusation that they had been responsible for nearly all of the problems of American Indians, they also decided that they could purchase indulgences for these sins by funding the Indian activists to do whatever they felt necessary to correct the situation. By early 1971, almost every major Christian church had set up crisis funds to buy off whichever Indian protesters they might arrange to have visit them.[3]

Depression and Silence

Guilt and anger are not only ineffective as motivators of lasting change; they are also quite exhausting. The furor of guilt and anger that typified relationships in the early 1970s was replaced gradually in the second half of the decade by an eerie silence, both in the church and throughout society. A deep depression born of frustration and fatigue began to set in. The civil rights movement had been costly: most of the leaders were dead, in jail, or in exile. Apathy replaced the enthusiasm and excitement of the 1950s and 1960s over the possibilities of change. A very tired body of people needed rest and time for introspection and interpretation before returning to the fray. In the church as well as in the rest of society, communication around issues of race and racism came almost to a standstill. In retrospect, it is clear that no new positive steps toward the future could be made until the depression lifted and the process of grieving moved to further stages.

When depression sets in, the underlying issues go undercover but they do not go away. Guilt and anger are still present, brooding silently underneath the surface. In some ways depression doesn't feel like a new stage of grief, as much as a return to the first stage of denial. But denial requires more energy than depression allows. In the late 1970s pessimists wondered if the movement was over while optimists kept looking for signs of the movement's resurgence.

Grief experts recognize that for individuals the stage of depression can be very brief, or it can last for a very long time. Although I have not found any studies to confirm my intuition about this, I suspect that collective depression on a societal level does not last very long, and it is lifted by the natural movements of human affairs. Thus, it might have been predictable that it would be only a matter of time before the depression of the 1970s gave way to the next stage of grief. Strangely enough, the energy for this next stage came neither from the fringes nor from the undersides of society, but from the center, from society's respected institutions of businesses and industry.

Bargaining: The Temptation of Diversity

The next stage in grief is bargaining. Many persons facing the approach of their own death or the death of a loved one will bargain with God, asking "Can we make a deal? If I do such and such, will you change your mind?" Or, they will search the world over for new cures: "If I try this medicine or that new approach, can I change my fate?"

In grieving the threat of the approaching death of racism, bargaining began to emerge on the national scene in the early 1980s. The nation's businesses and industries offered a bargain to people of color, an offer that was very difficult to refuse. The offer was called "multicultural diversity and inclusiveness," or "diversity" for short. (The same bargain was offered to women and other minorities, but I will focus on the offer made to people of color.) Bargaining began with the business sector, but it caught on like wildfire, and soon virtually every other system and institution in our nation was involved, including the churches.

Here is the bargain: white society promised people of color the possibility of positive change, as long as the old order of things would remain in place, particularly the benefits of racism for white people. In effect, white society said to communities of color, "We will give you a share of our world, with new opportunities and greater participation, but we will stay in charge and we will maintain our white privileges." In the early 1980s, a friendly offer of new opportunities and greater participation sounded so good to many people of color that they hardly heard the side about white society staying in control and continuing to reap larger benefits.

At the time, many people felt certain that multicultural diversity and inclusiveness was a wonderful answer to the dilemma of how to restart the stalled process of the post civil rights movement. Exciting programs like "diversity in the workplace" and "managing diversity" were created in the world of corporations and industry, and from there, the idea of diversity spread to every part of society. By the end of the 1980s, the goal of multicultural diversity and inclusiveness was one of the top ten priorities of virtually every system and institution in the nation.

The church was no exception. During the 1980s and early 1990s, almost all mainline Protestant and Roman Catholic churches in the United States developed programs to become more multicultural and inclusive. Most of these programs included racial quotas for staff hiring and for participation in church departments, commissions, and committees. Many also added evangelism goals of achieving higher percentages of membership of people of color. In addition, many denominations created separate departments for people of color to carry out their own work and ministries.

Still Bargaining: Diversity in the Twenty-First Century

The phenomenal explosion of programs of multicultural diversity has been the most significant event in recent racial history in the United States. Most churches in the United States are in the bargaining stage of grief, still bargaining about diversity. At the same time, this diversity itself is being questioned and evaluated, with many people becoming increasingly aware of its shortcomings.

If present programs of multicultural diversity and inclusiveness are evaluated from the perspective of the analysis of racism that guides this book, the results will not be favorable. There are numerous positive results due to the presence of people of color in our churches, of course, but the key question is to what extent the presence of these programs has changed the inner life of our churches, particularly the degree to which structures of white power and privilege have been transformed. It is very important to be aware that almost none of these denominational diversity programs are designed to raise or deal significantly with the questions of racism or of the distribution of institutional power. In fact, my perspective is that they are designed to avoid these subjects. For this reason, I have portrayed programs of diversity employed as bargaining tools as a passing stage of grief rather than a solution to racism.

Remember, our focus is on the approaching death of racism. If our society is to find a new path to racial equity and racial reconciliation, racism must die.

If we are unprepared for its death and unwilling to participate in its demise, we will be caught forever in the first five stages of grief—denial, guilt, anger, depression, bargaining. In the second to last stage of grief—the bargaining process—multicultural diversity is being used to keep us from accepting the death of racism. Until we give up entirely any notions of recuperating, reforming, rehabilitating, or repairing racism and agree that it has to die for good, the final stage—acceptance—will elude us.

It is not that multicultural diversity is unnecessary or wrong; quite the opposite. But right now it is serving us all too well as a bargaining tool to keep things the way they are. The bargaining stage is the most tantalizingly deceptive and dangerous of all the stages of grieving the end of racism. We can escape only when we understand that bargaining stifles our movement toward acceptance. When we finally come to the stage of accepting the death of racism, we will see that multiracial and multicultural diversity were essential elements in moving beyond racism.

The Final Stage: Acceptance and Anti-Racism

According to Kübler-Ross, the last stage of grief is acceptance of the reality of one's own approaching death or of the death of a loved one. Acceptance does not mean that life is over and death has won, but rather that life can now be lived in a new and more effective way. Of course, reaching the stage of acceptance does not mean we will no longer be affected by previous stages. Even while gaining new strength from the viewpoint of acceptance, a person will often revert back through the previous stages of denial, guilt, anger, depression, and bargaining. But each time it is possible to return to the stage of acceptance with greater strength and certainty.

In the same way, acceptance of the approaching death of racism does not mean that the struggle against racism is complete. Rather, it means that we can now participate in bringing racism to an end in a new and powerful way. Keep in mind that because you or I may be ready to accept the death of racism does not mean that everyone else is. Indeed, it should be obvious that large segments of our denominations are variously in denial, dealing with guilt and anger, or mired in depression. But the majority are stuck in the bargaining stage, clinging tightly to the false hope that if our churches become more diverse and more culturally competent, the work will be done. Ostensibly we extend an open invitation to all people, but really by inviting "them" into "our" church we hope to avoid making any serious changes in our church.

Racial diversity has made us look more colorful, and in some ways, we seem to be getting along with each other much better than before. But measured in terms of power, participation, and equity, the results of diversity are still disproportional. Multicultural diversity and inclusiveness, as we have designed and tried to implement, are simply not working. For those who have eyes to see and ears to hear, it is clear that the bargain is falling apart. Many denominations are already searching for new paths forward beyond the fading lure of diversity. Many churches have already begun to use the language of anti-racism and are even developing programs of training and organizing to address the issue of racism and anti-racism. The jury is still out as to whether these recent denominational developments toward becoming an anti-racist church reflect serious new directions for the church or only new language for maintaining the comfort of an old way of being. If sincere, these new directions will become effective only insofar as they are supported and encouraged by an increasing number of church members like you, who are preparing themselves to be part of the movement forward—people who are ready to ask: How do we become an anti-racist church?

Diversity in Your Denomination.

Without some familiarity with how diversity programs function in a given setting, the rest of this book will be difficult to understand. Although the language and the goals of diversity are quite similar in various denominational settings, the process and the programs vary greatly. I encourage you to explore programs of diversity in your church. In addition to becoming familiar with the programs, take care to learn the results. Following are some questions to guide you in your research.

- In what ways have diversity programs changed your church?
- How much diversity has been produced?
- Has the membership of people of color in your denomination significantly increased?
- To what extent has there been change in the church's decision-making structures or its culture? Have people of color achieved collective power or have they been a token presence with little influence?
- Has there been significant change throughout your denomination, or has the reserving of a small corner of the church for the activities of people of color allowed the central part of the church to remain virtually unchanged?

We Have Come a Long Way and Have a Long Way to Go

If there is anything to be learned from this long history of the struggle against the evil of racism, it is that we *have* come a long way. Most Christian churches have taken great strides forward, especially since the 1960s. We have come a long way toward recognizing our misuse of God's name and our distortion of the Christian faith in defending racist hatred and exploitation. We have begun to express repentance for past deeds and to walk new paths of justice and reconciliation. We have opened the doors of the church significantly wider and welcomed the presence of a far more diverse membership. We can point to improvements in relationships among church members and to changes in structures and ministries.

But even as we celebrate the progress we have made, can we agree that we still have a very long way to go?

In the next section of the book we will turn to a critical discussion of how to identify racism in the church today. To prepare us for the task ahead, I have composed a list of the things that I believe we have accomplished and a companion list of the things I believe remain yet to be addressed. I encourage you to read through them and reflect on the things I have listed. Perhaps I have included some things that, in your estimation, should be deleted, or there are others that you would include. It is not necessary at this point to agree on each of these items, but rather to agree to an agenda of discussing them in the chapters that follow

We've Come A Long Way	We Have a Long Way to Go
• *Past policies and practices of intentional segregation in the churches have been eliminated in virtually all denominations . . .*	*. . . but 11 o'clock Sunday morning is still the most segregated hour of the week; despite desegregation, integration, and programs of diversity, churches are for the most part as segregated now as they ever were.*
• *As in the rest of society, explicit expressions of racism in United States churches have vastly diminished; a welcome inclusiveness is emphasized and access is guaranteed . . .*	*. . . yet, explicit racism in churches, as in society, has been replaced by forms of exclusion that are more hidden, more subtle, and sophisticated.*
• *Individual attitudes and actions have changed, with growing acceptance of all people based on a sense of equality . . .*	*. . . however, a "colorblind" ideology is popularly accepted and often formally taught as a way of avoiding the issue of racism.*
• *Affirmative action goals and quotas for racial representation have been instituted in most denominations . . .*	*. . . but, for the most part, these goals and quotas have not been met, generally are not enforced, and a backlash on their acceptance has weakened and/or eliminated many of them.*
• *Equal opportunity in the churches has resulted in a significant increase in elected and appointed leaders of color in local, judicatory, and national leadership positions, and the numbers of pastors/priests of color have also appreciably increased. . . .*	*. . . but the numbers of leaders, pastors, and priests of color are still disproportional to church membership; on almost every measurable level, equal opportunity has not produced equal results—not even close.*

• *There is increased emphasis on multicultural diversity and inclusiveness, and on the production of multicultural resources, which reflects a desire to become a more diverse and inclusive church . . .*	*. . . but programs of multicultural diversity and inclusiveness often provide a thin veneer of change that covers unchanging conditions and power relationships.*
• *Ministries among people of color and within poverty-laden communities are given greater emphasis and publicity in most denominations . . .*	*. . . yet ministries among people of color are a long way from receiving proportional support, and inner city ministries face continuingly diminished support.*
• *Anti-racism programs are being introduced in major denominations . . .*	*. . . at the same time, anti-racism programs are not popularly accepted, are often the basis for replacing new language for the same old programs, and are more often than not still focused on individual attitudes and not on institutional and cultural transformation.*

Part II

The Present:
Racism in the Church Today

A fter a somewhat long and winding path, we come to the heart of the matter: the task of exploring how racism functions in the church today. On the
way, we traced the trail of the history of racism and of resistance to racism in the
churches over the past five hundred years, and even reached back to the theological foundations that were laid in the church two thousand years ago.

In our look into the past we discovered two contradictory images of the
church. One is a painful depiction of the church's support of racism and its participation in racism's devastating activities. The other portrays a powerful and
courageous church leading the struggle to overcome and defeat racism. We need
to realize that these are portraits still being painted. The contradictory realities of
a church for and against racism still exist today. And our own faces and actions
are only now being added to the mix, contributing to the reconciliation and
healing.

The rest of this book focuses on two tasks that are before us in our pursuit of
becoming an anti-racist church. The first is examining the racism that still today
deeply infects the church. The other is exploring the work of undoing racism and
building an anti-racist church, recognizing that this work is a continuation of the
resistance to racism that was begun before us. Two questions will guide us in this

examination and exploration: How is racism present in the church today? What must we do to become a church dedicated to racism's elimination? These are urgent questions aimed toward Christian people who are strongly motivated to search for answers and are personally committed to participating in the struggle to bring racism to an end.

The Starting Point: A Common Analysis

In order to work together to examine and comprehend racism in the church today, we have to look at racism through a common lens. Our starting point must be a broad and comprehensive understanding of systemic racism and how it functions, not only within the church but in all of society. If we use different lenses, apply different definitions, or employ different analyses of how racism works, we will end up moving in confusing and conflicting directions.

There is a very specific analysis of racism that I bring to this book. It is not my private analysis, but one that is shared in common by many individuals and organizations around the country who are engaged in anti-racism work. It is this analysis that I am using as a lens for exploring racism in the church. Since it is not possible to start from scratch and present this entire understanding of racism here, I emphasize again how important it is for readers to bring some comprehension of it to the reading of this book. A detailed exploration of this analysis of racism is found in my book *Understanding and Dismantling Racism*, as well as in a number of other books and resources listed in the resource section of this book.[1] What follows in the next few paragraphs is a brief review of this analysis of racism.

Defining Racism: A Quick Summary

To begin with, there is a brief shorthand definition of racism that is used by many anti-racism training organizations in the United States: racism is race prejudice plus the power of systems and institutions. Racism = Race Prejudice + Power of Systems and Institutions. The central point of this definition is that racism is *more* than race prejudice. If we are going to understand racism in the church or anywhere else the first thing we need to do is get over the popular but false assumption that personal prejudices and bigotry are what racism is all about. If we confuse prejudice with racism, not only will we misunderstand the disease, we will also be confused about the cure for the disease. We will end up believing that the solution to racism is eliminating our personal prejudices and building personal interracial relationships. As bad and as hurtful as

> *Racism—Race Prejudice + Power (The Power of Systems and Institutions)*

individual race prejudice can be, and as important as it is for us to get along with each other, this is not the fundamental issue underlying racism. The fundamental issue is power.

Racism is about the disproportional distribution of power. It places too much power into the hands of white society and too little power into the hands of people of color. "Power" in this definition refers specifically to the control of and benefits from systems and institutions in a society. Racism happens when the collective prejudices of one racial group are enforced by the systems and institutions of a society, for the benefit and advantage of that racial group and to the detriment and disadvantage of all other racial groups.

While working on our personal prejudices is important, race prejudice is relatively harmless unless it is enforced by systemic and institutionalized power. If we are going to end racism, we need to focus on changing the systems and institutions of our society that are still structured in a way that keeps mostly white people on top and people of color mostly on the bottom. When we only focus on changing individuals, we end up with newer and friendlier faces serving as gatekeepers for institutions with more subtle and sophisticated ways of keeping things the same.

Further understanding of this definition and building an analysis of racism require extensive exploration of the concepts of prejudice, race, and power, as well as of the three manifestations of racism—individual, institutional, and cultural. In addition, it is critically important to understand how racism becomes internalized in all of us, white people and people of color alike. Through the internalization of racial superiority in white people and the internalization of racial inferiority in people of color, we are all socialized to conform to racism and to support its functioning to our advantage or disadvantage.

These are the central concepts in the analysis of racism. Part 2 seeks to apply this analysis to the specific situation of systemic and institutionalized racism in the church today. We will focus especially on the question of how the predominantly white mainline Protestant and Roman Catholic churches in the United States are designed to serve white people better than people of color, and how this design of racism plays out in everyday church life. As we move through the next few chapters, I will pause occasionally to review and summarize portions of this analysis, but I want to emphasize that this will not be an adequate substitute for readers digging deeper on their own.

Chapter 6, "Race, Prejudice and Power in the Church," explores systemic racism in the church, and especially considers how biblical and theological misunderstandings of race, prejudice and power support racism, both in the church and in society. In chapter 7, "Captive Christians in a Captive Church," we will look at how the church contributes to the internalizing of racial superiority in white people and the internalizing of racial inferiority in people of color. The focus in chapter 8, "Institutionalized Racism in the Church," is on how the design and structure of the institutional church disproportionately empowers white people and disempowers people of color. Finally, in chapter 9, "Cultural Racism and the Multicultural Church," we will reflect on how the multicultural movement has both helped and hindered the process of facing and eliminating racism in the church.

Chapter six

Race, Prejudice, and Power in the Church

"When the Spirit of truth comes,
he will guide you into all the truth."

—JOHN 16:13

The purpose of this chapter is to explore how racism is still embedded in the church today. We will do this by examining how the church relates to each part of our definition of racism—*race prejudice plus the power of systems and institutions*—first focusing on prejudice and the church, then on the concept of race and the church, and finally on racialized power in the church. When we have finished exploring each of these parts, we will be able to look again at the definition as a whole and see that we have laid the groundwork for a biblically based understanding of racism.

In an earlier chapter, I spoke of stolen sacred stories, lamenting the fact that the teachings of the Bible and the Christian faith are often twisted and distorted in order to make it seem as if God is in favor of racism. The truth into which the Spirit guides us has been turned into lies. We have now reached the place in this study where it is time to turn the Bible right side up again and focus on taking back stolen stories and reclaiming an anti-racist gospel. When we take back the stolen sacred stories that have been used to defend racism, a strong foundation emerges to help us understand and combat racism. An anti-racist gospel does not need to be invented; it is not something new. The truth has been there all along, and if we allow ourselves to be guided by the Spirit of truth, we will recognize and reclaim it.

The Church and Prejudice

Individual prejudice, bias, and bigotry are sinful manifestations of racism that cause devastating harm to the fabric of human relationships inside and outside of the church. In order to overcome prejudice, over recent decades, most of our churches have developed extensive programs that encourage people to build caring interpersonal interracial relationships and to welcome and support multicultural inclusiveness. The problem with these programs is that the concept of prejudice is usually narrowly defined in a way that does not relate it to the institutional power structures of the church. As we will examine more deeply in the following pages, changing individuals without changing institutional structures produces a fundamental contradiction with frustrating and even tragic results.

Individual and Collective Sin

In order to go to the roots of this contradiction, we need to understand how the Bible and the church's theology make a clear distinction between individual sin and collective sin, and how this distinction influences an understanding of racism. Many people think of sin as having only one dimension: a wrong done by an individual. But the Bible clearly describes social sins that are committed collectively through societal structures. From a biblical point of view, personal prejudice and institutionalized racism are both sins, but they are very different kinds of sins. Prejudice is an individual sin, while institutionalized racism is a collective sin.

Individual sin is a thought, feeling, or action by a single human being, motivated by selfishness, greed, or some other human failing. Examples of individual sin include one person killing another or stealing another person's property or discriminating against another person because of class, race, or gender. Collective sins, on the other hand, are the actions of multiple individuals acting collectively as a body to hurt or oppress other humans, providing benefits for individuals or groups as a result. The violence of war, the ravages of societal poverty, and systemic sexism and racism are illustrations of collective or structural sin.

There is a longstanding theological tension in the church between these two distinctly different dimensions of sin. In the United States, where individualism is especially emphasized, the notion of structural sin often seems foreign to us. We are willing to accept personal responsibility for our own individual sinfulness, but we frequently dismiss or deny our involvement in social sins that benefit us and withhold benefits from others. The ideology of individualism insists that individuals can choose to separate themselves from responsibility for the actions of a community even if they are indelibly a part of that community. An exaggerated individualism is often expressed as a principal doctrine of American civil religion, and is taught everywhere, all too often including in the church, even though in direct conflict with the central teaching of Christianity. The sacred relationship between the individual and the community is one of the stolen stories that need to be reclaimed if we are to understand racism from a biblical and Christian perspective.

When an individual sin, such as prejudice or bigotry, is committed, the responsible individual needs to repent and make personal amends. But when collective sin, such as institutionalized racism, is committed, more than one person needs to repent and make amends. When whole groups benefit from collective harm done to others, those same groups must take responsibility as perpetrators. The Rev. Dr. Safiyah Fosua reflects on the place of corporate repentance in the Bible:

> People of the Bible grappled with the concept of individual sin as well as that of corporate sin. Sometimes their prayers were for individual sin(s); and at other times, they all stood and confessed that their country had sinned. When their spiritual leaders stood and confessed the sins of their nation before God, we read nothing of individuals offering vigorous protests that they were not to blame. The people of Israel understood that they, as a group, took part in both the blessings that came to the nation for wise decisions and in the consequences that came from bad decisions made by their leaders. Rise or fall, they would experience life together as a nation. This is a difficult concept for us to wrap our Western minds around. We have been conditioned by culture to think of ourselves as sole beneficiaries of the benefits or consequences of our actions.[1]

Racism Is Collective Sin

By applying these two theological dimensions of sin to the definition of racism, we can see that it is not enough for each of us to accept responsibility for our sins of individual prejudice. We need to be clear as well about the ways in which white society acts together in collective or institutional ways to oppress people of color and to benefit collectively from that oppression. And we need to understand how to take collective responsibility for undoing what has been done. But many people find it very difficult to accept responsibility for the structural sin of systemic racism. It is not unusual to hear such comments as "I've never owned slaves or lynched anyone" or "I haven't got a prejudiced bone in my body" or "I am not responsible for the racism of other people."

According to this way of thinking, we are not responsible for sins of institutional racism if we do not participate personally in committing them. This is true especially if such sins are rooted in actions that took place before we were born, even if persons today are still reaping the benefits of past sins. Willingness to accept responsibility for individual prejudice but not for the ramifications of collective sin is evidence of a privatized spirituality that distorts and dismisses our involvement in systemic social racism.

Systemic racism is collective sin committed on behalf of white society and providing benefits, to one degree or another, for all members of white community.

It is not enough for a person to repent of prejudice and not take responsibility for systemic racism. A church that calls for a person to be free of prejudice but does not ask the same person to be accountable for the results of systemic racism is preaching only half of the Bible's understanding of sin. Even more importantly, the church must take responsibility for the ways in which its own structures produce systemic results that benefit white people and fail to benefit people of color. We cannot deal with individual prejudice and ignore the far more devastating reality of collective and systemic racism in the church.

The Church and the Concept of Race

A Racialized Society

Race is a false and misleading social construct without basis in science or theology. The idea of race was invented by sixteenth-century Europeans, imported by seventeenth-century American colonialists, constitutionalized by our eighteenth-century American forefathers, and perpetuated throughout the nineteenth and twentieth centuries as a tool to measure human worth and distribute power and privilege. The sole purpose of inventing the concept of race was to establish white supremacy and white domination over all other races deemed inferior and unworthy. In the twenty-first century the results remain an unbearable weight over a divided society. Race still means you get more if you are white and less if you are a person of color.

We all have been "racialized," meaning that we have been defined as persons who belong to one of six major racial groups in our society: Native American, African American, Latino/Hispanic, Asian American, Arab American, or White. Even with the increasing crossover into multiracial identities, we are forced to choose a primary racial identity, or to accept arbitrary placement in one or another of these groups. We all are racialized and categorized, and the result is the maintaining of racial division and hostility. To one degree or another, we all personally internalize and act out our own role within our own racial group in maintaining the race construct of our society. The shackles of racial identity can't be removed until the results of racialization are erased and the United States becomes an anti-racist nation.

A Racialized Church

It is the same story within the church. In an earlier chapter, we focused on the history of how the church became racialized. Even before emigration to North America, the church was subject to a "European captivity" that stripped it of its African and Middle Eastern roots. Christianity became essentially a white religion. The churches of Europe blessed the colonialization and racialization of the world. In North America, the churches sanctioned slavery and supported segregation. Only with reluctance did the churches finally support integration.

Still today, Christianity in the United States is racialized. Our churches are divided by color into red, brown, yellow, black, and white denominations and congregations. There are a few multiracial congregations, but these are exceptions, and, usually, they are part of a denomination that is mostly one color. Most multiracial congregations have to struggle to keep from becoming just another church in racial transition. Race is not a specter from the past; race haunts the church today.

Race not only haunts us; it defines us. Race defines our borders, our membership, our culture, our theology, and our mission. It imprisons us and prevents us from truly being the church. Our beliefs, our worship, and our religious lifestyles are all racialized. If you tell me the race of your church, I already know more than half of what there is to know about your church.

A Racialized Bible

Even the Bible has been racialized. Actually, this is the root of the problem. For centuries, the Bible was used to defend racism. Still today, it is accepted popularly that race and racism are based on the Bible. Understanding how the Bible has been wrongly racialized and used as a tool of racism is the most important step in understanding and eliminating racism in the church.

The first step in racializing our churches and our society was to racialize the Bible. In order for our forebears to sell the idea of race and racism to the society, they had to present it as an idea authorized by God; it had to be in the Bible. In order for a racial hierarchy to be accepted, with white people on top and everyone else on the bottom, it had to be demonstrated that white supremacy was predestined and preapproved by the word of God. The separation of God's people into superior white people and inferior people of color had to be proclaimed and justified in the Holy Scriptures.

All this had to be invented because it was never in the Bible in the first place. It wasn't there then, and it still is not there today. We need to be absolutely clear about this: the idea of race is nowhere to be found in the Bible. There are many different categories of humanity in the Bible, but there is no racial category. You can search the Bible's images of heaven, hell, and the earth in between and you won't find the idea of race. For example, in the heavenly vision described in Revelation 7, the throne of God is surrounded by all kinds of peoples—nations, tribes, cultures, religions, and languages—but there is no mention of race. These same categories—nations, tribes, cultures, religions, and languages—are named in other biblical descriptions of the peoples on earth, but race is never included. There are occasional references to color consciousness; for example, in Song of Solomon 6:10: "She was black and beautiful." Countries located in Africa, such as Egypt and Ethiopia, are named in the Bible, but the fact remains that there is no race in the Bible.

So, if the defense of race and racism needed to be based in biblical authority, but neither were found in the Bible, then the only thing to do was invent a racist Bible. And make no mistake, it *was* invented. Slave owners, politicians, and church leaders invented a race-based Bible that identified white people as the true people of God and all other people as something less than the people of God. They invented fantasy stories, including, for example, that Noah's son, Ham, who was condemned because of sexual sins, was a black African. This story was used to promote the idea that Ham's condemnation was a condemnation of all black Africans. Another example is that the Tower of Babel is a story about God dividing humanity into races. In addition to fantasy stories, they invented a twisted theology that the system of racial enslavement in the United States followed a plan approved by God.

These inventions by slave owners, politicians, and church leaders were incorporated into the official teachings of most Christian denominations of the day. And the teachings were passed on from generation to generation. When I was in seminary in the 1950s, many of these ideas were still being taught, or at least tolerated, in seminary classrooms. Today, far too many people still associate the idea of race with the Bible. I ask people in the workshops on racism that I facilitate where they think the idea of race came from. Time and again, the answer is "from the Bible." It is an untruth implanted deeply into the conscious and unconscious memories of the people of God. It is a lie passed on from generation to generation that race is in the Bible, that it is God's invention.

The existence today of red, brown, yellow, black, and white churches is rooted in the historical idea of God's approval of racial separation. The web of lies and intrigue that racialized the Bible also created a racialized church that still entangles and confines us. Until the predominantly white church in the United States becomes an anti-racist church, race and our racialized identity will continue to haunt and define the church.

De-Racializing the Bible and De-Racializing the Church

The idea of race with all its trappings of superiority and inferiority is a sinful lie blasphemously placed in the mouth of God. It is a lie that is still perpetuated, and if we are white, we are still benefiting from it. These false beliefs will not be undone until the church publicly, transparently, and repeatedly proclaims it to be a lie that originated in the church and now must be undone by the church. The truth is that there is only one race, the human race, the people of God. All other divisions are human inventions for the purpose of advancing one segment of humanity against the others.

The first step in de-racializing the church is to de-racialize the Bible. As long as the idea of race is given divine consent, it will continue. It is not enough to say that all races are equal; it must be taught that race is an illusion, a social construct, that it was invented by humans and exists nowhere in the Bible, and it should be nowhere in the church. Until it is taught in every confirmation class, preached regularly in sermons, repeatedly publicized, confessed, and re-confessed, the lie will be passed on. Just as in Germany, because of the unfathomable consequences of the Holocaust, it is necessary to guard every generation against the resurgence of anti-Semitism, so also in the United States, because the belief in race-based identity and race-based superiority and inferiority is inculcated so deeply and so profoundly, we must be willing to dedicate hundreds of years of teaching to the contrary in order to erase its effects.

But de-racializing the Bible is only the first step in de-racializing the church. Our separation into red, brown, yellow, black, and white churches has created a disfigured and dysfunctional family of God. Our long-range vision for the future must not be only an anti-racist church, but a church no longer defined by the specious idea of race.

The Church and Racialized Power

Biblical Reflection: The Goodness of Power

The principal ingredient in racism is power—institutionalized systemic power. Racism misuses power for oppressive and evil purposes. However, this does not mean that from the point of view of the Bible and Christian theology, power itself is evil. In fact, quite the opposite is true. In misusing power, racism misuses something that from God's point of view is very good.

Christians tend to be very confused about power. We are not clear about what power is, if it is good or evil, whether we like it or do not like it, or whether we should accept it or reject it. In workshops on racism, I often ask participants how they define power and how they experience it. Usually I get answers that are quite negative, like "Power is control," or "Power is making others do what you want," or "Power is oppressive." When I ask if they believe power is good, neutral, or evil, the overwhelming majority respond that power is neutral, but that it can be used either for good or evil purposes, depending on who has the power. I ask participants if they would like to have more power. They usually say that they would like to have more power, but they also seem to feel guilty about that. They seem to believe that it is wrong to want or to have power. It is quite humorous when I summarize what I have heard: that power is not good and power is not bad, that although they don't like it and shouldn't want it, they would certainly like to have more of it.

Many people are surprised at first to hear that from a biblical point of view power is good, exceedingly good, in fact, absolutely wonderful! Since God is omnipotent, the all-powerful One, and since God is absolutely good, then power can be nothing but absolutely good. Moreover, God wants us all of us to have power. In the act of creation, God endows all people with potential power. In Jesus' last conversation with his disciples he promised "you will receive *power* when the Holy Spirit has come upon you" (Acts 1:8). And the Gospel of John proclaims that, "to all who received him, who believed in his name, he gave *power* to become children of God" (1:12, emphasis added).

> *Power is the ability or the capacity to become all that God intends us to be, individually and collectively.*

What is power? Power is the ability or the capacity to become all that God intends us to be, individually and collectively. Power is not evil or neutral. Power is good. We should want power and not feel badly about having it. We should also share power, thank God for it, and pray that we will use it for the good purposes it was intended and not misuse it for evil purposes. Power is the ability or the capacity to become all that God intends us to be, individually and collectively.

The Misuse of a Good Thing

The main point I want to make is that although power is good, it can be misused. The Bible is very clear about the uncountable ways that God's good power when placed in human hands has been misused, greedily and violently misused. Power can be used for evil purposes, and that is exactly what racism does. Racism is the misuse of God's good power. Even while we are focusing on how power is being misused, we need to maintain our clarity that the misuse of power does not change the nature of power being good. This is emphasized by South African theologian Dr. Wolfram Kistner:

> Power in itself is not evil. It is a gift of God given to every person and every society. The corruption of power through the selfishness of [humans], resulting in the deprivation of power from his fellowman, is evil. Churches and church members denying their participation in power structures are prone to become instruments of oppression by overlooking the magnitude and depth of the sinful selfishness of [humans] which seeks to entrench itself in the structures of society.[2]

That which is being misused is still good. In the analysis of racism that is the foundation for this book, it is crucial to understand that power is the ability or the capacity to become all that God intends us to be, individually and collectively and that racism is the misuse of God's good gift of power. This idea of the goodness of power will become even more important in our later discussion of dismantling racism. We need to understand that ending racism does not mean losing power, but transforming the misuse of power into the *good and proper use of power*. The end of racism means the gaining of a new sense of anti-racist power and the reclaiming and redeeming of power by using it as God intends it to be used.

Racism Misuses Power in Three Ways

It is not enough simply to state that racism misuses power. We need to be clear about exactly *how* racism misuses power, especially in the church. In the analysis of racism that underlies this book, there are three ways that this happens.

1. By disempowering people of color. The list of burdens and hardships suffered individually and collectively by African Americans, Native Americans, Latinos/Hispanics, Asian Americans, and African Americans, including lower salaries, unemployment, inequities in education and employment, and ineffective services, testify to the truth that racism oppresses and disempowers people of color.

2. By empowering and providing privileges for white people. Racism provides and preserves power and privilege for white society. It is crucial to understand that *this is the primary reason racism exists*. In fact, the primary purpose for racism isn't to hurt people of color but to create a society in which white people gain power and privilege.

3. By imprisoning and destroying all people. Racism takes everyone prisoner. Racism has the ability to make everyone serve its purposes, and destroy everyone's humanity in the process. This is the most devastating and destructive power of racism, because it subjects all of us to its will, people of color and white people alike.

As further background for this discussion, I encourage you to read the material I present in chapter 2 of *Understanding and Dismantling Racism*. The rest of this chapter will be spent exploring how these three misuses of power by racism are present in the church.

How Racism in the Church Disempowers People of Color

Along with the rest of our nation, the practice of open segregation and blatant discrimination was ended in the churches at the time of the civil rights movement, more than forty years ago. Almost all churches have developed intentional policies, programs, and practices that are open and inclusive of all people, and they all seek to incorporate and celebrate multicultural values and traditions. On the face of it, oppression and control of people of color in the church seems to be rapidly disappearing.

But despite the appearance of change, the power structures of the church remain much the same as before. The answers have not changed significantly to questions like: Who holds power in the church today? Who sets direction? Who makes decisions? Who determines whether or not change is made? A cursory examination of the leadership of any mainline Protestant and Roman Catholic denomination in the United States reveals that overwhelmingly these powers remain in the hands of white people. Small numbers of people of color now serve in leadership roles, but their presence is not strong enough to make any significant difference in the overall exercise of power. In many situations, the opinions of people of color are seriously taken into consideration, but regardless of whether the decision-making process is democratic or hierarchical, most of the time it is white people who are doing the serious consideration, and final decisions are still in their hands.

Of course, adjustments have been and are still being made. In most denominations there are people of color who hold higher offices such as bishop, presiding officer, powerful pastor or preacher. Additionally, in the administrative offices of virtually every denominational, educational institution or social service agency, there are at least one or two administrative executives and even an occasional CEO. But at the same time, in almost every case persons of color who hold positions of relative power are still controlled by job descriptions, decision-making processes, hierarchical structures, institutional culture, and accountability arrangements that were historically created to serve the needs of a predominantly white church. As long as these controlling factors are in place, it is virtually impossible for leaders of color in the church to use their power any differently than their white counterparts.

The deeper questions we need to ask are, "What is the result of this continuing white power? How does it affect people of color and take away their power?" Following are a few examples in our predominantly white mainline denominations today.

A Disempowering Theology and Practice of Mission

Not too long ago, missionary outreach to people of color was expressed in explicit terms of superiority and inferiority. People of color in the United States and throughout the world were believed to be pagans and savages who needed to be lifted up to a higher humanity by being introduced to Christianity and exposed to white culture and civilization.

We have certainly moved far beyond such explicit racism, but in subtler and more sophisticated ways, people of color are still controlled by white understandings of mission. Our programs of "racial/ethnic outreach" label whole populations who are other than white as "outsiders." Even though we substitute inclusive language of "mission with" or "ministry among" people of color, we still live in a "we/they" world. It is inevitable that as long as the vast majority of "us" on the inside of our mainline Protestant and Roman Catholic churches are white, we will refer to people of color on the outside or on the edges as "them" or, even worse, as "those people."

Pronouns are theological words, separating insiders from outsiders. No matter how sophisticated we become in using inclusive language, we are still separated and segregated by geography, institutional boundaries, and historically constructed walls of mistrust and hostility. Our relationships today remain objectified and depersonalized by the walls that divide us. Racism still separates us, and no amount of linguistic artistry will change the overwhelming reality of the power of "us" on the inside—to whom the church belongs—in relation to "them" on the outside—to whom the church does not yet belong.

A Failed Multicultural Theology: Inviting "Them" into "Our" Church

An extension of the pronoun problem is inherent in the theology of multicultural inclusiveness that is articulated in most of our churches. Not only do "we" invite "them" into "our" church, we also reinforce the problem when we ask people of color and of other cultures to leave a large part of their identity outside when they come inside. All too often, our invitation infers: "We hope you will come into our church, but if you do, you will have to accept us as you find us and you will have to change in order to become like us, because we weren't thinking about *our* need to change."

This is quite similar to the experience of the early New Testament church described in Acts, chapters 10–15. The early Christians thought at first that anyone coming into the church had to be circumcised in order to fit into their new environment. In this story, Peter and the church leaders discover the meaning of the gospel's radical and unconditional inclusiveness. In Christ, people of every place and circumstance are welcomed to "come as you are" into the church. This unconditional inclusiveness asks not how new people need to change in order to "fit" into the church but how the presence of new people can bring exciting and creative change to the church.

As long as the church's multiracial and multicultural programs insist that new adherents fit into old molds of church membership, we will continue to see the tally of new members of color in our multicultural numbers game fall far short of projected goals and quotas. To the degree we are successful in getting "them" into "our church," we will continue to see the disempowerment of people of color and the replication of a white church.

A Patronizing Theology of Charity: Fixing People of Color

Another way in which the church still disempowers people of color is through social service programs. Social service is one of the things Christians do with great enthusiasm, and we do it marvelously well. We feed the poor, rescue the downtrodden, and house the homeless. Our programs of charity, relief, and service span the globe. Church World Service, Catholic Charities, Lutheran World Relief, and World Vision are just a few of the big names that are associated internationally with compassion and caring for people in need. All denominations have departments or divisions assigned with the responsibility of guiding the churches' programs of charity, and many local congregations are involved in community services for the poor and homeless in their own parish areas.

So, what is wrong with that? What do these excellent programs of social service have to do with a theology of mission that disempowers people of color? I suggest that there are two very important theological and practical ways that the church's programs of social service create the opposite effect of what is intended.

First, charity is all too often a substitute for doing justice. Frequently the needs addressed by programs of social service are caused by natural disasters, but more often the needs are a result of social injustice, especially racism. As necessary as social service might be for the immediate survival of victims of injustice, it easily becomes a palliative alternative for correcting the causes of injustice. Charity is a biblical mandate, but it becomes a twisted and stolen story when it is a substitute for dealing with the injustices that caused the need for charity in the first place.

Second, and even worse, is the tragic reality that in many cases those of us who provide charitable aid are more often than not also a part of the society responsible for causing the injustices in the first place. This is especially true in situations of racial injustice, where white communities and white churches provide charitable social services for people of color. False assumptions often underlie our acts of charity, assumptions about what in our society is broken and about who and what needs to be fixed in order to end poverty and racism. Often behind our acts of love are judgments that hold victims responsible for their situation. We assume that poor people and especially people of color are broken and need to be fixed, and our charitable actions are aimed toward repairing their brokenness.

Charitable social services often distract us from facing the fact that our own brokenness often causes brokenness and need in others. To end racism and its devastating results, we need to come to the realization that it is white society that is broken and needs to be fixed. The cure for racism lies in treating the disease of racism in the setting from which it emanates: the white community and the white church. Reaching out to and helping the victims of racism is not enough. Only by changing and transforming systems and structures of white power and privilege will it be possible to make significant progress in dismantling racism in the church and in the rest of society.

How Racism in the Church Preserves White Power and Privilege

The most important issue in understanding racism is not what it does to *hurt* people of color, but what it does to *help* white people. For many white people, seeing racism from this perspective is new and shocking. It is a major turning point to understand that an effective response to racism is not what can we do to fix people of color, but what can we do to end white power and privilege.

Applying this concept to the church suggests that it is not enough to ask how racism within the church hurts and disempowers members of color but how racism in the church undergirds unwarranted power and privilege for white members. Like every institution in our society, the church was created originally and structured legally and intentionally to serve and benefit white people exclusively. And as we will see more clearly in coming pages, that original design is still in place. The decision-making processes, along with the hierarchical structures, cultural values, and accountability arrangements in our churches were all historically created to favor the needs of the church's predominantly white membership. That is what needs to be changed in order to shape an anti-racist church.

White Privilege in the Church

Power and privilege are not the same, though they are related. "Who has privilege?" is a different question than, "Who has power?" Power is held collectively within systems and structures, but privilege is afforded individuals who are part of the power structure. Individual privilege is always the result of group power. In understanding racism, we need to be clear that white privilege is a consequence of white power. Individual white people receive advantages because white people control systems and institutions.

It is not difficult to identify white privilege in United States society. White people get better education, better jobs, better housing, better health care, better police protection, better almost everything than people of color. White people are accepted, trusted, believed, and given more respect than people of color. So too in the church a system of privilege for white individuals is a product of systemic white ecclesiastical power. What privileges do white people receive as a result of white power in predominantly white, mainline Protestant and Roman Catholic churches? I suggest the following for starters:

> *What examples of white privilege would you add to this list? What privileges do white people enjoy in your congregation?*

- We can expect that white culture, white norms, and white music will dictate the style of worship, and we can choose to add or not to add multicultural flourishes to our white worship style.
- The images of God, Jesus, angels, and other biblical figures are usually portrayed as white.
- We are taught church history and biblical and theological interpretations that are filtered through the historical European/white experience.

- We have bigger and more adequate church buildings.
- Educational materials and other resources are designed for us and in our language.
- Seminary education and the shaping of a pastor is a process tailored mostly to fit white definitions and white needs.
- A white pastor can far more easily be assigned to a white congregation.
- We are much better represented in decision-making gatherings and conventions of the church.
- Nobody asks me how long I have been a Lutheran (Presbyterian, Episcopalian, Roman Catholic, or other mainline Christian).

What examples of white privilege would you add to this list? What privileges do white people enjoy in your congregation?

How the Church Is Imprisoned by Racism's Power

Racism's most devastating power is that it takes all of us prisoner. It controls and threatens to destroy us all. People of color and white people alike are made to serve racism's will and do its bidding. Each and every one of us is incorporated into the structure of societal racism and is forced to support it.

Analysts of racism have become aware in recent years of the effects of the intricate process of socialization, through which persons internalize an identity particular to our own racial group and act out that identity like puppets on a string. Each and every person of color is racialized to be a part of a racial group that is socialized to accept the negative effects of racism and to behave according to a racist society's standards for people of color. It is an identity-making process called "internalization of inferiority." And each and every white person is racialized to be part of the white race, and is socialized to accept white power and privilege as a way of life, and to behave according to a racist society's standards for white people. It is an identity shaping process called "internalization of superiority." Both of these internalization processes are destructive of the human personality and represent racism at its deadliest. This misuse of power is the most destructive form of racism, and is the most damaging, devastating, hurtful way in which racism affects the church. The next chapter is devoted to exploring the imprisoning power of racism and how the concepts of socialization and internalization apply to the church. We will examine how Christian individuals experience this socialization process. More importantly, we will look at how the church is imprisoned by racialization and how it has been made into an instrument that assists in the racializing and socializing of individual Christians.

Chapter seven

Captive Christians in a Captive Church

"Very truly, I tell you, everyone who commits sin is a slave to sin."

—JOHN 8:34

I began this book with the observation that for the vast majority of Christians, the scandalous reality remains that even if our daily life is increasingly multiracial, when the work week is over and we head for church on Sunday morning, we walk through doors into congregations that are racially defined as red, brown, yellow, black, or white. No matter how hard we try, we remain locked away from one another, imprisoned in separate and segregated churches.

Prison bars and gates are fitting images, in fact, for what keeps white people and people of color separated from each other, not only in our churches, but in virtually every aspect of our lives. Of course, it isn't difficult to see that racism places prison-like restrictions upon African Americans, Native Americans, Latinos/Hispanics, Asian Americans, and Arab Americans. But for many white people, it is shocking to discover the imprisoning and destructive effects of racism in our lives, to recognize that *all* people are imprisoned by this evil power. The heart of the analysis of racism on which this book is based is that we who are white are prisoners of our own racism. We have held the power of racism in our hands for so long that we are unable to let go. We receive power and privilege from racism, but in turn, racism gains power and control over us. Despite all the goodwill in our hearts, despite our deepest desires and intentions to become nonracists, the reality we have yet to face is that we cannot stop. We have been taken captive and are oppressed by our own racism. The imprisoner is imprisoned; the victimizer, victimized. We are prisoners in the racist structures of our society, and we need to be set free. In the words of the late historian C. Eric Lincoln: "The same fetters that bind the captive bind the captor, and the American people are captive of their own myths, woven so clearly and so imperceptibly into the fabric of our national experience."[1]

Willingly or Unwillingly, We Are All a Part of Racism

Before considering racism's captivity of the church, which is the focus of this chapter, let's recall briefly how it is that we all are captive to racism. White individuals and people of color are made to be a part of the collective structures of systemic racism through a process of racialization. Our nation was constructed with clearly defined racial structures, whose primary purpose was to separate all people of color from white people but which also served to separate people of color from each other by placing them into categories of Native American, African American, Latino/Hispanic, Asian American, and Arab American. Even today, with the current emphasis on recognizing and affirming multiracial identities, racism's evil goal is to make a sharp distinction between "white" and "non-white" and to be very clear that the first is superior to the other.

Through a complex multi-generational identity-shaping socialization process, we were assigned at birth to a collective racial group and were taught to participate in society according to our particular racial identity and role. For people of color this socializing process is called the "internalization of inferiority." No matter to which of the racial sub-groups they are assigned, people of color are taught to believe and accept negative societal definitions of self and to live out inferior societal roles. For white people, the comparable socializing process is called "internalization of superiority." White people are taught to believe superior societal definitions of self, as well as to accept white power and privilege as a way of life. As a result of this internalizing of racial identity, we all, like puppets on a string, support the construct of systemic and institutionalized racism. This internalizing process is incredibly destructive of the human personality and represents racism at is deadliest. We cannot comprehend racism if we do not understand this overwhelming shaping of our identities and our actions.

It is particularly important for white people to recognize that we are not immune to the destructive identity-shaping effects of racism. One of the reasons this is so hard for we who are white to comprehend is that part of our socialization is designed to keep us unaware of our collective racial identity. We are taught to defend fervently a concept of individualism and private initiative. But there are no "get out of jail free" cards that will release us from racism's imprisoning power. Willingly or unwillingly, wittingly or unwittingly, white Americans are all collaborators in the corporate acts of a society that victimizes people of color and rewards the perpetrators.[2]

The Captivity of the Church

At the heart of our analysis of racism is that all people, regardless of color, are prisoners of racism. Imprisonment is also at the heart of our analysis of racism in the church. We now turn our attention to examining how this is possible and to what extent the church is imprisoned by its own racism.

In its message of life and salvation, the church has clear and illuminating language by which to understand the sin of racism and to equip people to struggle to overcome it. But the imprisoning power of racism has stripped the church of its ability to understand the message that it proclaims and has severely limited its ability to carry out its mission of freedom.

The starting point for examining this contradiction is the history documented in the earlier chapters of this book and your own research into the history of racism in your denomination, congregation, or church institution. The church's participation in racism, as evidenced in the open and intentional involvement of mainline Protestant and Roman Catholic churches in support of our nation's systemic racism, is staggering. Decades after the end of legal segregation, our churches today remain mired helplessly in racial separation and isolation. The question is why. What is there about the nature of this captivity that keeps us perpetuating the past and makes us unable to shape new and effective paths into the future?

The Church's Internalized White Identity

Part of the answer to this question can be found in the reality that the mainline Protestant and Roman Catholic churches have internalized a white racial identity that reaches to our very foundations. As we explored in chapter 3, the Europeanization of a triumphal Christian church led to its identification with colonializing and racial dominating European nations. It was inevitable that the church in colonial America and in the United States of America self-identified as white and became closely associated with and dependent on societal systems of white power and privilege.

And after centuries of receiving power and privilege from racism, it was just as inevitable that racism would gain power and control over the white church. After holding onto the power of racism for so long, the church is unable to let go. Despite all the good that churches have tried to do during the post–civil rights decades, despite the deep desire within the church to change and to become a non-racist church, the reality the white church has yet to face is that we continue, willingly or unwillingly, to be an instrument for the construct of racism. C. Eric Lincoln's words ring just as true when directed toward the sacred sanctuaries of our land; churches are captive of their own myths, woven so clearly and so imperceptively into the fabric of their ecclesiastical experience.

It is difficult to imagine a greater contradiction than that the Christian church, called by God to be a messenger of freedom and liberation, is itself in bondage to racism and virtually powerless to preach its own most central truth. Even more troubling is the fact that not only has the messenger been taken prisoner, so has the message—the gospel of Jesus Christ. More than any other institution, the Christian church has been wounded deeply and destructively by racism. Of racism's many victories, the captivity of the church is among the most tragic. Certainly there can be no more worthy or important goal for the twenty-first-century church than wresting itself free from racism's imprisoning power and reconciling with those from whom racism has separated us.

The Sin of Racism: A Theological Issue

Any conversation about the church's imprisonment needs to be articulated in the church's own theological language. Since captivity and freedom are profoundly theological concepts, we need to probe how racism has affected the belief systems of various denominations and families of churches. In order to get to the question of captivity, the central theological question that needs to be raised is the Christian understanding of the relationship between sin and human freedom.

There are two central ways that the Bible explains how and why sin exists. From one perspective, human sinfulness (in this case, the sin of racism) is portrayed as freely chosen. From another perspective, sin is seen to be the result of captivity; it is a condition of human brokenness. We need to understand these two perspectives in order to make a judgment about the extent to which the church, as well as each of us, is culpable for or captive to racism.

Sin as Intentional Rebellion

The first way sin is described in the Bible is as a deliberate act on the part of an individual sinner. In other words, sinners sin because they want to; sin is a choice made freely and intentionally. For sin to be rectified, the sinner must admit to the sin and accept full responsibility for it. The sinner must repent and receive forgiveness. In this way, sinners become ex-sinners, unless and until they freely choose to sin again. This understanding of sin has been highly emphasized by the western church and is therefore most familiar to western Christians.

We find examples of this understanding of sin throughout the Old Testament in the rebellion of the people of Israel against the will of God and in the call of the prophets to repent and return to the covenant. In the New Testament, Jesus' suffering and death on the cross is a redemptive sacrifice; Jesus, himself without sin, willingly accepts the punishment due guilty sinners. Because of the atoning sacrifice of Jesus, God is willing to forgive and restore the repentant sinner. From John the Baptist's ministry, recorded in the Gospels, to accounts of the development of the early church found in the New Testament epistles, the call and command to sinners is to "repent and believe."

For our discussion of racism, the theological implication of this explanation of sin is that racism is a sin freely chosen and able to be freely rejected. If this were the case, the elimination and eradication of racism would be a relatively simple process that could be accomplished through acts of contrition, repentance, confession, and absolution. However, when we add the second explanation of sin, things become far more complex.

Sin as Captivity

The second way the Bible portrays sin is not as an intentional act, but as captivity foisted on humanity by forces of evil. In this instance, the sinner has far less choice in the matter. Sinners commit sins because they are prisoners of sin. Sinfulness is the result of captivity by forces beyond one's own power, akin to how we describe the overpowering control of addiction to alcohol or drugs. From this perspective one must be rescued and liberated from sin, set free by the powerful hand of God.

Examples of this understanding of sin are found throughout the Old Testament, particularly in Israel's history of enslavement in Egypt and liberation by the hand of God. Later, the Hebrew people were taken into captivity in Babylon, and, once again, their return from exile was made possible through God's liberating power. The theme of captivity and freedom is also prominent in the New Testament. In his first sermon, Jesus proclaimed his mission was to free prisoners and liberate the oppressed, a mission that is clearly visible in the Gospel writers' stories of Jesus' ministry and in their interpretations of his crucifixion and resurrection. Moreover, in the letters and stories in the rest of the New Testament, the theological self-understanding of the early church is repeatedly expressed in terms of rescue and liberation from the enslaving power of sin. Thus, throughout the Bible and in the early church, the theme of captivity and liberation became one of the central ways of understanding sin and brokenness.[3]

This understanding of sin puts an entirely different perspective on our discussion of racism. From this theological perspective, involvement in the sin of racism is not simply the free choice of an individual but participation in a collective evil that may not be in accordance with one's personal will; it reduces or eliminates one's freedom to be or to act differently. Repentance and desire for change is in a face-off with imprisoning forces that dominate one's will. But racism is not simply an individual sin; it is a collective and social sin. Ending racism requires rescue, liberation, healing, and rebuilding. To better understand the difference between the two categories of sin present in the Bible so that we can apply them more clearly to our discussion of racism, I encourage you to study the side-by-side comparison detailed in the chart below.

Intentional Sin	Imprisoned by Sin
• **Deliberate Choice**—Sin is portrayed as a free and deliberate choice by humans to disobey and rebel against God.	• **Helplessly Captive**—Sin is portrayed as humans being held captive and imprisoned by an oppressive evil power.
• **Individual Sin**—Its emphasis is more on the sinful condition of an individual person than on the condition of the people of God collectively.	• **Collective Sin**—Its emphasis is more on the sinful condition of the people of God collectively than on the condition of an individual person.
• **Solution: Repentance**—The message of salvation from this point of view centers on a sinner's repentance and seeking of God's forgiveness.	• **Solution: Rescue**—The message of salvation from this point of view centers on God's liberating power over sin's oppressive captivity.
• **Love and Mercy**—God is seen in both the Old and New Testament as a God of love and mercy who is willing to forgive and restore us.	• **Power and Might**—God is seen in both the Old and New Testament as a God of power and might who liberates us and sets us free.
• **Redemptive Sacrifice**—Jesus' suffering and death on the cross is portrayed primarily as accepting punishment in our place as a redemptive and atoning sacrifice for sin.	• **Liberating Victory**—Jesus' suffering and death on the cross is portrayed primarily as an unjust oppression that is overturned by the liberating victory of his resurrection.

Both of these explanations of sin are strongly present in the Bible. They are intended to be complementary to each other, not in conflict or competition with each other. Both are necessary for a comprehensive understanding of the nature of sin and how it is overcome. On the one hand, sin is an intentional act against God and against humanity that requires personal acceptance of responsibility, repentance, and forgiveness. On the other hand, sin is committed because humans are driven by an evil power that takes us captive and from which we must be liberated. If either of these understandings of sin is lifted up as more important than the other, a great deal is lost.

It is no accident that members of mainline Protestant and Roman Catholic churches are likely to be far more familiar and comfortable with the understanding of sin as individual rebellion, calling for personal repentance and God's forgiveness, than with the understanding of sin as collective oppression and captivity, requiring God's rescue and liberation. Sin as captivity isn't emphasized in mainline Protestant and Roman Catholic churches, except in the narrowest connotation of rescuing individuals through "soul salvation." In addressing moral, ethical, and social issues and other concerns of everyday life, for all practical purposes, this theological understanding of sin has been made to disappear or it has been distorted, submerged, underemphasized, depoliticized, and overly spiritualized by the western church. It has become a stolen story that needs to be reclaimed.

One of the most important theological movements of our day is the theology of liberation. Representatives of liberation theology seek to restore the biblical perspective of captivity and liberation, particularly in understanding the struggles of poor and oppressed peoples for social and political liberation. The implications of liberation theology for the issues of racism are far greater in scope than we have space to address here, so I encourage you to use the resource list at the back of this book to further pursue this subject. The particular point that I want to emphasize here, which is strongly reinforced by liberation theology, is that our understanding of racism is greatly distorted if this second understanding of sin as captivity is de-emphasized or excluded. To the degree that this has taken place in our churches, it has resulted in an inability to comprehend the nature and effect of racism.

Application to Your Own Situation.

Since each denomination has different historical and theological thrusts in dealing with issues of sin and human freedom, the following four questions to help you make accurate judgments about your denomination's understanding of these issues:

1. To what extent does your church teach an understanding of sin as a free act of the will, which can therefore also be removed whenever the sinful individual or the sinful church chooses?
2. To what extent does your church have an understanding of sin as a product of captivity by evil forces beyond ourselves, which cannot be altered simply by sinful individuals or a sinful church choosing to do so?
3. How does your church apply these two dimensions of sin to collective and social sin?
4. To what extent are these two perspectives considered when your church addresses the task of assessing and ending racism?

Response to Racism: Repentance or Rescue?

How then do we understand the task of ending racism when seen from these two theological perspectives? Can it be accomplished simply through acts of contrition, repentance, confession, and absolution? Or, does ending racism require our being rescued and liberated, set free by the powerful hand of God?

This much is clear: the first call of the gospel is to repent. The starting place to deal with the racism of the church is to understand racism as intentional sin. The reality is that we have been unfaithful to the gospel and we must accept responsibility for the sin of racism. The gospel calls the church to own up to its sins, to repent, to apologize, to ask for forgiveness, and to work for reconciliation.

But, haven't we already done that? Over recent decades, public apologies for past sins of racism have been made by almost all denominations; the United Church of Christ has apologized to Hawaiians; the Episcopal Church has apologized to Native Americans; and Baptist churches have apologized to African Americans. Churches, governments, and other organizations have made hundreds of formal apologies to people of color for oppressive acts against them.[4] Yet, while it is embarrassing to admit, not much has happened as a result of these apologies. After the initial enthusiasm wore off, things pretty much returned to the way they were before. For a brief moment, the sense of responsibility that the white church felt for past sins was somewhat relieved, but the separation and isolation of white churches from churches of color has hardly been reduced, and mistrust and misunderstanding are present still.

Why has so little changed? Perhaps the repentance was inadequate or lacking in true sincerity. Maybe the officials of the church who spoke the words of apology were not really representing the convictions of the membership. Or perhaps, in the words of John the Baptist, we have only been trying to flee from the coming wrath and have not yet produced fruit that demonstrates true repentance.[5] It is quite revealing that while willing to apologize, most churches drew a sharp line in the sand when the subject of reparations, as a sign of true repentance, was raised.

But even if these acts of repentance have been sincere, even if complete absolution has been received, and even if reconciliation has been deeply felt, it is quite clear that the problem has not been solved. We are still a deeply divided people of God unable to represent a racially unified body of Christ. Racism has not been sufficiently dealt with because the problem goes much deeper than simple guilt and repentance. We have yet to face the issue of captivity.

It is not that we cannot be forgiven of the most despicable of sins, including the worst forms of racism. The problem is that even after we have repented, confessed, and been forgiven, churches and individuals alike continue to face the same state of collective imprisonment in systemic racism as before. Evidence of that captivity is manifested unmistakably in the isolation, separation, hostility, and mistrust between white churches and churches of color.

Repentance is important, but it is not enough. Our analysis of racism insists that the situation is too complex to be solved by repentance, and our theological understanding of captivity to sin confirms it. There are clear reasons why acts of repentance and assurances of forgiveness are insufficient to bring about racial reconciliation and why more is required to free white churches from the tangled knots of our racist past. The reality is that the church is being held captive by the very system of racism it helped to create. Regret is not enough to end the systemic patterns and practices that perpetuate white power and privilege and imprison perpetrators of racism and victims alike. Churches, like all other institutions of our society, are ensnared by their own history. Yes, we need to repent, but we also need to know where the church's culpability ends and its captivity begins.

Freedom from racism is possible only through the liberation and transformation of the systems and institutions that hold us all in captivity.

A Captive Church in Denial of Its Captivity

There are two consequences of not understanding sin as captivity and lacking the ability to understand and deal with social issues through the lens of a theology of captivity and liberation. Both are catastrophic in nature. First, it becomes impossible for predominantly white and middle-class churches to understand the spiritual and political bondage of the world's poor and oppressed people, the vast majority of whom are people of color. Instead of identifying captivity and oppression as a cause, the church provides a variety of alternative explanations for their condition: they are underdeveloped, they are simply unfortunate, they are themselves sinful and at fault, and so forth. Churches may even confess their own sinful involvement as explanation. They may, for example, confess the sin of negligence or overindulgence, or even confess to being guilty of intentional racism *in the past*. But the sins confessed by the churches will not include an admission of racism's captivity and control. Consequently, churches will be limited in their ability to participate in finding solutions to the conditions of oppressed people. Churches will support relief programs, provide development aid, and even get involved in advocacy, but support for liberation struggles is not theologically or politically acceptable. When theologians of liberation insist that responsibility for the conditions of the poor and oppressed lies at the feet of the nations of the western world, including the churches aligned with them, there are few if any theological handles for mainline Protestant and Roman Catholic churches to comprehend or respond.

The second consequence is even more catastrophic than the first. In the absence of a theology of captivity and liberation, it is impossible to perceive, understand, or deal with our own spiritual, social, or political bondage. Without an understanding of captivity to sin, our own imprisonment by sin can be denied or ignored. And that means the churches have the option of being in denial of their own captivity to racism. Unless we reclaim a biblical theology of captivity and liberation and apply it to the perpetuator as well as to the victim of racism, we will remain patently and painfully ignorant of our imprisonment in racism. There can be no resolution of racism in the western church until it is able to deal with its own captivity.

Liberation of the Oppressor

If we understand that the system of racism causes us to be racist against our own will, we will understand too that we are being oppressed by our own racism. The oppressor is also oppressed. Those who are the cause of racism and who benefit from it are no freer than those who suffer from its deprivations and inequalities.

This becomes especially obvious when we consider the self-perpetuating nature of racism that afflicts generations over decades and even centuries.

We need to grasp this notion that all of us are oppressed; our state of being oppressors is also a state of captivity, a state of oppression. We need to grasp the biblical perception of a deeper evil power at work rendering both oppressor and oppressed powerless, making everyone into helpless pawns of diabolical evil. In the face of evil and its power over all of us, everyone is oppressed and none are free. We need to become clear that even while we who are white participate in and benefit from racism, we are also oppressed by our own racism and we ourselves need to be set free.

From this point of view, the distinction fades between the oppressor and the oppressed, between the captive and the free. The only distinction is between those who are aware and those who are in denial of their imprisonment. The ability of the church to be an effective participant in the struggle to end racism depends on our being able to comprehend the oppression of racism over all of us. We need to be concerned about freedom for people of color, but we need to be concerned about our own as well. We need to be aware that we too lose because of racism; we lose our humanity, our authenticity, and our freedom.

We must come out of our denial of our own captivity, especially if we want to be open to God's powerful liberating word. A theology of captivity and liberation insists that God's first option is for the broken, the captive, and the oppressed. If we are all captive and oppressed, then God's option is for all of us. There are not two gospels—a gospel of liberation for the oppressed and a gospel of forgiveness for the oppressor. There is only one: a gospel of forgiveness *and* liberation for all. There cannot be one gospel for those who are down and out and another for those who are up and about. There is not one Christianity for those who need freedom and a second Christianity for those who are already free. There is not one version of Christianity for those who need liberation and another version for those who only need forgiveness. Not only is God's first option for the broken and the oppressed, this is God's *only* option. There is only one gospel of Jesus Christ. It is the gospel of liberation *and* forgiveness offered to those who identify themselves as sinful *and* oppressed. That is all the gospel there is!

The simple reality is that the gospel claims that we are all broken and oppressed. In his dealings with the upstanding, righteous, educated, superior, religious upper class people of his day, Jesus' goal was to help them understand their own sickness, their own brokenness, their own enslavement. This was the only way he could bring healing, wholeness, and freedom to them too. When he confronted the Pharisees, he tried to make them see their slavery. When he addressed the rich young ruler or those from the upper classes or from the military, Jesus knew they had need of healing and wholeness. It was to these people that he said, "Those who are well have no need of a physician, but those who are sick; I have come to call not the righteous but sinners to repentance" (Luke 5:31-32).

From the perspective of this biblical and theological understanding of sin, beneath the political divisions that separate oppressors from oppressed, is a greater enemy who takes both the powerful and the powerless captive; a greater enemy who is responsible for turning humans against each other in the first place and dividing us into opposing camps. This powerful, evil foe is at large in the world, imprisoning the hearts and minds of entire peoples and perpetuating destructive beliefs and behaviors from one generation to the next. This is the evil one, whom the Bible names "Satan" and "Devil." It is impossible to comprehend, much less overcome, the forces that drive humans to acts of such malicious evil as war, genocide, and racism unless we come to grips with the understanding of sin as captivity.

We are living in a time of very serious confrontation in the Christian church between two theological frameworks for understanding the sin of racism. As we have seen, one theological framework proclaims that individuals are free to choose anything we want, including whether to sin or not to sin, to be racist or not to be racist, to repent or not to repent, to be forgiven or not to be forgiven. The other theological framework emphasizes a theology of captivity and liberation that understands racism as a product of oppression and captivity and proclaims the power of God to lead its captives into freedom. Instead of seeing these two frameworks as complementary, they are made to be competitive and placed in opposition to each other. A breakthrough in this theological standoff is desperately needed for the church to break free from the prison bars of racism.

Captive Members of a Captive Church

Christian Identity Formation

For those of us who are white to understand the full effects of the church's captivity to racism, we need to put ourselves personally into the picture and explore the role of socialization that the church plays, for good and for ill, in our lives. For each of us, our identity as white Christian individuals has been shaped in part by the teachings, worship rituals, and community life of the church. In fact, identity formation for all of us—the process of coming to see ourselves as beloved children of God—is central to the mission of the church. In baptism, whether as an infant or an adult, a person's identity as a part of the family of God is celebrated. In programs of education, Christian identity is nurtured and values are internalized. In the rite of confession and absolution, identities broken by sin are restored to wholeness. In Holy Communion, the family of God is fed and family bonds are strengthened. In the rite of burial, eternal preservation of a person's identity is assured. These examples and more are part of the sacred calling of the church to socialize and shape Christian identity.

Christian Identity Formation and Racism

We have received many positive things from these experiences, but we have received negative things too, including many aspects of our racial identity. Using the language of our analysis of racism, the church has contributed to our being racialized as white people. Growing up in a white church, we developed a deep consciousness of the family of God as a white family. We learned to live out white racial roles and to internalize racial superiority. Of course, the church alone is not responsible for our racial socialization. As we have seen in our analysis of racism, schools, government, media, family, and a hundred other institutions play a part. Within each of us a mentality is created—consciously and unconsciously, intellectually and emotionally—to accept race and racism as fact and to buy into our role in furthering them. Here are some examples of how this socializing process works in the society in general:

- We grow up isolated from people of color (the United States is more segregated today than it was in the days of legal segregation).
- We are taught to see a distorted racial picture of ourselves, as well as a distorted picture of people of color and the world in which they live.
- We are socialized to accept the privileges of being white without learning that they are benefits of racism.
- We are taught that everyone is supposed to be equal, while also learning to accept and be comfortable with the fact that we are not.
- As personnel who work for (or in other ways represent) societal institutions, we become gatekeepers of institutionalized racism, unequally distributing society's resources.

In similar ways, this racial socializing process is supported and furthered by the church. How does the church participate in this internalizing of racial superiority? For starters, here is a list of ways:

- We are received into and learn to be comfortable with a church family that is visibly white, or predominantly so.
- We live our Christian life in a segregated church, separated and isolated from Christians of color. The teaching that Jesus loves children of all colors equally is contradicted by the normalized experience of a white church.
- We learn to be comfortable with white religious culture, music, and art, including images of a white God, a white Jesus, white saints, and white angels. Even when we are exposed to multicultural experiences, there are usually clear messages about white as normal and superior.
- We are wrongly educated by what we are taught and by what we are not taught. For example, we are not taught an understanding of racism that goes deeper than the sin of prejudice. Usually we are taught a "colorblind" approach to racial differences.

- We are taught to understand sin from the theological perspective of individual choice, repentance, and forgiveness. We are not taught the lost theology of captivity and liberation, thereby making it virtually impossible to comprehend the imprisonment of the church or ourselves in the sin of racism.
- Seldom is the long history of the church's racism spoken of. Nor are we taught that the major difference between the white church and the church of color is caused by a system of white Christian power and privilege.
- A Christian self-image as a loving and caring people is often used to disguise the church's privileged position and the church's blessing of military force to protect our "Christian way of life."
- Apart from offering encouragement to respond charitably to the needs of people affected by injustice, the church does little to challenge societal injustices, including the injustice of racism. More often than not the "blessings" of a predominantly white society are identified as gifts from God rather than products of white power and privilege.
- We have progressed beyond a time when people of color were viewed as savage and pagan in need of missionary evangelism. Instead we are socialized (especially by church media) to see people of color as distant objects of charity and concern.
- We may be taught the history and theology that separate our churches denominationally, but we are not taught the history and theology that separate our denominations racially.

This short list could be expanded to many pages. In what ways have white people internalized the racialized identity of a white Christian? In what ways have people of color internalized the racialized identity of a Christian of color?

It is important to note in closing that the internalization of racial inferiority among people of color is not carried out only by the white church; churches of color contribute to this socialization as well. Both white churches and churches of color have been tools of white racism. However, it is not within the purview

> *In what ways have white people internalized the racialized identity of a white Christian? In what ways have people of color internalized the racialized identity of a Christian of color?*

of this book nor is it the task of this white author to describe internalization as experienced by people of color. The resource list at the end of the book includes resources for learning more about this. In addition, I encourage readers of color to explore and share their own experiences of this deadly phenomenon.

In the next two chapters, we will examine the imprisonment of the church more closely by studying the institutional structures and the culture of predominantly white mainline Protestant and Roman Catholic churches.

chapter eight

Institutionalized Racism in the Church

Now you are the body of Christ and individually members of it.

—I CORINTHIANS 12:27

Remember our definition: racism is race prejudice plus the power of systems and institutions. Racism is far more than the prejudices of a single individual and even far more than the collective prejudices of any one racial group. In fact, as we just finished exploring in the previous chapter, racism is so powerful that it can take individuals and entire racial groups captive and, like puppets on a string, make them do what it wants them to do.

Racism is based on systemic and institutional power. Racism persists in the United States because of the way institutions in this country are designed to provide and maintain white power and privilege. Our systems and institutions are more effective and efficient in serving white constituencies than they are in serving constituencies of color because they are structured to do so. Racism is also self-perpetuating, a giant machine designed to go on and on, over and over again providing more of everything for white people than for people of color. Racism's purpose and power are written into the genetic code, structure, and design of every societal system and institution—political, economic, educational, cultural, and religious.

Thus, the inevitable conclusion is that racism cannot be ended without fundamental transformation of our society's systems and institutions. In the 1960s, significant institutional changes were made with regard to laws against segregation and discrimination, but these changes did not go to sufficient depth to transform the institutional structures that are responsible for racism's misuse of power. Despite new laws, new opportunities, and new intentions, our systems and institutions—including our churches—are still structured to ensure control by white people and to provide far greater access to their benefits by white people than by people of color.

Institutions and Institutionalized Racism: A Quick Summary

Before exploring how it functions specifically in the church, it is important to review a basic understanding of institutionalized racism in any institution. Following is a quick summary.[1]

The Nature and Purpose of Institutions

Institutions are a good and necessary part of any society. Although we tend to be critical—sometimes even cynical—about institutions, they serve a very positive and irreplaceable function: to create, produce, manage, and distribute the resources of a society. A veritable galaxy of millions of small and large institutions in our society—each of them systemically functioning in an interrelating and cooperating way with other institutions—makes it possible for us to live together collectively and interdependently, to have adequate provision of food, health, clothing, and shelter, to fulfill our vocations, to share in community, and theoretically, to live together in peace and justice.

The Good and Bad in Every Institution

On the other hand, while institutions fulfill a good and necessary purpose, all kinds of problems and difficulties with them are unavoidable. The size and the scope of their interrelated tasks, coupled with the inevitability of human frailties and foibles, guarantee that despite all efforts to correct and improve them, institutions do not function fully to meet our expectations. While we work to make them better, flawlessness and faultlessness escape our reach.

Institutional Accountability

A central issue in improving and correcting institutions is accountability. In theory, institutions are accountable to the people they serve. The constituency of an institution is supposed to be able to evaluate and control its behavior. When an institution is accountable to us, we are able to affirm and encourage its good actions and require that its ineffective actions and negative behaviors be changed. When an institution is not accountable to its constituency, it goes easily out of control and its primary products are inequality and injustice.

What Is Institutionalized Racism?

Institutionalized racism takes place when an institution is shaped and structured in a way that it effectively serves and is accountable to only one racial group, while at the same time, it does not effectively serve nor is accountable to other racial groups. The institutionalization of racism is the result of intentional acts that can be traced historically in any institution. In the United States, every system and every institution were created originally and structured legally and intentionally to serve white people exclusively. Conversely, with the exception of organizations and institutions that were created specifically to resist racism, no institution in the United States has ever been designed or structured to serve effectively or be accountable to people of color. Even institutions of color are ultimately accountable to the oversight of white structures and systems.

> *Institutionalized racism takes place when an institution is shaped and structured in a way that it effectively serves and is accountable to only one racial group, while at the same time, it does not effectively serve nor is accountable to other racial groups.*

Dismantling Institutionalized Racism

When racism is institutionalized, it becomes a part of an institution's design and structure; thus, it should be obvious that dismantling institutionalized racism requires changing the design and structure of an institution. It is not enough simply to replace or provide better trained personnel or change institutional intentions or increase opportunities for persons of color. All these changes are good and necessary, but they are not sufficient. As I describe in greater detail below, such changes as these are only "transactional" in nature. What I call "transformational change" is the in-depth redesigning and restructuring of an institution at its deepest levels.

Part three of this study details the step-by-step process of dismantling institutionalized racism and bringing about transformational change in the church. However, it is important to state in advance, as we begin to identify and analyze the design and structure in the church that produces and maintains institutionalized racism, that our ultimate goal is the creation of a design and structure that redistributes institutionalized power and accountability directly into the hands of people of color. There is no other way to dismantle racism.

Biblical Reflection: The Institutionalized Body of Christ

The church is a spiritual community, a sacred society called to be the people of God. But it is also an institution, and in order to understand racism in the church, we must understand how the church functions as an institution. Because of the particular nature of the church as a spiritual community, we must also be clear about its special purpose, language, structure, and function. At the same time, it must be our intention to understand thoroughly the church as an institution in order to equip ourselves with the skills to guide the church through the process of dismantling institutionalized racism.

In order to understand the institutional nature of the church, we need to go all the way back to the time of its creation, when it began as a small secret religious movement, hidden on the back streets of Jerusalem and other cities in the Middle East. It is the nature of every movement, including religious movements, to start off without much internal organization. However, as movements start to grow in size, both numerically and geographically, the need emerges for organizational structure, and soon an institution begins to emerge. That is what happened in the early church. Although it started out as a religious movement, the church very quickly became institutionalized. The following is Paul's theological—and organizational—description of the church as the body of Christ from his letter to the Romans, written around A.D. 58.

> For as in one body we have many members, and not all the members have the same function, so we, who are many, are one body in Christ, and individually we are members one of another. We have gifts that differ according to the grace given to us: prophecy, in proportion to faith; ministry, in ministering; the teacher, in teaching; the exhorter, in exhortation; the giver, in generosity; the leader, in diligence; the compassionate, in cheerfulness. (Romans 12:4-8)

This text is very revealing about the growth of the early Christian community. It illustrates clearly two aspects of the early church. First, the church is a profound spiritual community, a movement with a mission, struggling to see itself theologically though the eyes of Christ. The idea of a body flowing together as one is movement language. Second, as the Christian movement grew and matured, it inevitably became an institution with structure and purpose. Within the unified body, as early as A.D. 58, there were leaders and an organizational structure, with lines of authority and accountability.

Thus, like any other movement, the church became institutionalized. There was an evolving need to carefully define increasingly complex relationships. While there were gains to be achieved in this developing of organizational structure, inevitably, there were also losses. Increasingly in Paul's epistles, we hear of interpersonal tensions as some people took more easily to change than others, especially as it became necessary for members to learn to understand their roles in relation to the whole and conform to mutually defined and mutually accountable relationships.

Some people might say that institutionalizing the church meant putting the Holy Spirit in a box, restricting the natural flow of energy and movement. Others might respond that the movement of the Holy Spirit was being impeded by impulsive individual actions, which called for a higher priority to organize the community for greater efficiency and efficacy in guiding the Holy Spirit's movement. Either way, the process was inevitable, and once it took place, some of the free-flowing movement was replaced by institutional design and structure. Of course, there remained a strong sense of the church still being a religious movement full of inspiration and flowing of energy led by the Holy Spirit. But it became important to recognize that both movement and institution are gifts of the Holy Spirit, both a piece of what God intended the church to become.

Nevertheless, with institutionalization also came struggles around issues of power, control, and authority, as well as the need to deal structurally with issues of inequality and injustice. The widows and orphans were not getting the care they deserved. Some groups were getting more benefits than others. Some leaders were making too many decisions on their own and needed to be called to accountability. Long before racism became institutionalized, there were other forms of institutional oppression in the church.

Then, as noted in chapter 2, the church became nationalized; it became a part of the state. If we return to the image I introduced earlier of the Ruler's Church, it is not difficult to imagine the jockeying for power as the church became increasingly friendly with the emperor and engaged in political maneuvering for greater favor and positions of power. The church may have started as a small movement of believers practicing communal sharing, but it was not long before it became an international organization, seeking to preserve the purity of the gospel in the context of hierarchy, authority, and institutional expansion.

How the Church Institutionalized Racism

In previous chapters, I traced what has been called the European captivity of the church and the subsequent support by various denominations of European colonial expansion throughout the world. Inevitably, the churches of the United States institutionalized a white identity and an organization that was designed and structured to serve and be accountable exclusively to white people. For the most part, the relationship of the church to people of color reflected values of white supremacy and domination almost exclusively. There were, of course, many missionaries who objected to the cruelty and inequality expressed toward people of color. But their voices were silenced for the most part. Along with every other institution in our society, the colonial Protestant and Roman Catholic churches were created and structured, legally and intentionally, to serve the white society exclusively. When we speak of racism being institutionalized, we need to be clear that this meant explicit and deliberate creation of an organizational design and structure of a church that was thoroughly white in its self-identity, authority, membership, programs and services, and accountability.

Is It Still That Way?

Having determined the historical origins of institutionalized racism, the primary goal of this chapter is to help readers examine their church's current design and structure. Our goal is to determine the degree to which the original structure and design of institutionalized racism is still in place, and to understand how institutionalized racism is still determining the life and mission of your church, including especially its distribution of power, authority, and accountability.

In chapter 6, I suggested that in the past forty or more years since the end of the civil rights era, the churches of our nation, along with other institutions, went through many positive changes, but at the same time they did not alter the underlying structures of institutionalized racism. I suggested that although we have passed through progressive stages of grief—denial, guilt, anger, and depression—in order to ready ourselves for the end of racism, the present stage of bargaining has brought us to a standstill as we are confronted by the imprisoning chains of underlying institutional design and structures that have not changed and still perpetuate a church for white people.

We are now at a point where it is necessary to test the accuracy of the assertion that institutionalized racism still controls your church today. Remember that we are not looking for the old forms of institutionalized racism that publicly and explicitly discriminated against people of color and insisted upon their segregation. We are also not looking for the outmoded forms of institutionalized racism that created and perpetuated negative feelings of prejudice and bigotry in white people toward people of color. Rather, we are looking for the far more subtle and sophisticated ways in which white power, authority, and accountability are still being preserved in the church.

It is also not enough to make generalized assertions about institutionalized racism in ecclesiastical structures. Like good investigative reporters, we need to be able to point to the structures and specifically describe how and where the racism is present and how it is perpetuated. We cannot just point broadly to an organizational chart and assert that it is all racist. Rather we must be able to look at each and every part of the organizational chart and clearly explain how each particular expression plays its part in keeping racism alive. To do this, we will look at five distinct institutional levels or structural layers of a church as presented on the chart on page 121:[2]

- *Personnel:* The staff and volunteers of the church who make the organization function.
- *Programs and Services:* What the church does for its constituency.
- *Membership and Community:* The people whom the church exists to serve.
- *Organizational Structure:* The way the church is put together and is managed.
- *Mission, Purpose, and Identity:* The "foundations" of the church; the formally stated reason the institution exists, along with its history, traditions, and culture.

LEVELS OF INSTITUTIONALIZED RACISM IN THE CHURCH		
Level	Explanation	Examples of Racism
THREE VISIBLE LEVELS—INTENDED TO BE SEEN BY THE PUBLIC		
Level 1: PERSONNEL	• Paid staff and volunteers within the church • People who are authorized to speak, act, and implement programs in the church's name • People who act as gatekeepers for church members and the general public	• Racial inequality in numbers, positions, and salaries • Ineffective training on racism, race relations, and cultural competency • Different treatment for white people and people of color • Lack of community and trust
Level 2: PROGRAMS and SERVICES	• What a church provides for its constituency: worship services, religious education, spiritual guidance, counseling, social services, serving opportunities, etc. • Designed to attract members and to help them grow in mind and spirit	• Different quality of programs and services for white people than for people of color • Programs are not designed to reflect commitments of the church regarding anti-racism or multiracial diversity • Policies regarding racism and race relations are absent, inadequate, or not enforced
Level 3: MEMBERS and COMMUNITY	• People who belong to the church • Community people who make use of the church's programs and services • Decisions and actions of the church are made in the name of and on behalf of the constituency	• Members are racially disproportional to the surrounding community • People of color in surrounding community are not adequately or equally served • Evangelism/outreach is discriminatory

	TWO LESS VISIBLE LEVELS—INTENDED TO BE SEEN MORE BY INSIDERS	
Level 4: **ORGANIZATIONAL STRUCTURE**	• Where the power of the church is: bishops, pastors, church councils, board of directors, managers, etc. • The hierarchy of authority and accountability: where decisions are made, the church's boundaries are drawn, budgets are decided, personnel is hired and fired, programs are approved, etc.	• Geographic or organizational boundaries exclude or ineffectively represent people of color • People of color do not have power or authority in the church • Church structures are accountable to white people and not accountable to people of color
Level 5: **MISSION, PURPOSE, and IDENTITY**	• Why the church exists; what it exists to do • Mission, purpose, and identity are defined by the church's constitution, by-laws, mission statement, belief system, worldview, history, and tradition	• The original mission, purpose, and organizational structure of the church in the United States was to serve white people exclusively • The identity, values, and worldview of the church today still reflects a commitment to serve white people better than people of color

This chart can be used to understand the structure of a congregation, a denomination, or any agency of the church. Take a moment to study the chart to see if you can identify the organizational levels of the part of the church you want to understand more deeply. For each of the five levels, there is a brief explanation of what is included at that level, and there are several examples of what institutionalized racism might look like at that particular level.

Also note that the first three of these institutional levels (Personnel, Programs and Services, and Constituency) are quite visible from the outside. They are intended to be seen by the public and are "dressed up" to make the institution inviting and attractive. The last two levels of an institution are far less visible from the outside. They reflect the inner working of an institution. Most of the information about these two lower levels is "insider information" and is known best by the personnel within the institution

The following pages explain each of these institutional levels in greater depth to enable readers—either individually or in study groups—to use this chart and the explanatory paragraphs as a basis for documenting how institutionalized racism is part of the design and structure of the congregation, denomination, or agency you are studying. Once again, I want to remind readers that we are not looking for the prejudicial attitudes and actions of individuals, but the ways in which the design and structure of the church cause it to serve more effectively and be accountable to white membership, while at the same time to serve less effectively and be less accountable to other racial groups.

The Most Difficult Levels of Institutionalized Racism

As we examine these five levels, it should become clear that racism may be operating simultaneously at any or all of them. At the same time, the more deeply racism is embedded in the lower levels, the more difficult it is to expose and eradicate. In recent decades, in efforts to help the church become more welcoming and multicultural, many church leaders have been willing to acknowledge the existence of problems with racism on the first three levels—in personnel, in programs, and in the constituency. It is on these levels where racism is most visibly expressed and most easily exposed, and where significant changes have in fact already taken place.

However, church leaders tend to be far more reluctant to recognize and deal with the racism that exists on the last two levels—organizational structure and mission, purpose, and identity. It is on these bottom two levels that self-perpetuating racism is most deeply institutionalized and entrenched, and where racism is far more serious and difficult to deal with. Thus, it is on these last two levels where most churches have made very little change, and where we need to focus in order to transform the deepest levels of institutionalized racism. Let's look at one level at a time.

Racism on the Level of Personnel

Personnel are the people who work for the church. They may be paid or volunteers; they may be ordained or laity. However, in their assigned roles they are authorized by the church to speak for it and to represent it to the constituency or to the public. Because their roles are officially endorsed, when a staff person or volunteer speaks and acts in the name of the church, that person's words and actions are no longer individual, but become institutional words and actions.

The most recognizable manifestations of racism among church personnel are expressions of prejudice or bigotry by individual persons. What turns prejudice into racism, however, is institutional power. Since a staff person or volunteer's words and actions officially represent the church, if an individual person speaks or acts in a racist way, that person's individual prejudice automatically becomes institutional racism. Whether it is a priest or pastor, a church secretary or a Sunday school teacher, the bigoted behavior of an individual has the effect of painting the entire church with a racist brush. The actions of a single individual are all it takes to communicate a message that the entire church is racist.

Another important measure of racism at this level is the extent to which a church's personnel have become racially diverse. Since the days of the civil rights movement and especially since the 1980s, there has been a great emphasis in the church on racial diversity and inclusiveness in institutional personnel. It is important to affirm diversification of personnel as a sign of progress and positive change. Not only have churches developed hiring policies and practices to enhance staff inclusiveness and diversity, but progressive education and training programs have also often been created to help multicultural staff relate better to one another. In multiple ways, churches are becoming increasingly effective in projecting an image that on the personnel level racial inequality is being overcome and progress is being made in overcoming racism.

At the same time, new problems emerge quite quickly when personnel in an institution become racially diverse. For example:

- Often there are conflicts between white personnel and personnel of color. When this happens, efforts to present an image of compatibility and harmony become more important than identifying and resolving conflict.
- People of color are usually required to assimilate into a white organizational culture, and are subjected to standards that are unequal and racist.
- Often there are serious limitations as to how high within the organizational structure personnel of color are permitted to ascend. As will become much clearer when we examine the organizational structure and focus on the offices of the church's decision makers, the more powerful positions are still reserved for white people and especially for white men.
- The biggest problem is that racial diversification of personnel is frequently the only institutional level where significant change is attempted. In fact, change on the level of personnel can all too easily be a cover for racism that is embedded in other levels of an institution. The result is that all the pressure to prove that the church is free of racism is placed upon the church's personnel.

Racism on the Level of Programs and Service

This level deals with the programs and services the church provides, such as worship, education, counseling, nurturing, social services, and the like. As with personnel, the church's programs and services are also highly visible and intended to be seen by the membership as well as by the general public. They are designed with an aim to attract, nurture, and retain the church's constituency. Promotional material and media advertisements are directed toward the public with the intent of gaining new members. Official policies and procedures guide the production and delivery of the church's programs and services in the achieving of these goals.

One way of identifying racism on this institutional level is to compare the programs and services in congregations of mainline Protestant and Roman Catholic denominations that are located in the white community with the programs and services in congregations of the same denomination that are located in communities of color. More often than not, this comparison will reveal dramatic differences. In the church, just as with other institutions, economic status affects the quality and quantity of the distribution of goods and services. The simple fact is that churches in white communities have historically received and still receive today more and better of almost everything than churches in communities of color receive, and the cause of this reality is directly related to the relative economic power of the white community compared to communities of color. Besides the immediate effect of disproportional distribution of goods and services, an even more important concern is the long-term effect of this economic inequality: it perpetuates the power of churches in the white community and perpetuates powerlessness of churches in communities of color. Power begets power and perpetuates itself, and powerlessness begets powerlessness and perpetuates itself.

In addition to this central issue of institutionalized economic disempowerment, a myriad of other problems of racism in the church exist at this level of programs and services. For example, educational materials designed for white churches often are distributed to communities of color with little or no adjustments for cultural realities in those communities. And even though history courses and special days and months are added to emphasize the realities of people of color, these superficial changes are seldom integrated into the continuingly dominant white history and reality at the center.

Of course, we need to acknowledge that many corrective efforts are being implemented to solve problems of racism at this institutional level, and such creative efforts certainly need to be continued. However, it is crucial to emphasize again that if such changes are made without examining the underlying structures and foundations of an institution and without confronting racism in its deepest institutional expression, the result will continue to be like using Band-Aids to cover up cancer. As we shall see more clearly when we explore the levels of organizational structure and mission and purpose, the continuing control and favoring of white power and privilege goes much deeper than an institution's programs and services.

Racism on the Level of Constituency and Community

Most churches exist in clearly defined geographical jurisdictions, such as a neighborhood, city, region, state, and so forth. For example, a congregation may exist to serve a neighborhood or an entire community, and a diocese or district is designed to serve a larger area. At the same time, a congregation or even an entire denomination may have a history of serving a specific ethnic or national constituency, such as German immigrants or rural farming communities. The changing demographics in the United States have challenged these old alignments and call for adjustments of churches to reach out to new constituencies. This has been certainly true for most mainline Protestant and Roman Catholic denominations in the past half-century, as they have been reaching out across racial lines in efforts to build multiracial constituencies.

White churches in this country were created and structured intentionally to serve exclusively white communities and white constituencies. Even if they were not totally white, they were usually strictly segregated, with people of color receiving far less quality of service and having little or no power. With the passage of civil rights laws, churches also desegregated and redefined their community and constituency. From this perspective, a great deal of progress has been made with regard to overcoming racism in local and national denominational constituencies. There are very few churches in the United States that, at least theoretically, have not redefined their constituency in multiracial terms.

But it must be kept uppermost in our minds that this is only theory. Despite the end of legalized segregation, de facto segregation is still the predominant reality in our nation, and therefore most churches are still serving segregated communities and constituencies. In racially changing neighborhoods, when white residents leave and people of color move in, churches still tend to close and move away or in other ways change the quality of service they offer, without consultation with their new constituency. The opposite experience is seen within neighborhoods that experience "re-gentrification," when people of color are forced out by racist economics and politics and white people return to "reclaim their community." When re-gentrification takes place, churches return to serve white constituencies.

It also needs to be understood that a church's decision to open its doors to people of color has not automatically resulted in people feeling welcome to come through them. How often the cry is heard: "We have opened the door for those people, but we don't know why they don't come in." It needs to be said that an anti-racist church seeking to be multiracial must also develop its cultural competency and make many cultural changes before it can adequately serve people of another racial, cultural, or ethnic background.

Transformational Change: Going Deeper Where Power Is Exercised

As noted above, many positive changes have been made in our churches on the first three institutional levels. And those changes have been important. The effects of the changes, however, are quite limited if change does not also take place in the two remaining institutional levels of the church. Despite manifold efforts to recruit and train racially diverse church personnel, despite endeavors to make the churches' programs and services more multicultural and distribute them more equally, and despite serious attempts to build multiracial membership, in most denominations the pattern of racial disparity created over the centuries continues to manifest itself in ways that are simply beyond the control of those working for change. Addressing issues of race and diversity in the church on visible and public levels, and not on the less visible levels where power is exercised, turns out to be superficial and ineffective.

Specialists in systems change make an important distinction between "transactional change" and transformational change. Transactional change refers to minor changes and transformational change refers to major changes in an institution. If we are satisfied with what a system or institution is producing, we need only to make adjustments, or transactional changes that will improve—but not significantly alter—the product or the method of production. However, if we are not satisfied with what a system is producing, transactional change will have no permanent effect, and will actually help to cover up the deeper problem. Deeper, transformational change is required to obtain a different product.

Any system or institution—*including the church*—will produce what it is designed to produce. If an institution is designed to produce racism, it will produce racism. If an institution is designed to produce white power and privilege, it will produce white power and privilege. And if an institution is designed to subordinate people of color, it will subordinate people of color. Transactional change on the three institutional levels of personnel, programs and services, and constituency may make institutionalized racism look better or feel softer, or even make it seem like it is going away. But it will not eliminate institutionalized racism. If we want any system or institution—*including the church*—to produce something different, transformational change is required in order to produce a new design.

Making transactional change in the church when transformational change is needed will inevitably be very frustrating. As long as we depend upon transactional changes to produce transformational results, we will not have true transformation. In fact, they will even cover up temporarily the need for transformational change, ultimately making the need for transformational change to be felt more severely. Institutionalized racism can only be eliminated if transactional change on the institutional levels of personnel, programs, and constituency is accompanied by transformational change on institutional levels of *organizational design and structure*, and *mission and purpose*. Let's take a closer look at these other two less visible levels.

Racism on the Level of Organizational Structure

Every institution and organization, including the church, has a formal institutional structure. Knowledge of the church's organizational structure is primarily insider information; it is not often familiar to the general membership. A person has to be an insider, usually an elected or assigned leader, to know its details and its complexities.

The center of institutional power. The organizational structure of the church is usually hierarchical in nature, to one degree or another. At the peak of the organizational structure is the center of power. This is where the bishop or presiding officer of a judicatory or the pastor of a congregation is in charge and exercises power. Depending upon the denomination, along with the bishop or presiding officer or pastor, a church council or board often shares decision-making power. It is at this place in the organizational structure that:

- policies of the church are defined and implemented;
- programs of the church are created, altered, or ended;
- personnel of the church are appointed or hired and fired;
- the church's programs and services are designed;
- budgets are approved;
- parish boundaries are demarcated or changed; and
- institutional accountability is defined and enforced.

Institutionalized racism is most deeply embedded where power is exercised. Our definition of racism is race prejudice plus power by systems and institutions. If the center of power is at this level of organizational structure (and, as we shall see in a moment, also at the level of *Mission and Purpose*), then this is also where the center of racism's misuse of power also will be found, and where it needs to be addressed. This is where we need to spend a lot of time analyzing and transforming institutional racism.

The opposite is usually the case. In fact, most churches quite specifically and intentionally avoid changing the center of power when issues of race relations and racial conflict are identified, analyzed, or addressed. In most churches, racial issues are addressed only on levels that are visible to the outside, because the goal in addressing racial issues is to look good, to look racially just and fair. Unfortunately—*and this is the major point of our analysis of institutional racism*—when efforts to deal with racism are addressed only on levels of personnel, products and services, and constituency, then institutional power structures will stay the way they were when they were originally created. This means that the organizational structure of most churches remains still virtually all white, and they are still structured to serve a white constituency. While less powerful personnel positions may have been to one degree or another diversified, the more powerful positions of management, and especially the highest positions of decision-making power, remain virtually unchanged.

Everywhere one looks in mainline Protestant and Roman Catholic churches, the vast majority of the seats of power are still occupied by white men. Of course, there may be a token presence of women and people of color to give it the flavor of change. But it must be noted that "position" is not necessarily the same thing as "power." Positional presence of people of color does not change power; in fact, it tends to support and extend white power, and it even prevents deeper change. Even if a few persons of color are given entrance to this level, it is quite simply not enough.

Accountability. It is also on the level of organization that the issue of accountability becomes central. One of the primary means of reducing or limiting the power of people of color in such positions is the continued absence of accountability to communities of color. No matter how many persons of color occupy leadership positions within church structures, the continued racism of those structures is assured if the institutions remain exclusively accountable to the white community.

Thus, the two central issues for understanding racism on this level of organizational structure are first, the limited presence and power or leadership of color; and second, the absence of accountability of the organizational structure to communities of color inside and outside the institution. Designing and shaping anti-racist churches in the United States begins with restructuring positions and power at the center of the organizational and institutional structures of our churches in such a way as to permit them to be led by people of color on the same parity with white people, and with making the church's institutions as formally accountable to communities of color as they are presently formally accountable to white people. It is to these two issues we will return in part three, where we will address the task of shaping an anti-racist church.

Racism on the Level of Mission, Purpose, and Identity

We have now arrived at the foundations of the church, the level of Mission, Purpose, and Identity, where the church's reason for existence is not only defined but preserved and defended. At this level, some core documents and traditions play a major role:

- *Identity Documents*: A church's identity is reflected in its mission and purpose, and is expressed in formal theological "identity documents," that were created at each denomination's inception. These identity documents reflect the church's worldview, its belief system, and its values.
- *Mission Statement*: Nearly every denomination and congregation also develops and often revises a mission statement, which is a brief summary and contemporary reflection of what lies deeper within an institution's foundations.
- *History and Tradition*: Besides its formal theological and legal identity documents, other marks of identity are built into a denomination's history and tradition. Tradition can be as powerful as theological documents in determining a church's identity.
- *Logos, Music, and Art*: Denominations, as well as many congregations, have their identity symbolized in a logo, in music, or in other artistic representations.

This level of mission, purpose, and identity is the deepest expression of power in a church. This level determines what will happen on all the other levels. Ultimately, all other levels are accountable to this level. In a real sense, a church's purpose and identity are sacred and unalterable. If any part of the church wanders away from its purpose stated in its identity documents, ultimately it will face church discipline or even expulsion. When a denomination or a congregation does find a need to make substantive changes, however, as is the case with dismantling racism, those changes need to be reflected ultimately in the purpose and identity documents.

It is on this deepest level of the church that historic racism has been most securely preserved. I hope the principle has been clearly established in each reader's mind that every institution in the United States—including every church—was created with a mission and purpose to serve white people exclusively. This mission and purpose was nurtured and deepened for centuries. Every mainline Protestant and Roman Catholic denomination has a white racist institutionalized identity that was created and is still preserved and protected on this level. All identity documents, theological self-definition, belief systems, and mission statements, along with traditions, symbolic logos, music, and other artistic expressions, were shaped to be consistent with this racist mission and purpose. Based on this racist identity, the other institutional levels were created and shaped to serve and be accountable to a white membership and to take advantage of the subservience and powerlessness of people of color. Racism became institutionalized and self-perpetuating in the church because it was inscribed in the church's identity, in its DNA. It began centuries ago with intentionality and deliberate design. Then it was passed on to generation after generation. Thus, this is the most important level where transformation must take place. In the twenty-first century, we are finally coming face to face with the responsibility and the opportunity to work for institutional transformation on this level, where true change can be initiated.

Of course, such a profoundly inscribed and embedded identity is not easily or quickly transformed. Over the past fifty years, we have softened the descriptive words of our mission statements by removing offensive words about exclusion, and we have added our intentions of implementing diversity, inclusiveness, and equality. In some cases our mission statements are even beginning to use the language of anti-racism. But these words have come from our mouths too easily and have become disguises to cover up a white identity that is still present and functioning to guide our nation's institutions.

Summary

When we focus on the lower levels of the institutional chart, a clear picture emerges that reveals the need for transformational change:

- Membership in mainline Protestant and Roman Catholic churches is still disproportionately white and still segregated. Jesus loves all the little children—

but in the twenty-first century they are still confined to their separate and unequal places of worship.

- Most churches have programs of multiracial and multicultural diversity and inclusiveness that on one level make people of color feel welcome but also result in little change in the power and decision-making process.
- Structures of authority, power, and accountability are still primarily in the hands of white people (mostly male).
- Where there are new leaders of color, the style and structure of their leadership is still defined by job descriptions, decision-making processes, hierarchical structures, cultural values, and accountability arrangements that were created historically to favor the needs of a predominantly white church.
- Primary decisions about ministry by and among people of color are still made within mostly white structures and mostly by white people.
- The cultural values, theological assumptions, belief systems, and models for ministry of the churches still reflect white historical reality.
- The programs and services of the churches are still aimed primarily toward a white audience, with the exception of programs of charity, which are still paternalistically aimed disproportionately toward people of color.
- Programs of social service have a continuing priority emphasis on charity to deal with needs created by injustice, with little increase in emphasis on dealing with the injustices that create the need for charity.

We will return in part 3 to these two lower institutional levels—Organizational Structure and Mission, Purpose, and Identity, when we begin to face the transformative work of designing and structuring an anti-racist church that will effectively serve and be accountable to all people. Before that, however, there is one final step in exploring racism in the church, and for that we now turn to a chapter on cultural racism.

Looking at Your Church.

How does this general list compare to the lists you have been compiling as you moved from level to level in examining your denomination, congregation, or religious institution? What is missing from your list, or what is on your list that is not on this one?

Chapter nine

Cultural Racism
and the Multicultural Church

"In our own languages we hear them speaking about God's deeds of power."

—ACTS 2:10

Have you been in church on Pentecost Sunday and heard the story from Acts 2 read aloud in one language and then in another and another by congregational members? God speaks to us in many languages. Hearing the gospel in each other's language is one of many exciting symbols of an increasingly multilingual, multiracial, multicultural church in the United States. It may be a small step—for some a first step—but it is a very important step on a path that we all need to walk.

The Christian church today is in the midst of a multicultural movement. We have a passion, a yearning, to repeat the experience of the first Pentecost. Denominations and congregations, aspiring for a multiracial, multicultural identity, study the Gospel stories of Jesus as he courageously and lovingly crossed divides and communicated across cultural boundaries. We attempt to emulate him in dealing with our own racial and cultural boundaries. As we work toward our goal of becoming a multicultural church, we carefully keep count of the different races, ethnicities, nationalities, languages, and cultures represented in our congregations. We proudly display our altar linens made from African kente cloth and our stoles from Central America. We sing new songs and hymns from all over the world, even as we remember the "old days" and honor the "old ways" with the music and festivals from the country or region where our denomination originated. In all of this we hope and pray that we are in some way repeating the Pentecost experience.

Is it happening? Yes! Are we there yet? No, not yet. We are on our way, but we are still a very long way from authentic multiculturalism. In fact, we have taken only the first steps of a journey to traverse racial and cultural boundaries. The journey began only a few decades ago but it is already taking us to new places we scarcely dreamed of. This journey toward a multicultural church is exciting and exhilarating and sometimes frightening. Above all it is a mission to which we have been called by God, who speaks through every language and acts within every culture.

Multicultural Hits a Wall: Cultural Racism

The path we are following toward a multicultural church is not an easy one. There are a multitude of obstacles in the way, none of which is more ominous or more dangerous than cultural racism. Cultural racism—the domination of one racially defined culture over others—stands alongside individual racism and institutionalized racism as the third manifestation of the systemic racism that overpowers us and prevents us from becoming the church that God intends us to be. While we are attempting to replicate Pentecost, we need to be aware that multicultural diversity can be practiced in a racist way. It can even be a means to try to cover up our racism. True multicultural diversity cannot happen until we have done all that is necessary to be free of cultural racism.

Before exploring cultural racism in the church, it is important to pause for a moment to summarize the analysis of cultural racism we bring to this book, as this is the starting point for our discussion. There are five important concepts that need to be included in understanding cultural racism. Let's take a brief look at each of them.[1]

What Is "Culture"?

Culture refers to the values, worldview, ideas, beliefs, behaviors, language, art, literature, religion, rituals, holidays, food, clothing, and dance that constitute the collective lifestyle of a society or a group of people in a society. Culture is our "way of life." It is important to remember that culture is collective. There is no such thing as the culture of a single individual apart from the large group of which an individual is a member. Culture is learned and passed on from generation to generation through a socializing process. At the same time, culture is not static. It changes and evolves over time and is influenced by encountering and interweaving with other cultures.

What Is "Race-Based Culture"?

As we have seen, the enforced process of racialization in the United States created six main racial groups: Native American, African American, Latino/Hispanic, Asian American, Arab American, and white. One major effect of this racialization has been the gradual receding of antecedent national, ethnic, and cultural identities and the surfacing of new "race-based cultures," which are cultural identities based on race. From the amalgamation of many cultures within each race has emerged a Native American culture, an African American culture, a Latino/Hispanic culture, an Asian American culture, an Arab American culture, and a white culture. In the United States, a significant part of the cultural identity of every person is "race-based," and within each racial group, everyone is socialized to accept the cultural norms associated with his or her racial identity.

What Is "Cultural Racism"?

A short definition of cultural racism is the domination of one racially defined culture over others. In the context of the United States, this applies to the domination of white culture over Native American, African American, Latino/Hispanic, Asian American, and Arab American cultures. With any definition of racism, the use of power is central. There are two ways that power has been used in implementing cultural racism in the United States. The first is the use of force by white society to create the segregated circumstances that produced six separate race-based cultures. The second is the power of white culture to continue to impose itself and maintain a dominant and controlling position over all other cultures. This focus on power is key. According to a definition employed by Crossroads Ministry, cultural racism is *when a racially defined societal group uses systemic power to establish its cultural way of life as dominant and superior and simultaneously imposes its cultural way of life onto other racially defined societal groups, destroying, distorting, discounting, and discrediting their cultures, while appropriating aspects of their cultures without accountability to those groups.*[2]

What Is White Cultural Identity?

Generally speaking, while there is great awareness of race-based culture among people of color, white people do not usually think of themselves as being part of a racial or cultural group. Nevertheless, despite this lack of awareness, there is a collective white racial and cultural group that is dominant and controlling in our society. In fact, one sign of the power of white cultural identity is its ability to exist and to dominate while at the same time remaining hidden from white consciousness and awareness. All of us, but especially those of us who are white, need to become aware of the white culture that collectively dominates our society.

As it does for people of color, cultural racism has negative and destructive consequences for white people. These effects can be seen clearly throughout history and today. Racialization forced European Americans into a "melting pot" experience that merged their national, ethnic, and cultural identities into a single racial identity called "white." Stripped of their European cultural heritage in order to shape a culture based on power and privilege, white people have lost much of the past. Like all other races in our society, white people live in cultural isolation, imprisoned by the very same power that imprisons others.

What Is Multicultural Diversity?

Multicultural diversity refers to the promotion of societal inclusiveness on the basis of race, ethnicity, gender, sexual orientation, and human physical differences in order to counteract the effects of historical exclusion and discrimination. The modern multicultural diversity movement began in the early 1980s, and since then virtually every institution and community in our society has placed multicultural diversity among their highest organizational priorities. While multicultural diversity refers to many areas of inclusiveness, we are focusing here on efforts to overcome exclusion and division by race, and to become a multiracial/multicultural society

Culture and Cultural Racism in the Church

The Culture of the Church

In order to understand cultural racism in the church, we need to think about how the church experiences culture. Let's begin with a question: Is it obvious that every denomination and every congregation has its own unique culture?

Many denominations in the United States have roots in European churches and are heavily influenced still by their particular culture of origin. For example, Methodists and Episcopalians in the United States are marked by their English beginnings. Presbyterians are shaped especially by their Scottish origins. The various Lutheran cultures are greatly influenced by their roots in Scandinavian countries, Germany, or Eastern Europe. And while there is a common culture that binds all Roman Catholics, the church in the United States is influenced by the cultures of the countries from which its members immigrated, including Ireland, Poland, Italy, and Spain.

Many other denominations, including Baptist, Adventist, Christian Church (Disciples of Christ), Church of God, Christian Science, Jehovah's Witnesses, and Mormon (Latter Day Saints), were either "born in America" or have developed a uniquely American religious culture.

Despite a variety of origins and differing cultural characteristics, to some degree, all churches in the United States have become culturally "Americanized." Even if churches maintain distinct theological and liturgical differences, predominantly white mainline Protestant and Roman Catholic churches are increasingly similar culturally. Bound together by commonalities of race, language, political loyalties, and middle- to upper-class lifestyles, these predominantly white churches are culturally very much alike despite denominational differences, especially when compared to denominations of color.

The culture of denominations and congregations of color is very different from white denominational culture. Churches of color are heavily influenced in terms of organization by their parent church bodies, but they differ considerably from their white counterparts with regard to their primary cultural identity. Of course, this is due in part to their global origins in Africa, Asia, Latin America, and other parts of the world. But to an even greater extent, the cultural identity of churches of color is due to the cultural racism of white churches who enforced centuries of isolation and refused to recognize or value any culture other than their own as "American." Consequently, there is a unique and markedly different culture in these "other American churches."

The Culture of Your Church.

How would you describe the culture of your denomination or your congregation? In what ways does it share a common culture with other white mainline American denominations? What is distinct about it? Was it originally rural and now becoming more and more urbanized and suburbanized? Was it earlier more countercultural and now increasingly accepting and influenced by the world and culture? Does it reflect the European culture of the past, the amalgamated white culture of the melting pot, or the culture of color of the "other American cultures"?

If you are from a denomination or congregation that is other than white mainline Protestant or Roman Catholic, how would you describe its culture? In what ways is it different from the common culture of other churches? Has the culture remained the same over the generations or is it in transition? How is it influenced by cultural racism?

The Church and Cultural Racism

In the context of a church's cultural identity, it is possible to move to the central question of this chapter: How has the church been affected by cultural racism? We need to consider how the problem of cultural racism is a barrier to efforts today to become a multiracial/multicultural church. To begin to address this question, we need to be clear that the historical path of racism followed by each of our denominations is very little different from the path that has been followed by the rest of society. Despite what our churches have taught about Christians keeping ourselves pure and separate from the world, the fact is that all of our churches have succumbed to the ways of the world by adopting and imitating the world's cultural racism. There is no way to soften the reality that our history of racism and the resulting racial divisions within the churches of the United States are mirror images of the history of racism and the racial divisions of the society in which the church exists.

This is no accident. As documented in previous chapters, mainline predominantly white Protestant and Roman Catholic churches in our society participated very enthusiastically and intentionally in shaping the racial divisions and racism that we find in the world and in the church today. Moreover, they remain still overwhelmingly identified with and defined by the dominant white culture. Just as our churches are captive to institutionalized racism, so are they imprisoned by white cultural racism. Consequently, we live in virtual isolation from churches of other races and cultures. Like the rest of our society, Christians are imprisoned by racial and cultural barriers that divide us into red church, black church, brown church, yellow church, and white church.

Identifying Cultural Racism

It is important to be able to document and describe precisely how cultural racism is being experienced in the church and how it negatively impacts both white people and people of color. Using this documentation, it will be possible to clarify further what keeps us locked in cultural segregation and isolation and to understand why our efforts to shape multicultural churches have failed thus far to unlock these prison doors. Following are a few examples of how cultural racism can be identified within most predominantly white mainline Protestant or Roman Catholic churches:

- The style of worship (usually exclusively in English) is rigid and relatively unemotional. The images, symbols, rituals, practices, and artistic expressions within the churches reflect the dominance of western culture over all other religious cultural expressions. Examples: God, Jesus, and other biblical figures are represented artistically as white; religious music is predominantly from a European and white heritage.
- The power to define, decide, set or change the cultural beliefs, norms, and practices in the church are overwhelmingly in the hands of white people.
- As with all other institutions in the United States, the church has a white organizational culture, reflected in decision-making processes, communication and management styles, use of time and space, and so forth.
- The history of the church is told by predominantly white historians from a white point of view, with little emphasis on the history of churches of color—despite the fact that Christianity is originally a Middle Eastern and African religion.
- Biblical interpretation, theological doctrines, and ethical teachings express for the most part a white/European perspective and are controlled by predominantly white male theologians. Because of this, issues of justice receive low priority. Particularly appalling is the silence of white theologians and white theology on issues of race and racism.
- Because evangelistic and missionary outreach has historically reflected white cultural supremacy, the beliefs and cultures of other Christians and other religions have been discredited, discounted, distorted, and, in the worst-case scenario, destroyed entirely.
- The beliefs and values of American civil religion (such as excessive individualism and nationalism) are reflected in the popular beliefs and values of the church.

Often Christianity and national loyalties are virtually inseparable, as is illustrated by the presence of the United States flag in many church sanctuaries.

- The churches' agenda for participating in the ecumenical movement is dictated from a white point of view. Consequently, the issue of the racial separation of churches is not given a very high priority in our efforts to understand and overcome denominational divisions.

Cultural Racism in Your Church.

The examples listed above provide a starting point for examining cultural racism in denominational settings, including your own. If you are from a predominantly white congregation or denomination how does this list compare with your experience? What practical examples of cultural dominance and oppression in your church would you add to the list?

If you are from a denomination or congregation of color how have you felt the influence of white culture imposed in your church's life? What examples can you offer of how the culture of your church of color has been discredited, discounted, distorted, or destroyed by this influence? Where have you seen the culture of color appropriated by white churches?

Turning Point: The Multicultural Movement in the Church

With this initial list of marks identifying cultural racism within your church in hand, the next step is to place this list into the context of current efforts for change in your denomination or congregation. Fifty years ago, such a list would have been relatively static, the items largely unchanging, because few if any efforts were being made to address issues of institutional and cultural racism. This is no longer the case. As I have emphasized repeatedly, our nation and our churches have been going through an extensive process of change over the last five decades. In chapter 6, using stages of grief as a matrix, we charted this process noting how our nation and its churches moved from denial to guilt, anger, and depression, before getting stuck in the bargaining stage. In each stage, we moved forward ever so slowly toward the goal of eventual acceptance of the end of racism, even while facing strong resistance to change at every step along the way. By and large, our churches and our nation are now in the bargaining stage, which is the second to the last stage of grief. The central feature of this stage is the great effort being made to achieve multicultural diversity and inclusiveness. We turn our attention now to looking more closely at programs of multicultural diversity and analyzing their effect on our churches.

In the 1980s—twenty years after the doors of our segregated churches had been thrown open—predominantly white mainline churches were faced with the reality that despite our efforts to integrate, very few people of color were crossing the thresholds of our sanctuaries. So, in the hope of furthering goals of racial integration, the churches joined in the nation's multicultural diversity movement and developed a major effort to build an inclusive church. Eager to break out of self-constructed racial prisons, all mainline Protestant and Roman Catholic churches in the United States began to commit themselves to the gospel's unifying call to become multiracial and multicultural churches. The multicultural movement is still present in the churches today, reflecting the high priority we give to overcoming the racial walls that divide us. But now, nearly thirty years after its beginning, it is time to evaluate these efforts to shape multicultural diversity. We need to assess what is working in our diversity programs and what is not. We need to ask which features of the churches' approach to diversity should be preserved and expanded. We need to ask why it is that the central goals of multicultural diversity and inclusiveness are yet to be achieved. Why have we not yet been able to break down the barriers that separate us into red, yellow, brown, black, and white denominations? What is keeping us from building a truly multiracial/multicultural church?

The Beloved Community: Reconnecting with God's Vision

To begin our examination of multicultural diversity programs in our churches, we must look at the biblical and theological framework that distinguishes our diversity programs from diversity programs in our nation's secular institutions. In most ways, diversity efforts, whether religious or secular, are much alike, both in their strengths and weaknesses. The programs have similar objectives, strategies, and timelines. Nearly all establish some form of racial quotas, mandate diversity training programs, develop extensive publicity and promotional efforts, and have significant budgetary commitments. It is the recovery of a biblical vision of inclusive community that sets apart the churches' multicultural diversity programs from all others.

Underlying the central message and images throughout the Bible, but particularly in the New Testament, is the unifying vision of the oneness and wholeness of God's creation. At the center of this vision is the reconciled community of all people, a community surpassing divisions of gender, race, class, and nation, where all receive the gift of unconditional acceptance, peace, and justice. In past centuries this vision was distorted and suppressed in a convergence of political and ecclesiastical power, resulting, tragically, in the will of God being taken hostage and used to grant divine permission for the unjust rule of white supremacy. In recent decades, we have rediscovered the New Testament proclamation that all people are one in Christ Jesus. The recovery of this vision has enormous significance for the transformation of our churches. In our renewed emphasis on God's call that we be reconciled with one another and freed from all that divides us, we dare to proclaim and to dream that one day "every valley shall be lifted up, and every mountain and hill be made low; the uneven ground shall become level, and the rough places a plain. Then the glory of the Lord shall be revealed, and all people shall see it together" (Isaiah 40:4). The churches' gradual reconnection to this dream is the unique and driving force behind our programs of multicultural diversity and inclusiveness. Step by step, this reconnection has been taking place, but the longest and most difficult steps are still before us.

Diversity's Tentative Beginnings

The first step in uncovering and rediscovering this ancient biblical vision was reversing the churches' shameful support of racial oppression. Only then could we begin to establish principles of inclusiveness as the theological foundation for programs of diversity and inclusiveness. It must never be allowed to be forgotten that until just recently the churches blasphemously permitted and often encouraged the use of the Bible and doctrine for the support of racism, as well as exclusion on the basis of gender and sexual orientation. Only by remembering centuries of blindness and unspeakably painful violation of these core beliefs of the Christian faith can we be assured that they will not be repeated, and that we need even more strongly to affirm the biblical vision of justice and reconciliation.

In recent decades, denominations have developed official statements and proclamations that create a biblical and theological framework for their programs of diversity. A key passage from Paul's letter to the Galatians has become the biblical foundation for understanding the Christian principle of inclusiveness: "There is no longer Jew or Greek, there is no longer slave or free, there is no longer male and female; for all of you are one in Christ Jesus" (3:28). This single passage summarizes with great clarity all that is meant by the oneness, unity, and inclusiveness engendered by the Christian faith, and it illuminates the many other expressions of this central New Testament theme.

There are two main points I want to emphasize here. The first is that our churches are trying hard to bring about change. And not only trying; it is also clear that there has been progress in moving toward the goal of becoming an inclusive church. It is important for us to celebrate the strength of these efforts. The second point is that we still have a long way to go. In fact, we have in many ways run aground and nearly stopped making forward progress. We have yet to discover the full meaning of inclusiveness. Like the early New Testament church, we have to learn that God's acceptance and inclusiveness is far more radical and far more unconditional than we could imagine. We need to be clear about the weaknesses and the danger of failing in our efforts, for the reality is that the changes we are seeking have remained elusive and unmet.

Why Multicultural Diversity Programs Are Not Succeeding

In chapter 6, we began to discern and describe the barriers to success of our diversity programs. We need to continue that effort now. I will use my own denomination, the Evangelical Lutheran Church in America (ELCA), as an example of what I believe are the difficulties being faced by every denomination. In 1987, a goal was set to increase the membership of people of color within the ELCA by 10 percent in the next ten years. In the decade that followed, we achieved only about 1 percent gain, and only a little more since. A parallel goal of achieving 10 percent representation of people of color on church staffs, committees, and commissions, and at church meetings in convention or assembly, has been met on church-wide levels, but only irregularly on regional and local levels. Still greater difficulties have been encountered in efforts to manifest a multicultural atmosphere and identity in worship, educational curriculum, and meeting styles. An important strength of ELCA multicultural diversity programs is the Commission for Multicultural Ministries, which supports direct ministries among various people of color communities. However, these programs have little effect on overcoming the separation and isolation of communities of color from the main programs of the predominantly white churches.

I am taking little risk in making the judgment that the diversity programs in other denominations have met similar obstacles and seen similar results. Despite investments of enormous amounts of time, energy, and money into multicultural diversity, progress is extremely limited and forward motion is very difficult and frustratingly slow. Why is this the case? Because we do not know how to do it; we fall back constantly into the grinding wheels of cultural racism. All too often, instead of overcoming cultural racism, our efforts have provided a protective screen that allows cultural racism to continue and even to increase. For example, our attempts to welcome people of color into our churches are carried out in a manner that often results in our trying to assimilate them into white religious culture rather than opening ourselves up to becoming multicultural. Our message to new members is: you can come in, if you are willing to be like us. People of color are asked to leave their culture outside and to adopt the white culture of the church they are joining. Even though alternative hymnbooks and liturgies and observance of holidays such as the birthday of Dr. Martin Luther King Jr. give an occasional different cultural flavor, in most other ways the basic cultural life of our denominations and congregations remains unchanged. Some denominations provide alternative organizational space and financial support for people of color to have their own cultural experiences, but usually not in ways that influence or change the dominant white culture. The message we often seem to be giving is that the culture of each denomination is part of its essential identity and belief system, rather than a context that is able to adapt and change. We seem unable to acknowledge that true diversity must allow for and be open to the transformation of culture.

When we do attempt to incorporate the culture of other religious traditions into our worship services, programs, and educational curriculum, we often do so in an embarrassingly awkward and sometimes even unethical manner. One of the most aggravated forms of cultural racism is the misappropriation of images, symbols, rituals, practices, and/or religious expressions of any culture, without permission, acknowledgment, or accountability to those groups from whom we are "borrowing." Examples include imitating Native American rituals, such as vision quests and sweat lodges, or adapting aspects of African American holidays, such as Kwanzaa. Marjorie Bowens-Wheatley, a Unitarian Universalist minister, writes:

> Upholding European American ideas, values, and assumptions as the norm is as much a part of sustaining racism as segregation, scapegoating, or the lack of equal opportunity. Dismantling racism begins with saying that we can no longer do business as usual. . . . Our first task in approaching another people, another culture is to take off our shoes, for the place we are approaching is holy. Else we find ourselves treading on another's dream. More serious still, we may forget that God was there before our arrival.[3]

On the positive side, our efforts to attract people of color into our churches have not been completely without success. But when two or three people of color are present in our midst, we often feel ill at ease and do not know how to relate. We are ill equipped to deal openly with issues of racial identity and race relations, so we adapt a "colorblind" approach, pretending that we do not see color and that we are all the same under the skin. Or, alternatively, we overreact. To ensure that people of color are visibly present everywhere within our church structures, we turn to the same few people of color again and again until they are completely worn out. The reality is that "tokenism"—the symbolic presence of people of color—is not a substitute for adequate representation.

It's the Power Thing Again

Our difficulties with diversity are actually symptoms of a far deeper issue—the issue of power. Racism is always about power. If cultural racism has resulted in people of color being either assimilated or isolated in our churches, then the underlying causes are bound to have something to do with the issues of power and accountability. Take another look at the institutional levels chart on page 121. Do you recall that the power of an institution is concentrated in the bottom two levels of this chart, the levels of organizational structure, and on institutional identity? Cultural changes on the upper three levels of personnel, programs, and constituency produce superficial adjustments but do not represent serious transformation. Even when the presence of people of color in our churches increases, there is very little change in the levels of institutionalized power and accountability. The decisions are still made by white people who are in charge of a white system and a white organizational culture, and measuring of the effectiveness of the decisions and of the system continues to be carried out via accountability processes dominated by white people.

Sometimes even the rules of democracy work against us. There is an underlying tragic contradiction in democratic process, whether in our nation as a whole or in our churches, that has allowed racism to be enforced for centuries by the rule of the majority. We are still caught in this contradiction. Even though we may be making serious efforts to do justice, there are no alternate processes for making decisions other than by the rule of the majority. This means that as long as white people are in the majority, both the wrong decisions and the right decisions will be made by white people. And as long as people of color are in the numeric minority, they will not have the democratic power in the church or anywhere else to determine their own destinies.

There is urgent need for new forms of decision making that take into consideration the fact that as long as race plays such a strong role in our lives, our democratic system will reinforce racial dominance. No matter who is in the majority, so long as race is a factor, the manner of making decisions will always be based upon racial dominance. We will not reach the final stage of accepting the end of racism without the creation of anti-racist forms of decision-making that will change the way we deal with power and accountability.

Still Stuck in the Bargaining Stage of Grief

The present state of affairs in our programs of diversity is that our churches are offering an unequal multicultural bargain at an unequal multicultural bargaining table. This is bound to produce unequal and disproportional results. The unequal bargain is that white churches, along with the rest of society, promise positive change for people of color, while keeping the old order of power and decision making in place. In offering this bargain, the white society says to communities of color: "We will give you a share in our world, with new opportunities and greater participation, while we will maintain our white privileges and stay in charge."

The only way to resolve this problem is to realize that we are not yet fully prepared for the death of racism. It is a great and dangerous temptation to pretend that bargaining is the last stage in the process and that programs of multicultural diversity as they are presently designed are a way of helping white-controlled church structures to look more colorful. As long as our current programs are designed to keep old structures and relationships of power in place, we will be stuck in this next to the last stage of grief. We need to be glad for all that has been achieved in this bargaining stage and through programs of multicultural diversity, but unless we are prepared to move to the next stage, our present path toward shaping an anti-racist church will lead only to failure.

Part III

The Future:
Shaping an Anti-Racist Church

While I was working on this final section, I heard from the Rev. Willard Bass, an African American Methodist pastor, community organizer, and friend from Winston-Salem, North Carolina, who has been helping me think about the content and style of the book. He wrote:

> The challenge I continue to think about is to be able to have hope. It is not enough to be convicted, ashamed and disarmed by the truth about racism in the church. I think that for white people and for people of color who are Christians, embracing the whole truth about our faith requires a rethink of what it means to be Christian in America. I hope by the time you are finished with this book, your readers will be able to have hope in tackling this huge challenge.

Decades ago the motto *¡Si Se Puede!* (Yes, We Can) originated in the Farm Worker Movement to reflect the confidence of a strong community struggling for justice. More recently it was a progressive political slogan in Barack Obama's campaign for the presidency. As we prepare for the next steps of organizing for change in the church we need to claim the attitude of confidence and strength and hope expressed in *¡Si Se Puede!* We need to keep these affirming, hopeful words in mind as we move into the next pages, believing fully that it is possible to overcome racism. Our churches *can* become anti-racist in their deepest foundations. We *can* be strong leaders and participants in these efforts. You and I *can* shape anti-racist churches that are dedicated to dismantling racism in church and society. We can overcome racism. Yes, we can! In this final section, we take up the task of how to go about doing this.

God's Call to a New Beginning

Throughout this book, we have been following a path to action, a journey toward change and transformation. We have now come to the final step on that path. Before us waits the most important task of all: defining, describing, and planning the action of shaping an anti-racist church. I am delighted to join you in this exciting, demanding, spirit-led, risk-filled, life-giving, restorative, hope-filled, gospel-centered task.

It is a calling from God for Christians to take up the unfinished task of overcoming racism. For those of us who have hoped and prayed for an end to complacency and who long for new commitment to racial justice in our churches and society, today is a new beginning. We have seen that for centuries people have responded to God's call to stand against the evil forces of racism and to work for a racially just world. It is that history that brings us to this moment when the baton is passed to us. Now it is our responsibility and our task to respond to God's call to join the "great cloud of witnesses" before us in running the race, persevering in resisting racism, and organizing to change church and society.

Making a Path by Walking It

As we focus in these final chapters on the crucial work of creating new momentum for change within mainline Protestant and Roman Catholic churches, we need to be clear that there is no established path toward our goal. We are creating the path by walking it. It is a risky journey that at times can lead to dead ends, forcing us to turn around and retrace our steps.

While the anti-racism work already under way in a number of our churches can be affirmed, it also needs to be critiqued. Many programs of anti-racism are very limited and severely flawed. Good words and intentions have not translated into effective action. Too often programs are disguises for change that allows things to remain the same. Our churches, like virtually all institutions, are stuck in the bargaining stage, refusing to acknowledge that real change is needed. Until we are prepared to accept the end of racism, even the strongest programs of anti-racism will be no more effective than the programs of multicultural diversity on which churches have focused their efforts in the post–civil rights era. This focus will not lead to transformation of institutional racism, which is all about power, access, and accountability. It is not possible to achieve our goal of racial equality while holding on to white power and privilege. The two are mutually exclusive. Nothing short of an anti-racist identity and new structures of power and accountability will bring us to the ultimate goal of the ending racism.

God has called us to this task and promises to lead us and guide us along the way. We *can* shape anti-racist churches that are dedicated to dismantling racism in the church and in society. *¡Si Se Puede!* Yes we can!

Steps along a Continuum toward Change

The chapters that follow present a practical step-by-step process for moving beyond multicultural diversity to defining, designing, and creating an anti-racist church. The primary tool that I use to depict the path forward is the *Continuum on Becoming an Anti-Racist Multicultural Church* on pages 148–49.[1] This is an adaptation of a tool developed by Crossroads Ministry to help institutions and communities understand where they have been, where they are now, and how to organize for the next steps toward institutionalizing anti-racism. The continuum, adapted here to apply specifically to the church, measures gradual movement through a series of six stages as a church deals progressively with institutionalized racism in creating a path to becoming an anti-racist/multicultural church.

The continuum is divided into two parts. The left side describes conditions of past and present racism in the church along a continuum from monocultural to multicultural. The right side describes the church's future along a continuum from anti-racist to anti-racist multicultural. In addition, each side is divided into three stages, with the six stages of the full continuum spanning from a segregated church to a changing church in a changing society. I offer a few introductory comments below. Please take a moment to review the continuum.

CONTINUUM ON BECOMING AN

WHERE THE PREDOMINANTLY WHITE CHURCH IS NOW
MONOCULTURAL → → → MULTICULTURAL → →

1. An Intentionally Segregated Church	2. A "Club" Church	3. A Multicultural Church
• Pre-1960s—legally and intentionally structured segregation • Intentional and public exclusion of African Americans, Native Americans, Latinos/Hispanics, Asian Americans, and Arab Americans • White power and privilege and dominance of people of color is inscribed throughout the church • Intentional and public enforcement of racist status quo throughout the church • Institutionalization of racism includes formal policies and practices, teachings, and decision making on all levels • The church usually has similar intentional policies and practices toward other socially oppressed groups such as women, gays and lesbians, Third World citizens, etc.	• Publicly obeys the laws of desegregation; removes signs of intentional exclusion • Tolerant of a limited number of people of color with "proper" perspective and credentials **But . . .** • White constituency is still exclusive and paternalistic in its attitudes and actions, and often declares, "We don't have a problem." • Continues its organizational structure, mission, and self-understanding as a white church serving a predominantly white constituency • Continues to maintain white power and privilege through its de facto policies and practices, teachings, and decision making on all levels of church life • May still secretly limit or exclude people of color in contradiction to public policies	• Develops official policies and practices regarding multicultural diversity and inclusiveness • Sees itself as a "non-racist" church with open doors to people of color • Carries out intentional inclusiveness efforts, recruiting "someone of color" for committees or staff **But . . .** • "Not those who make waves" • Little or no contextual change in power structure, culture, policies, and decision making • Is still relatively unaware of continuing patterns of white privilege, paternalism, and control • Increasing discord about diversity, and signs of failure of programs of multicultural diversity • People of color increasingly express dissatisfaction or leave the church

ANTI-RACIST MULTICULTURAL CHURCH

WHERE THE PREDOMINANTLY WHITE CHURCH NEEDS TO GO
→ → ANTI-RACIST → → → ANTI-RACIST MULTICULTURAL

4. Identity Change—An Anti-Racist Church	5. Structural Change—A Transforming Church	6. A Changing Church in a Changing Society
• Programs of anti-racism training are instituted throughout the church, resulting in a common analysis of systemic racism and a growing understanding of racism as a barrier to effective diversity • A consciousness of internalized racial oppression and white power and privilege emerges within the church, along with an increasing commitment to eliminate inherent white advantage • Cross-racial relationships are deepened and white people begin to develop accountability to communities of color • Through auditing and evaluation, the analysis is applied to all levels of the church • A critical mass of old and new church leadership and membership claims an anti-racist identity and a vision of an anti-racist institution • A transition to Stage 5 is initiated by a formal decision to institutionalize an anti-racist identity throughout the structures and culture of the church	• The church commits to the new stage of redesigning, restructuring, and institutionalizing an anti-racist identity • Restructuring ensures full participation of people of color in decision making and other forms of power sharing on all levels of the church's life and work • Inclusion of worldviews, cultures, and lifestyles of people of color is ensured in all aspects of church life • Authentic and mutually accountable anti-racist relationships are structured between people of color and white people within the church • There are similar institutional changes toward other socially oppressed groups, including women, gays and lesbians, Third World citizens, etc. • There is within the church a sense of restored community and mutual caring	• The church commits to participation in the struggle to dismantle racism throughout society and rebuilds and redefines all relationships and activities between the church and the wider community on the basis of anti-racist commitments • Clear lines of mutual accountability are built between the church and racially oppressed people in the larger society • The church builds anti-racist relationships with other churches, particularly with churches of color, with emphasis on mutual accountability, reconciliation, and reparations • Alliances with allies in church and society ensure links to all aspects of social justice, particularly to issues of global interdependence and international structures of justice and equality

Stages 1–3: "Where the Predominantly White Church Is Now"

The left half of the continuum represents the historical path that churches have been following since the beginning of the civil rights movement until the present time. Currently all mainline Protestant and Roman Catholic churches are located somewhere on the left side of the continuum. While it is true that over the last fifty years virtually all have moved from stage one (formal segregation) to various expressions of stage two (club church) and stage three (multicultural church), it is important to understand that the basic power structure does not change as long as the church is on this left side of the continuum. Although a church looks like it has become multicultural, it is still segregated in terms of who has power. By attempting to become diverse without dealing with underlying issues of structure based on white power and privilege, churches have created a dilemma of racist multicultural diversity. Ultimately, all attempts to become multicultural without changing structures of power, access, and accountability are destined to fail. Confronted with this failure, many churches are beginning to realize the need to move toward the second half of the continuum, but, at the present time, it is only small groups of people from any church who are actually exploring doing so. The rest of the church's membership, programs, and organizational structure remain anchored in the first half of the continuum.

Stages 4–6: "Where the Predominantly White Church Needs to Go"

Our focus in the chapters that follow is on the right side of the continuum. In moving from the left side of the continuum to the right, the first important principle to grasp is that the structural changes of stages five and six cannot be made effectively until there is readiness in the church to make and accept these changes. For this to be the case, the church's identity must be transformed gradually from a racist church to an anti-racist church, which is what happens in stage four. In describing a concrete plan of action in the next three chapters, we will focus first on the immediate goal of shaping an anti-racist identity and then we will move to the step of institutionalizing that identity and shaping an anti-racist church.

In preparation for the structural changes that are to come, chapter 10, "God's Call to Become an Anti-Racist Church," explores the need to develop and internalize an understanding of racism within the church and its members. Chapter 11, "Getting It Done: The Organizing Task," outlines the process to accomplish the task of shaping an anti-racist identity. It includes examples of how this is beginning to happen in some denominations and proposes ways to overcome the barriers that prevent completion of the task.

The last chapter, "Institutionalizing Anti-Racism in the Church," focuses on developing a step-by-step process of institutionalizing new structures of power, access, and accountability, which includes linking the churches' anti-racism work to the anti-racism work of other churches, institutions, and communities.

chapter ten

God's Call to Become
an Anti-Racist Church

"You must be born again."

—JOHN 3:7 NIV

New Identity: A Birthing Process

The first and most important task in shaping an anti-racist church is to give birth to an anti-racist Christian identity. Stage four of the *Continuum on Becoming an Anti-Racist Multicultural Church* describes this process in step-by-step detail. As with any birth, this includes a long period of pregnancy and gestation that is risk-filled, often painful, and has many potentially dangerous complications. And likewise, as in any other birthing process, when it is completed, the exciting and joyful celebration of the newborn will far outweigh the agony of the delivery. Six steps in giving birth to an anti-racist identity are outlined in stage four of the continuum, which we will explore more carefully in this chapter. Only when these six steps are completed and an identity transformation has taken place will it be possible to move to the next stage and institutionalize permanent changes in the design and structure of the church.

Taking this birthing metaphor one step further to the biblical imagery of rebirth, this identity-transforming process can be understood in no less powerful terms than what Jesus described as being "born again"—a complete spiritual transformation. The church's understanding of rebirth in biblical terms is linked to baptism. The most fundamental and unifying teaching of Christianity is that in baptism everything dies that does not belong to God, and in its place a new person is born—a new person whose central identity is "child of God" in the "family of God." Each day is a day of rebirth, a day of cleansing, a day of re-establishing that we belong to God and to God's whole and holy family. In the same way, the rebirth and renewal of mainline Protestant and Roman Catholic churches as anti-racist multiracial/multicultural churches, after centuries of imprisonment in racism, is nothing less than a death and resurrection experience. Not only individual members of the church, but the church itself must be born again.

Go Home and Free Your Own Church

The pathway we have been following toward ending racism leads directly to the doors of our home churches, to face our congregations at their segregated Sunday morning worship services. We need to go home and free our own people. Contrary to earlier thinking, the mission to build a multicultural church does not begin with "outreach" to people who are not yet in our churches, but rather it begins with "inreach" into the center of our sanctuaries. We cannot escape the painful realization that our own people and our churches are imprisoned by racism and are not free.

But at the same moment of this realization comes a message of new hope and freedom. The message is the unchanging gospel that although we are enslaved by sin, we are freed by grace. And that is good news for all people—for people of color and white people alike. Along with this message of freedom comes a mandate for mission, a mission to shape an anti-racist church. An anti-racist church promises to all of us a renewed and restored life together in the beloved community. The starting place is to return to our segregated and imprisoned churches, with a commitment to the task of transformation and liberation from racism.

In many denominations this mission of anti-racism has already been initiated; the shaping of an anti-racist church is already starting to take place. Most mainline predominantly white denominations, including Episcopalian, Lutherans, Presbyterian, Roman Catholic, Disciples of Christ, Methodist, Mennonite, and many more, are already engaged in some form of anti-racism work. It is important to acknowledge and celebrate that this work is not a mere projection of what may happen in the future. It is something that has already begun to happen.

Examples of Hope

What are some examples of this anti-racist activity? Many denominations are holding anti-racism training workshops. Some denominations have already organized anti-racism transformation teams that are equipped to work toward systemic change. Others have passed church-wide resolutions that call for a commitment to become anti-racist churches. One denomination, the Episcopal Church, requires that every diocese be involved in intentional anti-racism work. Other denominations with less centralized authority are "enthusiastically encouraging" that the work be done regionally and congregationally. In the Roman

Catholic church, not only are a number of dioceses developing anti-racism programs, religious orders are also leading the way (for example, the Sisters of Notre Dame de Namur, the Dominican Sisters of Springfield, Illinois, and the Sisters of Providence of St. Mary in the Woods).

Some denominations have given descriptive names to their anti-racism work. For example, the Unitarian Universalists, who have been doing anti-racism work longer than any other church, call it "Journey Toward Wholeness." The Mennonites have named their anti-racism work "Damascus Road." The Roman Catholic Archdiocese of Chicago calls it "Dwell in My Love." Other denominations just call it "anti-racism"—but are no less innovative in their approaches.

Early pioneers in anti-racism training were already at work in the mid-1980s and early 1990s, trying, learning, failing, learning from their mistakes, and picking themselves up to try again. It was during these years that the Peoples Institute for Survival and Beyond, Crossroads Ministry, and a handful of other anti-racism training groups began to develop their workshop styles, team-training models, and organizing strategies for community and institutional transformation.

Churches, along with universities, social service agencies, and local communities, were the scenes of living laboratories, as anti-racism workshops were designed, critiqued, improved, and incorporated into ongoing programs. Anecdotal histories are yet to be written to record the multiple workshop experiences that were simultaneously wonderful and painful, as white people and people of color together experimented and learned how to teach effectively about systemic racism and its ability to continue to manifest itself in ways that preserve white power and privilege and disproportionately exclude and disempower people of color.

As the new millennium approached, the importance of anti-racism training began to be recognized increasingly as an agenda item for church leadership. By the year 2000, within the course of little more than a decade, a transition had begun to take place in many church settings, from an exclusive focus on multicultural diversity to a new focus on anti-racism. Without dismissing the goal of multicultural diversity, a new and critical understanding that anti-racism is a necessary prerequisite to diversity's success was being seriously considered within many denominations. It is impossible in the space of this book to describe in detail the many ways that programs of anti-racism currently are being explored and incorporated in various denominations and religious organizations. However, I have placed in the resource section a list of all the programs of which I am aware, along with contacts, email, and website information, if available.

The Testing of Hope

From the perspective of the analysis being presented in this book, these new directions continue to be signs of hope in the struggle to dismantle racism. At the same time, each of these anti-racism programs needs to be tested with a critical eye, by placing them under the lens of our anti-racism analysis. While celebrating that the work of anti-racism has begun, we need to also ask how well it is being done. Will it be able to stand the test of time? The mission of anti-racism is only in its early stages of development. As we shall see more clearly, the shaping of an anti-racist church requires a long-term, decades-long commitment. And after its initiation it needs to be institutionalized as an ongoing transformation process that is permanently a part of the church's work. If we do not have this long-term, high-priority commitment, we will be faced with the great danger of anti-racism becoming another superficial institutional adjustment, providing new language to take the place of the failed programs of multicultural diversity.

> *What anti-racism work is being done in your denomination? Compare the process being followed with suggestions given in this chapter.*

The sad truth is that many denominational anti-racism programs are already beginning to slow down. Part of the reason for this has been the effect on the churches of the national economic crisis in 2009 and 2010. As is usual in budgetary cutbacks, less popular programs such as anti-racism are the first to suffer. But we are not only facing a problem of economics; it is a question of how deep is our commitment, and how serious is our yearning for freedom. It is a testing of hope. What anti-racism work is being done in your denomination? Compare the process being followed with suggestions given in this chapter.

Characteristics of an Anti-Racist Identity

Although many readers may have come to this book with a prior introduction to and understanding of the idea of an anti-racist identity, it will still be helpful before proceeding further to recall and summarize its major components.[1]

Anti-Racist Identity Is a New Way of Being

Although anti-racism requires *action* against racism, it also requires a new *identity* for individuals and for communities. As an individual, anti-racism is not only something I can *do*, but it is someone I can *be*. Anti-racist is a new name for a person or community that develops an analysis of systemic racism, becomes committed to dismantling racism, and will not rest until ultimately escaping from the prison of racism.

Anti-Racist Identity Is the Opposite of Racist Identity

"Anti-racism," not "non-racism," is the opposite or the antithesis of racism. As long as systemic racism controls the lives and actions of white people and people of color, there is no such thing as "non-racism." Anti-racism is the exciting and powerful work of tearing down the systemic and institutional barriers of injustice that divide us. Anti-racism is long-term work that has been carried out by anti-racist people in our society for centuries and needs to be continued until the prison of racism has been completely eliminated.

For white people attempting to comprehend anti-racism, the crucial question is not whether we can escape our identity as racists but what more we can be *in addition to* being racist. Robert Terry, one of the earliest white leaders in understanding anti-racism, put it this way:

> I am not personally offended when someone says being white in America makes me a white racist. That is true. I *am* offended, however, if someone says that is all I am. That is not true. I am both a racist and an anti-racist, and, as an anti-racist, strongly committed to the "elimination of racism."[2]

Anti-Racist Identity Is a Positive Identity

It is very important to understand and affirm that anti-racist is not a negative but a very positive identity. It is fairly common for people who are exposed for the first time to this concept of anti-racism to ask: Why do we have to express it so negatively? Isn't there a term that is more positive? I don't want to be "anti" anything; I want to be "for" something.

There is a simple response to these questions: anti-racism is positive. It is very positive to be against something as evil as racism. It is a very important affirmative activity to resist racism and to work for its demise and its deconstruction and to build something new in the place where it once stood. Being against racism is a good thing. Before we can work for additional positive expressions of relations between white people and people of color, we have to affirm our opposition to racism.

The Goal: "Anti-Racist Institutional Identity"

Just as it is impossible for individuals to be "non-racist," so also there can be no such thing as a "non-racist institution." A racist institution cannot just simply decide not to be racist anymore. A declaration by an institution that it is non-racist is an act of denial that will inevitably be crippling and paralyzing, making true change impossible. The inherited designs and structures of our institutions ensure the preservation of white power and privilege. So long as those designs and structures remain in place, public declarations of non-racism will only provide new cover for the original disease.

Anti-Racist Institutional Identity Calls for In-Depth Transformational Change

Turn back for a moment to pages 121–22 and review the chart showing the structural levels of an institution. Recall that the three upper levels of the chart—Personnel, Programs and Services, and Community and Constituency—are the outwardly visible levels of an institution. It is on these levels where superficial or "transactional" change is often attempted in order to look more colorful, while seeking to avoid more in-depth or "transformational" change on the levels where real power resides. The change I will be discussing here, and even in more detail in the next chapter, focuses on the lower levels of the chart, on transformational change at the heart of the institution in its organizational structure and in its mission, purpose, and identity.

Change in Thought and Action

How does identity change take place? It has often been said that we act ourselves into new ways of thinking just as much as we think ourselves into new ways of acting. For all of us as individuals, as well as in the way we function collectively, changing the way we think and act are both components of an identity shift.

It is possible to name a number of illustrations from recent decades of ways in which we as a society are going through identity transformation by collectively changing our ways of thinking and acting:

- Reflect for a moment on the process of our gradually becoming a society of non-smoking people who increasingly think of smoking as inappropriate and unhealthy behavior, leading to our accepting the restrictions on smoking to smaller and smaller locations.
- Consider how we are learning to accept handicapped/differently abled people as part of what is normal in our society rather than abnormal. We now accept wheelchair ramps, designated parking areas, and Olympic-style sports activities as a necessary and ordinary part of life.
- Think of the ways we are gradually changing our understanding of gender identities and roles, and are reconstructing our values and societal standards of behavior for men and women as a result.

In each of these illustrations, it is possible to see that social transformation involves changes in our attitude and consciousness, as well as in our behavior, all of which result in our internalizing a new sense of identity. These same ideas about identity transformation are also true about race, racial identity, and racism. Over the past four or five decades, we have learned to think and act very differently than in former years. Even though we are still imprisoned by old categories and old ways of thinking and action, we have already made significant changes in our ideas about and our acceptance of each other. Yet, a deeper sense of identity change involves continuing to shift our self-perception and our collective perceptions of who we are.

An Identity Crisis

Each of the above illustrations of identity transformation, and certainly the case of racial identity change, involves the experience of "identity crisis." This crisis comes when old self-perceptions no longer fit and there is awareness that new ones must be created. In fact, a new identity cannot be created as long as the old identity is comfortable and acceptable. Shaping an anti-racist identity is possible only when there is a sufficient crisis with regard to our existing racist identity and it is no longer tolerable to remain the way we are. When shaping a new anti-racist identity in the church, an identity crisis with regard to the old racist identity is both essential and unavoidable.

Here I am referring not only to an individual identity crisis but also to an institutional identity crisis. Drawing from our discussion about institutional and cultural racism in the previous two chapters, we need to focus on the need for collective and institutional identity change. During the past few decades, as mainline Protestant and Roman Catholic churches have attempted to become more multiracial and multicultural without reforming and restructuring institutional structures of white power, a full blown, church-wide identity crisis became increasingly inevitable. It is impossible to end racism while at the same time continuing the systems of white privilege that for centuries maintained the churches as segregated white institutions.

In the first half of the *Continuum on Becoming an Anti-Racist Multicultural Church*, this identity crisis is portrayed as moving steadily toward an inescapable dead-end at the conclusion of stage three, where we are stuck with what I have called "racist multicultural diversity." Moving past this apparent dead-end can only happen by discovering the second half of the continuum. It is only as we acknowledge how racism has imprisoned all of us and made us do its bidding, and that "racist multicultural diversity" is an impossible contradiction, that the resultant identity crisis will impel us toward the transformation of our identity from racist to anti-racist.

The path toward resolving this identity crisis is opened up when the church makes the decision to cross over into the second half of the continuum. The rebirth of mainline Protestant and Roman Catholic churches as anti-racist churches is a movement toward renewal. Shaping an anti-racist church means giving birth to a new church identity (or perhaps better said, to be restored to its original identity) as God's family, engaged in the struggle to undo the racism that has established itself as an evil identity and a divisive power within the church. Before the church can redefine, redesign, and institutionalize new structures of power and accountability, it must first enthusiastically and unequivocally claim its identity as an anti-racist people of God. In New Testament language, such a time of crisis and resolution of crisis is also described as a *kairos* moment, a moment when an inescapable dilemma is turned into a new and exciting opportunity. A *kairos* moment is the startling realization that just when it seems clear that life cannot continue on its current path, a new path becomes available. In the church's dealing with racism, it is a *kairos* moment when awareness that superficial change is no change at all is followed by the discovery that deeper transformation is a gift of rebirth that is ours for the asking. When the church is no longer able to avoid consciousness of the failure of racist multicultural diversity, it will at that moment be able to begin the step-by-step process of shaping a new anti-racist identity and becoming an anti-racist multicultural church.

Is Your Church Having an Identity Crisis?

In the research you have done while working your way through this book, have you perceived an identity crisis in your church about racism and about racist multicultural diversity? What have you learned about the lengths to which your church has gone to avoid awareness of its racist identity and behavior, or to deny that either exists? Can you offer examples of how your church has used multicultural diversity as a cover-up for systemic racism?

Motivation for a New Anti-Racist Identity

The most significant and dramatic movement in the transformation to becoming an anti-racist church is the crossing the line from the first to the second half of the continuum, from stage three to stage four. This is the movement that results from dealing with the church's racial identity crisis. It is the moment when rebirth begins. It is the beginning of white peoples' rejection of a racist identity and the first steps of moving toward acceptance of an anti-racist identity.

Very often during a workshop on racism, a participant of color will raise the question: "Why would white people want to give up their racism? You've got it all working for you. You have all this power and privilege. I can't understand why you would want to change." This is exactly the question that white Christians in a predominantly white church need to answer. Why would we want to give up the status and position that racism gives us? What is our motivation for becoming anti-racist Christians in an anti-racist church? As organizers of change, what is the motivation that we will draw upon to lead people forward? What will make white Christians want to cross the line into the second half of the continuum in order to become anti-racist?

There is more than one answer to this question, more than one single motivation that might impel us to deal with leaving behind all that racism has provided for us and move forward across the line to claim an anti-racist identity. Three answers come to mind.

1. A Combination of Love and Fear

A mixture of love and fear is part of the answer. From one end of the motivational spectrum, many of us are moved by the ideal of love for others. As Christians, we hold a deep belief in the unconditional love that we ourselves experience from God and seek to imitate by the way we act toward others. But from the other end of the motivational spectrum, many of us are also motivated by fear, especially our fear of what will happen if we do not end racism. As people of color gain in political power and as white people in our nation draw closer and closer to becoming a minority, the plain reality is that our ability to sustain white control diminishes. Thus, to one degree or another, both love and fear are leading us to change.

2. The Failure of Multicultural Diversity

In earlier chapters, I have argued that most of our programs of multiracial and multicultural diversity are failing badly. The reason is that they offer conditional acceptance instead of unconditional acceptance. We have said to people of color: "You are welcome to come into 'our' institutions; you can come into 'our' churches, but they still belong to us." I named this conditional acceptance "racist multicultural diversity." This form of racist diversity is bound to fail. We are gradually coming to the realization that stage three on the anti-racist continuum is highly volatile and unstable, and we cannot stay there. We have to either move forward or backward.

3. For Our Own Sake

There is a third, and I believe even more powerful, motivation at the center of our desire to give up racism and become an anti-racist people: our own self-interest. Earlier we had an extensive discussion about the power of racism to take each of us captive, along with the entire church, and to imprison us, even against our will, in an identity as racists. If we are racist against our will, that means both our freedom and our humanity are being taken from us. Even though we may accept the power and privilege that racism gives us as payment for our imprisonment, in the end we lose a great deal more than we have gained. Racism strips us of our humanity. It steals from us our identity as children of God. But with the end of racism, our humanity is restored. It may appear that with racism we gain, and with the end of racism we will lose what we have gained. But that view is a deception and a lie. In fact, with racism we as white people are also oppressed, and we lose far more than we gain. And with the end of racism we will gain enormously.

Why would white people want to give up their racism? For me the answer to this question is "in order that we might live again." With racism, we lose our humanity, our authenticity, and our freedom, and with the end of racism we can regain our humanity, our authenticity, and our freedom. The ability of white Christians and the white church to be effective participants in the struggle to end racism depends on our being able to anticipate the freedom from the oppression of racism over us. It is not only the freedom of people of color we need to be concerned about; we need to be concerned about our own. In addition, we need to be clear that the church also will experience liberation by ending racism. With the end of racism, the church will once again be able to understand its own message and carry out its mission of freedom.

As we will see in the next chapter, when we deal with the subject of organizing to make change take place, all of these motivations are important in creating the energy to cross the line from stage three to stage four of the continuum. Only when there is a greater need to move than there is a desire to stay put, will we be ready to cross the line. To be an organizer for change means to help people want to move forward.

Building Blocks of Anti-Racist Identity: Moving through Stage Four

Shaping an anti-racist institutional identity is not easy. Crossing over the line from stage three to stage four of the anti-racist continuum is just the beginning of a long path to freedom. We have entered a process that requires time, energy, programmatic organizing, and a large budget. It is a step-by-step process that needs to be implemented throughout an entire denomination, ultimately involving all of the leadership and all of the membership. Programs of education and training must focus on undoing old beliefs and practices, developing new understandings, redefining interpersonal and institutional relationships, and building a new collective consciousness as part of the church's self-understanding.

Identity Change--An Anti-Racist Church.

Take a moment to re-read the six steps in stage four of the continuum outlined below.

- **Building a common analysis:** Programs of anti-racism training are instituted throughout the church, resulting in a common analysis of systemic racism and a growing understanding of racism as a barrier to effective diversity.
- **Undoing internalized socialization:** A consciousness of internalized racial oppression and white power and privilege emerges within the church, along with an increasing commitment to eliminate inherent white advantage.
- **Learning accountability to communities of color:** Cross-racial relationships are deepened and white people begin to develop accountability to communities of color.
- **Auditing and evaluation:** The analysis is applied to all levels of the church through auditing and evaluation.
- **Reaching a critical mass**: A critical mass of old and new church leadership and membership claims an anti-racist identity and a vision of an anti-racist institution.
- **Institutionalizing the anti-racist identity:** A transition to stage five is initiated by a formal decision to institutionalize an anti-racist identity within the institution's identity documents and throughout the structures and culture of the institution.

These items constitute a step-by-step process to give birth to this new identity. As we proceed to reflect on each of these steps, each item should be considered as part of a carefully organized and implemented process of transformation. And also keep in mind that the completion of this stage is a prerequisite to the task of institutional restructuring that is described in stage five. A conscious anti-racist institutional identity must be established before formal and permanent changes in the design and structure of the institution can take place.

Step One: Building a Common Analysis

The most important first step in building an anti-racist identity is for the church to learn and agree upon a common analysis of racism.

This common analysis will be a new and ongoing lens for the church to view racism's reality and the basis to work collectively on racism's dismantling. Through anti-racism training workshops and other educational programs, the church's leadership learns together and eventually agrees upon, claims, and proclaims a common analysis of systemic racism.

Anti-racism training must be required for all, and not just some of the leadership; and the common analysis of racism must ultimately be shared and affirmed by all of the church's membership. Only when a critical mass of the church's leadership and membership shares in this common understanding of racism will it be possible to make the kind of structural changes in the church that are required in order to become an anti-racist church.

It is very important to understand that this common analysis cannot come about simply by reading a book or though some other form of individual personal change. Rather, it requires the collective sharing of the experience of together acquiring this analysis of racism and being enabled to collectively speak with one voice about their common understanding.

The introductory model of anti-racism training used by Crossroads and by the People's Institute for Survival and Beyond, as well as other anti-racism training organizations, is usually a two- or three-day workshop. The workshop presents an analysis of racism based on the teaching and experiential reality of communities of color and includes an understanding of historical and systemic racism as it is manifested individually, institutionally, and culturally. For large national denominations, the process of involving leadership in these workshops will require a number of years to complete. During this time, not only is a consensus built about an understanding of racism, but a new consciousness and a new identity gradually evolves. There are no shortcuts to this process; only as the leadership and membership of a church are given opportunity to struggle and grow together in their understanding of racism will the transformation of consciousness and understanding take place that will give birth to an anti-racist identity.

Step Two: Undoing Internalized Socialization

The second step in building an anti-racist church identity is to deprogram internalized beliefs and behaviors.

We discussed earlier in the book the socializing effects of racism, using the phrase "internalization of racist oppression," which results in internalized inferiority in people of color and internalized superiority in white people. Our socialization has caused all of us—white people and people of color alike—to have distorted self-understanding and dysfunctional relationships within and across racial lines. The ongoing process of building an anti-racist identity must serve the function of deprogramming our socialization and enabling new self-understanding and new cross-racial relationships to be strengthened. Many groups have found it essential for white people and people of color to organize separate "caucuses" in order for each group to explore and to learn to counter the forces of socialization that have led to internalized inferiority and superiority.[3] As the analysis of racism is shared more broadly and especially as internalized racial oppression is dealt with, there should develop among church leadership and among the membership a new and deepening awareness of structures of power and privilege that disproportionately empower white people and disempower people of color. With this new consciousness, it will begin to be clear that one of the first priorities in stage five will be the elimination of structures that foster white advantage.

Step Three: Learning Accountability to Communities of Color

The third step in building an anti-racist church is learning to be accountable.

Shaping an anti-racist identity also involves working very hard at developing new cross-racial relationships. As white people work side-by-side with people of color to develop a common analysis of racism, cross-racial relationships and new accountability relationships will begin to deepen in several ways that have almost never before been present between these two groups:

1. Since white people will be learning an analysis of racism that originates from communities of color, they will develop a new ability to listen to, learn from, trust, and follow the leadership of people of color.

2. White people will learn to be answerable to communities of color in ways that counteract the one-sided accountability of people of color to white people that has defined cross-racial relationships throughout the centuries. For white people, it is an entirely new learning to be responsible to communities of color. Learning these new skills is a first step toward building mutually accountable relationships between white communities and communities of color, as well as structuring mutual accountability at the deepest levels of our institutions.

3. At the same time, for communities of color, participating in authentic mutual sharing of power and accountability is often a first-time experience and does not come easily. Shaping an anti-racist institutional identity involves people

of color increasingly overcoming the effects of their own socialization and of the experience of accepting being dominated and of having their roles and functions within the church structures be defined from white perspectives.

Step Four: Auditing and Evaluation

The fourth step in building an anti-racist identity is for the church to apply the analysis and ask honestly the question, What needs to be changed?

At all structural and geographic levels of the church, processes of auditing and evaluating every aspect of the church need to be initiated, resulting in an increasing awareness of how white power and privilege and dominance over people of color have been institutionalized within the church's institutional design and structure as well as developing a long-term commitment to reverse this reality. Applying the analysis throughout the church is the means of identifying where change is needed. As auditing progresses, it will reveal many ways in which a new anti-racist identity is needed in order to transform the church, including a new understanding of the Bible and theology, of worship content and style, of Christian education, evangelism, social justice, and so forth. Only when there is a comprehensive picture of what needs to be changed is it possible in the next stage to develop a strategy for changing it.

Step Five: Reaching a Critical Mass

Step five in building an anti-racist identity is to develop new anti-racist leadership in the church.

The transformation of established church leadership is essential in the shaping of an anti-racist identity. Equally essential is the developing of new leadership, especially among young people. White youth and youth of color need to be recruited and prepared for taking positions of leadership of an anti-racist church. An unequivocal qualification for all new leadership must be anti-racism training, acceptance of the common analysis, and a commitment to join the long-term process of shaping within the church an anti-racist identity.

I use the phrase "reaching a critical mass" as a way of describing the point when enough people have changed individually so that collective decisions can be made that will allow the entire institution to change. Some analysts of change have called this the "tipping point."[4] A critical mass may or may not mean 51 percent of the voters. It could require much more than that and it could require much less. When a critical mass is reached, structural change will be perceived as that which will strengthen the church, rather than threatening to destroy it.

Only when there is a critical mass of people within the church who share a common analysis of racism will it be possible to move to the next stage in the continuum and begin to institutionalize concrete and specific changes. Understanding and acceptance of the analysis must eventually expand to and be shared by clergy and lay leadership, the church's membership, and all other stakeholders in the church. From the experience of a number of denominations and other similar institutions, such a process requires a number of years of intense and intentional learning and growing together.

Step 6: Institutionalizing the Anti-Racist Identity

The final step in the transition to stage five comes when the church makes a formal decision to institutionalize an anti-racist identity throughout its structures and culture.

When a critical mass of the church's leadership and constituency have reached a consensus and broad acceptance of the shared analysis of racism, it will be possible to claim formally and proclaim publicly a new anti-racist institutional identity, and to inscribe officially this identity in the church's theological and legal identity documents—its statement of faith, constitution and by-laws, and vision and mission statements. The church will also now be ready for the long-term task of institutionalizing anti-racism by transforming its design and structure at every level. This formal process of declaring an anti-racist identity will complete stage four of the continuum and prepare the institution to move to stage five.

How Does It Work in Reality?

Whenever I introduce the *Continuum on Becoming an Anti-Racist Multicultural Church* in the context of a two-and-a-half-day anti-racism analysis workshop, someone usually asks, "Can you give us some examples of institutions that have worked their way to the end of the continuum?" My usual response is that as far as I know, no one has gotten nearly that far in their efforts to become an anti-racist church, but I can give lots of examples of churches and other institutions that are somewhere on the journey through stage four and are on the pathway toward shaping an anti-racist identity.

I have already mentioned that during the past ten years a very large number of mainline Protestant and Roman Catholic churches have been developing anti-racism training work. Most denominations have explored some sort of anti-racism program. Some of them, including among others, the Episcopal Church, the Evangelical Lutheran Church in America, the Unitarian Universalist Association, and the Mennonite Church, have been developing extensive anti-racism training and organizing programs since the 1990s. There are also a number of regional judicatories within these denominations (Lutheran synods, Methodist districts, Roman Catholic and Episcopalian dioceses, and so forth) and clusters of congregations within larger denominations that are independently engaged in anti-racism work.

Of course, this is wonderful news. It is exciting to watch the action at the leading edges of many of our churches, as they are crossing over the line from stage three to stage four of the anti-racist continuum, even if the initial movement is tentative and tenuous. Some are doing anti-racism training and trying to raise awareness of the need to be at this new place. Some have developed anti-racism teams but are still trying to figure out what a team should be doing. Some are trying to deepen relationships between the predominantly white church and people of color by making public confession of past sins, although few of these are as yet willing to seriously discuss reparations. All of them are still looking for ways to expand the work consistently and uniformly into regional jurisdictions and congregations. However, nearly every one of these denominations would describe themselves as being at least in the early steps of shaping an anti-racist identity.

At the same time, honesty and modesty would hopefully make each of them quickly affirm that only a small leading edge of their church has entered into stage four. The simple reality is that although most churches have taken some small steps in the direction of anti-racism, none has progressed so far as to be more than at the starting place of shaping an anti-racist identity. And it would probably not be an overgeneralization to say that all of them still suffer from lack of clarity as to where next steps should lead them. Those denominations that have been at it the longest would be the first to describe in modest terms the limited progress they have made and the barriers that keep them from moving forward.

Even while a small leading edge of a church may be doing anti-racism training in stage four, a significant part of their leadership and membership is still in stages two and three and are not yet aware of the impossible contradiction of trying to build multicultural diversity without shaping an anti-racist church. And even if the majority of a church's leadership and membership would affirm the multicultural goals of stage three, the unchanged institutional structures that are still designed to serve a white constituency languish in stage two, where they will remain until a critical mass of an anti-racist church is able to institutionalize new anti-racist structures and designs in stage five.

It is very important to both celebrate the positive steps that are being taken, as well as to be realistic about the long-term efforts that are required to complete the task. We need to be as forthright and honest as possible in describing the limits and the barriers that most institutions have met as they move through the early steps in stage four. One very important task is to explore the reasons why many anti-racism programs seem to be stalling, and even sometimes completely shut down at approximately the same place along the journey forward. And even when smaller groups within larger church judicatories seem to be moving faster and further along the pathway than their parent bodies, it also seems clear that they are limited in how far and how fast they can progress if they are not supported by a larger church-wide anti-racism movement.

The Pathway Forward: Breaking through Barriers and Limitations

To conclude this chapter on shaping an anti-racist Christian identity, I want to emphasize three items. They are particularly relevant to readers who want to engage in direct organizing within their denomination, local congregation, or religious institution.

1. The Skill to Go with the Will

It should be obvious that the steps I have described in shaping an anti-racist institutional identity in the church require a significant amount of organizing skill. This is not a task for individuals working alone, but rather one in which collaborative teams are needed to do long-term organizing for institutional transformation. The purpose of the next chapter will be to help readers understand the skills that are needed and suggestions for how to develop them. Along with building relationships with organizations that provide training in anti-racism and in institutional change, it is also important to build relationships with those who are doing this work in other church or community settings.

2. Reconciliation between White Churches and Churches of Color

In furthering the work of anti-racism in the churches, nothing is more important than the ecumenical work of rebuilding relationships between predominantly white mainline Protestant and Roman Catholic churches and denominations of color. For the most part, these relationships have been either non-existent or have been in a state of brokenness at least since the time of the Civil War. Since the 1960s, efforts to reconcile and/or re-unite white churches and churches of color—both within and between denominations—have been for the most part avoided or unsuccessful when they have been tried.

As a re-reading of the items under stage five of the continuum will reveal, serious efforts toward reconciliation between white churches and churches of color is not likely to take place until predominantly white churches have taken on the cloak of an anti-racist identity. It should be obvious from negative reactions in recent years to controversial subjects such as apologies for racism, reparations, and re-mergers that there is a lack of understanding and analysis required to participate in discussions and actions about them. Crucial issues such as these cannot be sufficiently understood and officially discussed without a common understanding of racism and until an anti-racist identity has been more fully and effectively established in the white churches. Nevertheless, it is inevitable that these subjects will continue to be raised. One measure of the progress a church is making in shaping an anti-racist identity might be an increasing maturity that white churches demonstrate when these subjects are raised. A more detailed discussion of these subjects will take place when we examine stage five in the continuum in chapter 13.

3. Anticipating a Critical Mass

Even though it has already been stated several times, it bears repeating as a conclusion to this chapter that transformational change is possible only when a critical mass of the leadership and membership of the church is prepared to take on an anti-racist identity. When we explore the task of restructuring and institutionalizing anti-racist power and accountability in chapter 13, it assumes the readiness of the church for in-depth change.

Chapter eleven

Getting It Done: The Organizing Task

Put on the whole armor of God
so that you may be able to stand against the wiles of the devil.
For our struggle is not against enemies of blood and flesh, but against the rulers,
against the authorities, against the cosmic powers of this present darkness,
against the spiritual forces of evil in the heavenly places
Therefore take up the whole armor of God,
so that you may be able to withstand on that evil day,
and having done everything, to stand firm.

—EPHESIANS 6:11-13

From a Christian point of view, to speak of racism is to speak of "the wiles of the devil" and "spiritual forces of evil." When we promised in our baptism to resist the devil and to stand against evil and all its empty promises, we were actually making commitments to resist racism. The goal of this chapter is to help us put on the whole armor of God by increasing our organizing skill in order to help the church shape a new anti-racist identity.

A friend of mine, Pamela Warrick Smith, has written and recorded a song about organizing, titled "Work, Fight, and Pray." In it she admonishes us to work to bring about freedom and fight for justice and pray for peace. According to Smith, "We must work to bring about freedom; / we must fight to have justice for all; / we must pray to have the treasure of peace. . . .; / We must work, we must fight, we must pray."[1] Throughout this book I have celebrated those who organized to resist the evil of racism throughout past centuries. Now we are preparing to become organizers who work, fight, and pray in order to help the church resist the evil of racism for years to come.

Learning to Organize to Change Your Church

Thus, it is time to talk in practical terms about how to make change happen in the church. In this chapter we need to think clearly about the organizing skills that we need in order to implement the six steps of shaping an anti-racist identity in our denomination, our local congregation, or our religious institution. It is not enough to know what kind of change is needed; we need to know how institutions and communities change and how to use organizing skills and methods to help that change to take place.

As I described in the previous chapter, a growing number of churches have begun to move across the line into the second half of the *Continuum on Becoming an Anti-Racist Multicultural Church*. The leading edges of these churches stand on the threshold that leads toward an anti-racist identity. We are on the edge of discovering a new path forward. We must not go backward, nor can we remain where we are. Yet, the dilemma is that anti-racism programs already begun are not yet effective enough to carry the churches forward. New organizing efforts and more effective organizing strategies are needed to move further ahead. In this chapter, readers can learn to become more effective anti-racism organizers in the church.

Organizing Is a Divine Calling

I have a strong belief that organizing for justice and social change is a holy calling and a sacred task. I not only believe that God calls us to organize for change, but even more importantly, I believe that God is our best model for organizing. Recall the words of the prophet Isaiah: "You are the potter; we are the clay" (Isaiah 64:8). God is the potter who molds and shapes us into being God's people. God is the divine organizer. When God called and led Moses and the people of Israel from slavery to freedom, God was organizing. Throughout the history of Israel, God not only organized, led, and shaped God's people but also called leaders to help with the organizing work. When Jesus came as God's representative on earth, he not only skillfully organized events to make revolutionary change happen, he also organized and trained disciples and apostles with the skills of organizing to ensure that change would be continued.

"You are the potter, we are the clay" is not an image of our being manipulated by God without power and without choices. Rather, the clay takes on life and becomes participant in its own creating, as well as helping to shape and organize God's world and universe. When God becomes our potter/organizer, we become co-potters, co-organizers, joining with God in molding the creation according to God's will. When we organize to change our communities and institutions in order to align them more closely with goals of justice and peace, we are living out this sacred calling to be co-creators with God.

The specific organizing task we are dealing with here is organizing to change the church. However, the subject of organizing belongs to a larger context of how to change any community or institution, or how to bring about social change in any area of life. While the central focus on the following pages will be organizing to bring about change within our churches, it is also important to understand our larger calling to community organizing and community change. This chapter seeks to help readers address five specific questions:

1. What is organizing for institutional change?
2. What does an organizer do?
3. What are the primary action principles of anti-racism organizing?
4. How can we assess the anti-racism organizing that is presently taking place in our churches?
5. What are concrete next steps of organizing in our churches?

As a result of our thinking together about these five questions, you hopefully will be much closer to being ready to take the next organizing steps toward shaping an anti-racist identity in your own churches.

What Is Organizing for Institutional Change?

We have already seen that institutional racism is quite different from individual prejudice and bigotry. It is relatively easy to wipe out personal bigotry, but it is the racism that is rooted in systems and institutions that prevents the great gaps between white people and people of color from closing. Institutional change must be our focus in order to take us to the next steps forward in overcoming racism.

Institutional change—whether in the church or any other institution—does not happen by itself. It must be carefully planned, organized, and strategized by well-trained organizers and leaders. When institutions are left to evolve and change without careful guidance, they will change chaotically and eventually break down or wear out like a car without maintenance.

Organizing for institutional change has a goal of creating in people who share the same new understanding, new mindsets, and a will to take common action. The process of changing institutions can be compared to a political campaign with a set date when everyone will vote. Political campaign organizers develop a strategic plan that targets Election Day as the moment when the largest possible number of people will vote for a candidate. Similarly, as we plan a course of action to make changes in an institution, we need to think about the organizing it will take to bring as large a number of people as possible to a common acceptance of those changes at more or less the same time.

For another set of comparisons, let's return for a minute to the illustrations I mentioned in the last chapter of the collective changes in attitudes and actions that have taken place in our society in relation to such issues as smoking or handicapped/differently abled people or gender roles. Think about the extraordinarily large number of people who have been involved in intentional planning and organizing to bring about and further those changes. The important decisions that were made about each of these issues could take place only at the conclusion of carefully strategized organizing campaigns to alter and unify the opinions, attitudes, and understandings of many people.

This same thing needs to happen to bring about change in the church in order to shape an anti-racist identity. Organizing to shape a new anti-racist identity includes unifying large numbers of people to:

- agree on common understandings and definitions;
- adopt new values and principles;
- shape new ways of thinking, feeling, celebrating, and confessing;
- create new cultural symbols, icons, and rituals;
- add to and subtract from the way we collectively do things.

A long-term organizing plan will include relationship building, decision making, consensus building, theological reflection, and leadership development. And implementing such a plan will require patience, encouragement, endurance, confrontation, and lots and lots of prayer and guidance by God's Holy Spirit.

There are no pre-existing roadmaps or magic formulas on "how to become an anti-racist church" that can be easily applied and will result in an automatic commitment to anti-racism. But skillful organizing will help us get there. The task of dismantling racism and of building anti-racist multicultural systems and institutions requires intentionally organizing a path of change that is carefully followed one step at a time.

Organizing for change is not a short-term project, but a long-term process. There is no quick fix. An anti-racist identity will not be created by passing a single resolution at the next church convention or by presenting a single workshop or series of lectures and discussions on racism for people to attend. Not just one, but many resolutions will need to be passed by many church conventions, and there will need to be many lectures, public discussions, classes, and workshops. And a large amount of educational resource materials will need to be produced, helping to create an understanding of and commitment to an anti-racist church—all this and much, much more.

Who Are Your Co-Organizers?

Picture the people in your denomination, in your congregation, or in your religious institution whom you would like to see working, planning, and strategizing together with you to accomplish a successful campaign to shape an anti-racist identity. What names of people, committees, or interest groups already working for change in the areas of race, race relations, or racism did you discover in your research? Make a list of these people, especially those with whom you would like to speak further about working together. Give this list a title: "Potential Co-Organizers of an Anti-Racist Identity in My Church." I strongly suggest that you put your name on top of the list. The ideas on these pages will speak to you more directly if you think of yourself as an organizer.

What Does an Anti-Racism Organizer Do?

People with experience in community organizing often name five things that an organizer does in order to achieve a specific organizing outcome: an organizer *educates, motivates, agitates, provides technical assistance,* and *helps people gain a sense of their own power.*

These five activities can be seen as if they were the sparkplugs of an engine, with the final result being that the engine has smooth running power to move a vehicle. Let's take a brief look at each of the components of this definition as they apply to organizing to shape an anti-racist identity in the church.

1. An Anti-Racism Organizer Educates

In the previous chapter, we stated that the first step in giving birth to an anti-racist identity should be to provide anti-racism training throughout the church with a goal of achieving a common analysis and understanding of systemic racism. Anti-racism workshops will be the first among many educational endeavors that organizers will need to initiate to meet the need for common understanding of racism and the task of shaping an anti-racist identity in the church.

Throughout the entire organizing process, teaching will be the most fundamental tool for change. Of course, it is absolutely essential that the context and content of all teaching about racism and about an anti-racist identity be grounded in the biblical and theological teachings of the church.

Who Are Your Allies in Educating?

Who are the educators in your church who can help with this task? Can you name five or ten of them that you believe could help in organizing anti-racism workshops and other educational activities? What needs to be done to invite them to be part of the process of shaping an anti-racist identity in the church?

How Do You Prioritize the Participants?

Who should be the first in your church to be targeted for educational programs, based on such factors as who is the most ready to receive information, who will have the most influence on the change process, and so forth?

2. An Anti-Racism Organizer Motivates

An anti-racism organizer in the church helps motivate people to be ready for change. First of all, it must be seen as the call of the gospel to change. It is also important for everyone to be aware of the positive rewards for change as well as the negative results of not changing. Dealing with the subject of racism in the church—as well as everywhere else in our society—inevitably raises emotions of fear, confusion, doubt, and reluctance. These negative reactions can be replaced by positive feelings of courage, clarity, faith, and enthusiastic support. It is the task of organizers to help people deal with their feelings and to feel positively motivated to participate in the process of change.

Who Are Your Allies in Motivating?

Who are the most powerful motivators in your church? Can you name four or five of them that you believe could help inspire people to commit time and energy to these organizing tasks? What needs to be done to invite them to be part of the process of shaping an anti-racist identity in the church?

3. An Anti-Racism Organizer Agitates

Please read this word as *agitate* and not *aggravate*! To be agitated means to be "stirred up" for action. In many churches, there are "stir up" prayers that historically have been part of the liturgy during the season of Advent. These prayers ask God to stir up God's people to make us ready for the coming of the Christ child. To agitate people around the subject of racism does not mean to make them defensive, but to stir them up for anti-racist action.

People usually are more ready for change when they are upset with the way things are. An anti-racism organizer in the church carefully helps people become aware of and understand the destructive power of racism over each of us individually and collectively, to the point that they are angered by the contradiction of racism in God's church and moved to action. Organizers for change need to develop the skill of helping people to be upset with the current status of racism, and to stir up the hearts of people so that there will be a common agitation for change.

Who Are Your Allies in Agitating?

Who are the people in your church who are agitated because of racism? Can you name five or ten leaders or potential leaders whose anger over racism can be transformed into energy for positive organizing? What kind of agitating needs to be done as part of the process of shaping an anti-racist identity in the church?

4. An Anti-Racism Organizer Provides Technical Assistance

An anti-racism organizer helps people get the skills that are necessary for bringing about anti-racist change. Equipping present leaders and developing new leaders must be high on the priority list. Like all other institutions, a number of technical skills are required to be a leader and to participate in the church's organizational structures.

Many people in the church are intimidated when confronted with the church's institutional and administrative functions. It is even more complex when engaged in deliberate and intentional processes of institutional change. Anti-racist organizers in the church need to help existing leaders and future leaders develop technical skills of institutional transformation as they join in the process of bringing about long-term change from an anti-racist perspective.

Who Are Your Allies in Providing Technical Skills?

Who are people in your church with the technical skill of understanding how the institution functions? Can you name five or ten people who could provide information and leadership training that will help bring about change? What needs to be done to be part of the process of shaping an anti-racist identity in the church?

5. An Anti-Racism Organizer Helps People Sense Their Own Power

An anti-racism organizer helps people gain a sense of their God-given anti-racist power, to enhance their ability to dismantle institutional racism and build new structures that counteract its power. In order to accomplish this, the people who are on an anti-racism organizing team first need to have a sense of their own anti-racist power and be committed to helping others discover their power to give birth to an anti-racist identity and to shape an anti-racist church.

Action Principles of Anti-Racism Organizing

The next few pages describe five primary anti-racism organizing principles that can help guide the work of organizing to shape an anti-racist identity in the church. These five organizing principles are the product of the shared experience of a very large number of people, and although the body of knowledge is growing with new learning every day, these principles continue to provide a foundation for moving forward.

Of course, these brief pages can only provide an introductory taste of the organizing principles and skills that we need to have to do this work. The resource section in the back of this book points to other books and resources on organizing. Most importantly, as the fourth organizing principle emphasizes, hands-on training is essential for people who wish to implement these principles within their own churches.

First Principle: There Must Be a Crisis

We change only when we have to change. It is the nature of institutions—including the church—not to make major transformative changes except by necessity. The concept of "homeostasis" is recognized by the medical and environmental communities as the human tendency toward constancy and need for stability. Human communities and organizations function best while maintaining normal and continuing patterns of organized behavior. Significant change usually happens only when a crisis occurs that interrupts normal patterns, making it difficult or impossible to continue forward without making adjustments. Earlier, I described the biblical concept of a *kairos* moment, a moment of crisis and opportunity, when a situation has come to the point where failure to act is no longer a choice and choosing to act is an occasion for new possibilities. Organizers take advantage of such a moment of crisis and opportunity in order to overcome resistance to change.

This concept is particularly applicable when dealing with controversial and difficult issues such as racism. Not only do we resist change; we resist exposing racism as an existing issue, keeping it as well hidden as possible. "Racism? No, we don't have a problem; we all get along very well, and we don't want people stirring up trouble here!" But when the crisis becomes large enough, the forces of denial can be overcome.

Historically, movement toward ending racism has taken place only when avoidance and denial have been forced aside by the emergence of a crisis. The end of slavery, the end of segregation, and the acceptance of integration happened because the way things were could not be continued. It is likewise true today that taking the next steps in overcoming racism—within the church as well as elsewhere in society—will only happen when we cannot stay where we are. Thus, organizers of an anti-racist identity know that there must be a crisis for change to take place. Shaping an anti-racist identity in the church will happen when we can no longer live with the identity we presently have—of a church divided and imprisoned by racism. The movement to cross over the line from stage three to stage four on the anti-racist continuum will not happen so long as the church can comfortably stay where it is. There must be a crisis. And the truth is that we do not have to invent one; a crisis is already here. We have seen that the biggest and most urgent situation currently facing churches is the failure of racist multicultural diversity. This is what is propelling us from stage three toward stage four on the continuum. This crisis does not have the outward calamitous appearance of disaster as did the laws of segregation; neither does it have the loud and confrontational expression of the civil rights movement. While far quieter, more hidden, and surrounded by denials that a serious problem even exists, it is a disastrous crisis nevertheless—a bomb waiting to explode.

The failure of programs of diversity is the most serious blow possible in our society's efforts to portray the successful overcoming of racial disparity. In our organizing to shape an anti-racist identity in the church, we must take full advantage of this crisis; we must expose its reality and stir up the hearts of leaders to move from inaction to action. When this *kairos* moment is perceived and the opportunity is acknowledged, church leadership can finally decide to move into the process of shaping an anti-racist identity as outlined in stage four of the continuum. As difficult as this decision can be, it will ultimately be a positive and energizing step. For it will provide new realization that the institution has not hit a dead end, but has found a gateway toward the common self-interest of moving forward in the struggle for racial justice.

Second Principle: There Must Be a Common Analysis

As shown on the continuum, the first step of organizers will be to provide anti-racism workshops with a goal of developing among leaders of the church a common analysis of the problem and a common analysis of its cause. There needs to be a clear understanding of systemic racism and the results it has produced. The analysis must be held in common by institutional leadership. The cause of the crisis must be concretely understood and addressed.

A common and collective analysis of racism does not come easily. It requires a carefully constructed process through which participants are guided to struggle together until there is growing agreement. Such an analysis does not get created by committee and cannot be based on the distorted perceptions of past socialization. I do not know of any more effective way for such an analysis to be developed than through participation in anti-racism training workshops. The purpose and function of anti-racism training workshops are to help a group of people deprogram distorted experiences and misunderstandings and then to shape new understandings of systemic racism.

Third Principle: It Is an "Inside Job"

We are preparing to do heart surgery, to bring about transformation at the heart of the church. Such in-depth institutional change can neither be forced nor implemented from the outside. The primary motivating energy and transforming power to shape an anti-racist identity must come from within. The energy to move forward on these next steps of our journey must come from people who are not only motivated by love for the church, but also by the knowledge that the church cannot survive without transformation at its very heart. If there is to be an effective response to the crisis, it will need to be generated by those who feel a sense of ownership of the church, who have a deep knowledge of the church, and by those who have the power to endorse, mandate, and bring the changes to fruition.

At the same time this work cannot take place without participation by and accountability to the community outside the church. The "world" to which we are sent to bring a message of justice and reconciliation is not a passive observer of this struggle within the churches. Rather, the communities surrounding our churches have a great self-interest in the question of whether we will deal with our continuing systemic racism. In a real sense it is a task in which intense cooperation and collaboration must take place between those who are inside and those who are outside the church.

Who are the "insiders" who can make this change happen? There are two answers to this question. The first has to do with who will be the initiators of change. Who will get the anti-racism work started in a church? More often than not it will begin with an ad hoc group of people who are the first to become aware of the impending crisis caused by multicultural diversity efforts that are superficial and dangerously support the continuation of racism. This is the institution's "early warning system." These are the people—people of color and white people—who will initiate an organizing process that increasingly brings the entire church to awareness of the crisis.

The second answer to the question of who will make change happen is that ultimately almost everyone needs to become involved. Persons from the top to the bottom of the church's organizational structure must participate, from regional and national offices to every local congregation, from the bishop to each and every commission and committee, from the local pastor to congregational members, from white people who are seeking a more authentic church to people of color seeking authentic power and participation in the church. The coming together of this wide range of people cannot be accidental or serendipitous. Rather it must follow a careful and intentional organizing and skill-building process. Most importantly, the church's highest leaders need to mandate and endorse an anti-racist identity, just as the entire membership will ultimately need to accept and embrace it.

Fourth Principle: Trained Organizing Teams Guide the Way

One of the best approaches to carrying out this organizing work is the creation and training of anti-racism leadership teams to develop long-term strategy and the short-term, step-by-step process that will provide guidance for its implementation throughout the institution. The anti-racism organizing team will plan, design, and guide the institution through in-depth transformation. These organizing teams must, of course, be mandated, endorsed, and supported by the central institutional leadership.

The creating of such teams to lead in a transformational process requires organizing skills that do not ordinarily come naturally to personnel and constituency of the church. As awareness of crisis and the need for transformation become increasingly clear, so also will there be a growing realization of the need for new abilities and capacities to lead through the process of change.

How does a group of persons in the church learn to become a team of effective anti-racism organizers? A number of networks have programs to train organizers that focus directly on organizing to address systemic and institutional racism. Two of these training groups with which I personally have been very much involved are Crossroads in Chicago and the People's Institute for Survival and Beyond in New Orleans. During the past thirty years, these two organizations have led anti-racism workshops and taught organizing skills to tens of thousands of people from hundreds of organizations, institutions, and communities throughout the United States, including a large number of churches. In the resource section, I have provided an extensive description of both the work of Crossroads and of the People's Institute. I also have listed a number of other anti-racism training organizations that do similar kinds of anti-racism training and organizing, both within churches as well as other parts of society.[2]

Fifth Principle: A Long-Term, Step-by-Step Process

How long does it take to reform or transform a church? We can learn a lot about the answer to this question from Martin Luther, John Calvin, or Pope John XXIII. We also can learn from those who have been working on anti-racism transformation in the church over the past thirty years. It certainly is clear that transformation is a long-term process that does not happen overnight. It requires years of education and organizing just to complete the six steps we have been discussing in stage four of the anti-racist continuum. And that only leads us to the lengthier process of structuring an anti-racist church that we will take up in the next chapter.

What is more important is that movement toward this goal can be achieved with a step-by-step process aimed toward completing a long-term plan and design for transformation. The continuum does not assume the job will be finished in a predictable period of time, but it does provide for a measuring tool to determine and evaluate progress.

Why is it so difficult and why does it take so long? It is extremely important to recognize that it is not only the insidious power of institutionalized racism, but also the nature of an institution that determines and controls the answer to this question. Transforming any institution—including the church—is always a long-term process. Institutions are *supposed to be* difficult to change. The purpose of an institution is to be an instrument of preservation, perpetuation, and protection. By their very nature, institutions seek stable existence and resist instability and change. Thus, the bad news may be that it will be a lengthy and difficult process to bring about these changes; but the good news is that when we have completed the creation of an anti-racist church, it also will be difficult to change!

Just as racism was institutionalized gradually in the church, so now we must reverse that process by de-institutionalizing racism and re-institutionalizing anti-racism. The institutionalized racism in the church that we are seeking to change was created over a period of five hundred years. During those five hundred years, within the church there evolved carefully designed racist ecclesiastical structures and processes of decision making, the training of white clergy and other white leaders, the creation of racist programs of worship, education, and other services, and the shaping of racist policies and practices, cultural styles, and values—all intentionally in the context of a mission and purpose to exclusively serve white Christians. Not only does all of this need to be undone and redone, but a new anti-racist leadership and membership in the church needs to learn about and accept these changes and then live with them long enough until they are as natural as the previous way of life.

A Practical Guide to Assessing Anti-Racism Work in the Church

How can we assess the anti-racism organizing that is presently taking place in our churches, whether on a denomination-wide level or within a specific region or judicatory, in a congregation or religious organization? Until such an assessment is made, it will not be possible to ask the next and final question of this chapter: How do you develop a plan to join and effectively participate in your church's anti-racism work?

This next section provides a practical guide for accomplishing this task, and will be presented as a suggested assignment for readers who are exploring anti-racism work in a specific setting. For these tasks, it will be far better if readers are working as part of a larger reflection/action group. If a reader is working alone, it will be more difficult to do effective and accurate evaluations or to make plans for next steps. I strongly recommend, wherever possible, to do this assessment with colleagues working together collaboratively.

Assessing Anti-Racism Work in Your Church

There are two steps to assess your church's anti-racism work:

1. *Research and Documentation*—First, it is necessary to have a working knowledge about the anti-racism work that is taking place in your church.
2. *Evaluation*—With this information in hand, the second step is to evaluate what you have learned.

Research and Documentation

If you brought this knowledge with you to the reading of this book, or if you have done the suggested research about your church during the reading of this book, then you are well on your way to being ready for the next step. If you have not yet completed this research, then a bit of work still lies before you. The two best resources for this research are first, direct communication with people who are already doing this work in your denomination, judicatory, congregation, or religious institution; and second, the Internet.

Direct Communication. Readers can follow a personal line of inquiry by communicating directly with leaders of anti-racism work in your church. In the resource section at the back of this book, there is contact information for many denominational and regional anti-racism offices. If information about your church is not listed and you are not already familiar with the names of these persons or the means of contacting them, that information is also usually available through on-line research. Besides contacting official representatives of your church's anti-racism process, in order to have a range of information and interpretation, it will be essential to also contact people in the "grassroots" who are most affected by the process and to receive their impressions of the effectiveness of the anti-racism strategy.

The Internet. Researching through the Internet is not complicated. For example, when I type the phrase, "ELCA anti-racism work," into my search engine, I am given multiple choices of files and data on anti-racism work in the Evangelical Lutheran Church in America, as well as in its synods and many of its colleges, universities, seminaries, and other institutions. Likewise, when I substitute any other denominational name in place of ELCA ("Methodist anti-racism work," "Mennonite anti-racism work," and so forth), similar data appears for each denomination. For some denominations, it may be more fruitful to name a particular diocese, regional judicatory, institution, or religious order.

The information you are seeking should minimally include the history, current status, and future plans of your church's anti-racism work. Beyond that, more specific and detailed data should include such items as how an analysis of racism is articulated and taught, the strategy for anti-racist leadership development, the extent of funding and future funding commitments, participation and power of decision making by people of color in defining and implementing the anti-racism work, and affirmation and resistance experienced across the church. The more information that is available, the more accurate will be your assessment. It may be helpful to acquire a geographical map of your denomination or region on which to draw the results of your research of what has been done so far, who has been doing it, and what they have been doing.

Evaluation

With the information about your church's anti-racism work in hand, the second step is to assess what you have learned. Your primary lens for this assessment can be the content of this book, both the analysis of racism contained in parts 1–2, and the goals, methods, and criteria to organize for change that are described in part 3. As a basis for doing your assessment, I have listed below eight areas and questions that will help to put your church's anti-racism work alongside the precepts and principles laid out in this book. For cross-referencing purposes, I have also identified the chapters referred to in each area.

1. What is your church's theological understanding of racism and anti-racism? To what extent is the anti-racism work in your church based on a theological understanding that is both consistent with your denomination's historical teaching, as well as providing an adequate biblical and theological understanding of racism and anti-racism? For example, does the theological approach get past the issue of guilt and provide energy and encouragement for positive action? Does it reflect an understanding of racism as an imprisoning power requiring a theology of liberation? (Chapter 1—"Reclaiming an Anti-Racist Gospel"; Chapter 7—"Captive Christians in a Captive Church")

2. How is history a part of the anti-racism process? How open and honest is the anti-racism process about your church's history of racism and its participation in the oppression of Native Americans, African Americans, Latinos/Hispanics, Asian Americans, and Arab Americans? In part 2, the historical section of this book, I stated that we cannot become effective in dismantling racism in the church in the twenty-first century if we do not recognize and keep in our consciousness the blasphemous ways in which our churches and our nation have misused God's name to support racism in centuries past. In your church's anti-racism work, is the historical involvement both in racism and in resistance to racism known, understood, taught, and taken seriously? In order "not to forget and not to repeat" the atrocities of the past and to acknowledge their continuing harmful effects on the present, is there an insistence, as well as a recommended process of "repentant remembering," to regularly recall this history and to keep it in the forefront of people's memories? And just as importantly, is there a celebratory process of recalling heroes and heroines who resisted racism in church and society, and that especially recognizes the role of the African American church in resisting racism and preserving a gospel of liberation from racism? (Part 1—"The Past: Racism and Resistance in Church History," chapters 2–4)

3. Is there a common analysis of racism? What is the content of the analysis of racism and anti-racism of your church's anti-racism process? Is it based on an understanding of systemic and institutionalized power in the church? Does it address the internalization of racist oppression? Is it comprehensive in its understanding of institutional and cultural racism? Has a plan been established to teach this analysis throughout the church as a strategic necessity for shaping an anti-racist church? (Part 2—"The Present: Racism in the Church Today," chapters 6–9)

4. Is there movement from bargaining toward acceptance? Is there a growing understanding and recognition that efforts toward change during recent decades (since the civil rights movement) have neither required nor sufficiently brought about changes in structures of power and accountability, and that programs of multicultural diversity have in effect been based on a bargain that allows white power and privilege to stay in place? Are there signs of movement toward getting past the bargaining stage, leading the church toward the stage of acceptance of the approaching death of racism? (Chapter 5—"Racism and Resisting Racism in the Post–Civil Rights Church"; Chapter 9—"Cultural Racism and the Multicultural Church")

5. Has a priority been established to shape an anti-racist identity? Is there an awareness or understanding that shaping an anti-racist identity in the church is a prerequisite to institutionalizing structural change? Is there a strategy and timeline that clearly defines the steps toward a "critical mass" claiming an anti-racist identity? Is there danger of discounting or skipping this most important step? (Chapter 10—"God's Call to Become an Anti-Racist Church")

6. What is the organizing plan? What is your church's anti-racism organizing strategy? Does it have a clear multi-year plan with measurable goals? What kind of organizing teams are being developed and what kind of training are they given? Is there clarity about roles of white people and people of color in the organizing process? Are there plans to engage all levels throughout the church, organizationally and geographically? Judging from the level of funding and staffing committed to the anti-racism work, what is the relative priority being given to anti-racism work? (Chapter 11—"Getting It Done: The Organizing Task")

7. Is the anti-racism process anticipating structural transformation? Where do you think your denomination presently is on its anti-racism timeline? Are permanent and transformative changes being anticipated? As we will see more clearly in the next—and final—chapter, each small step forward is focused on the long-term goal of institutionalizing permanent change. Assessing where a given denomination is in their anti-racism process needs to ask whether these larger, permanent changes are being anticipated. (Chapter 12—"Institutionalizing Anti-Racism in the Church")

8. Where is your church's growing edge? Finally, our assessment needs to ask not only how far we have come and how far we need to go, but also exactly where we are at the present moment and what will be the next step. Where do you locate your denomination, congregation, or religious institution on the *Continuum on Becoming an Anti-Racist Multicultural Church*? Is it clear that next step to be taken is the "growing edge" in your church's anti-racism process? (Introduction to part 3)

The Next Steps in Organizing to Change Your Church

As this discussion of organizing draws close to its ending, in my imagination I see readers of this book in either one of two groupings: those who are already involved in anti-racism work, or those who are ready to become involved in a way that you haven't been involved before. Depending on which group you are in, there are two different approaches to the question about where to go from here.

Already Involved?

If you are in this group, you have, to one degree or another, already identified with and engaged in the anti-racism work of your denomination, congregation, or religious institution. From within this group, your action questions are probably about whether this assessment of your anti-racism work is helpful, and how it might assist in determining your work's future directions.

As an active participant in your church's anti-racism work, you probably have already decided whether this assessment suggests the need for significantly new directions for your anti-racism work, or whether it provides helpful suggestions for fine tuning or "tweaking" your programs to make them more effective. Either way, I hope this book can become a new tool in your group's anti-racism toolkit.

I also hope you will discover and make use of new resources in the resource section, and especially that you will build new relationships with those you might discover in the resource section who are doing similar work in other churches or other institutions. Those of us engaged in anti-racism organizing, whether in the church or in other parts of society, have much to teach and learn from each other. And it is only with our combined strength that we will achieve our goal of becoming a truly anti-racist people.

Want to Become Involved?

If you have not yet taken an active role in the anti-racism work of your denomination, congregation, or religious institution, then your action questions might include how to find and join with others who either are already doing this anti-racism work or who might be interested in starting.

If you have not yet experienced a full anti-racism training workshop, I suggest that it be your next step. Perhaps such workshops are available through the anti-racism work of your denomination. If so, this is also a good way to begin a personal relationship with those who are responsible for leading the anti-racism work in your church. If workshops are not available from within your church, there are contact websites and telephone numbers for anti-racism training organizations in the resource section of this book. These organizations facilitate workshops all over the country throughout the year.

Secondly, I suggest that you contact persons involved in anti-racism work in your denomination, either nationally or locally, and explore the possibility of your joining in their work. If no such contacts are available, then perhaps you will want to initiate some new anti-racism work from within your congregation or from within your church institution (school, college, seminary, or social service organization). It is usually best to initiate new work such as this locally, and once foundations have been built, to expand them to broader geographical or organizational dimensions. Hopefully, you will be able to discover in the resource section other groups in other churches or organizations that are located geographically near you. Making contact with persons in these groups can provide additional direction and support.

One Final Step

Thus far we have dealt with the past and the present and have not explored the future. The final chapter in this book is future oriented—not the far distant future, but rather what might happen in the next couple of decades within churches that are successful in shaping an anti-racist identity. The *Continuum on Becoming an Anti-Racist Multicultural Church* has two more stages—stage five and stage six—that provide direction for the restructuring of the church to represent its anti-racist commitment as well as for the churches joining in the shaping of an anti-racist society. The purpose of the next and final chapter is to explore the organizing tasks to make this restructuring take place. As I hope has been made clear, however, there is one very important prerequisite before a denomination, congregation, or religious institution can enter into the work of this next chapter: it must wear around its shoulders the mantle of an anti-racist identity.

chapter twelve

Institutionalizing Anti-Racism
in the Church

*He has made both groups into one and has broken down the
dividing wall,
that is, the hostility between us. . . .
So then you are no longer strangers and aliens.*

—EPHESIANS 2:14, 19

Breaking Down Walls of Hostility

One of the most disturbing aspects of being human is our propensity to build
walls—hostile walls that divide us. The dividing walls of hostility that the apostle
Paul refers to in his letter to the Ephesians are not just spiritual. They also are
physical, like the Berlin Wall and the wall the United States has built between our
nation and the nation of Mexico. Dividing walls of hostility are also defined and
created by law, such as the walls of legal segregation in our history and the walls
of legal apartheid in South Africa's history.

Speaking directly to the subject of racism, we create walls of hostility that
institutionalize and perpetuate racial divisions. As we discussed previously, it is
the nature of institutions to be structured to function in self-perpetuating ways.
The way an institution works is to "institutionalize" its programs, services, policies, and procedures. When an institution is designed well and functioning cor-
rectly, this institutionalizing function serves and unites us. But institutionalizing
can also function as a wall to divide us and serve us unequally.

That is what has happened with the institutionalization of racial inequality. White power and privilege is promoted and protected by the structures and
design of our systems and institutions. Remember the sentence I have used
repeatedly in this book to describe institutionalized racism: every system and
every institution in the United States society—including the church—was created originally and structured legally and intentionally to serve the white society

exclusively. Although legal walls have been partially broken down, and although even spiritual walls have been partially opened, the racially restricting designs and structures of the dividing walls in our churches and other institutions are almost as tightly closed as they were when originally created. The decision-making processes, the hierarchical structures, cultural values, and accountability arrangements in our churches still favor the needs of the church's predominantly white membership. These are the dividing walls that need to be broken down in order to shape an anti-racist church.

Just as these walls were built, so also they can be torn down. Just as our churches were structured, so also they can be restructured. It is inherent in the church's beliefs and teaching that God has already acted, and "has broken down the dividing wall" between us. We are called to make God's actions visible, to transform our churches' design and structure so that they will serve all of us with equity. The exciting reality is that we are in a new moment in history when it is possible to make these actions happen!

Just as exciting, the institutional walls that divide and destroy can be replaced by institutional structures that unify and give life. Just as *racism* has been institutionalized, so also *anti-racism* can be institutionalized. This task of building something new is even more important than the task of tearing down that which is old and dysfunctional. Our goal is to create institutions that are designed to be self-perpetuating so that they will function over and over again in an anti-racist way.

Ready for Stages Five and Six on the Continuum

We now come to the point of describing in concrete action terms the institutional and systemic changes that are needed, and the transformation that is possible in order to reach the goal of shaping an anti-racist church. We will explore the process of transforming power structures, creating new accountability arrangements, and institutionalizing changes in the church. We will also delve into heretofore controversial and dangerous subjects such as apologies, reparations, and racial reconciliation. We are ready not only to better understand these concepts, but also to put them into action.

What has changed? What makes it now possible to explore and take action on these issues? The answer should be obvious. We are approaching these subjects from the point of view of an anti-racist identity. With new language and new understanding, it is possible to explore and act on these subjects in new and creative ways. Sustained and strengthened by the new identity of anti-racism, the church's leadership, constituency, and personnel—all of its stakeholders—now are able to take on the exciting task of step-by-step transformation of racist structures into anti-racist structures. It is the moment to transform the mission and purpose and the organizational structure of the church at its deepest levels in order to reflect its new anti-racist identity; and it is the moment, from an anti-racist perspective, to change its worship, its music, other expressions of culture, and its everyday life and programs of education and service.

We're ready for the payoff for the hard work and organizing that has moved us step-by-step through stage four of the continuum. The official proclamation that the church's life will now be based upon an anti-racist identity is a signal to all people that everyday life will be different. We are on the brink of redefining and restructuring the distribution of power. Having struggled with an analysis of racism and adopted a new anti-racist identity in stage four of the continuum, the church is now ready to make and institutionalize the long-term changes that will enable it to become anti-racist in all its organizational aspects and life.

Making New Paths by Walking Them

A word of caution: stages five and six of the continuum are uncharted territory. No churches, nor any other institutions, have fully been here, but this is the direction in which every church needs to be headed. If our society, in its communities and in its systems and institutions, is to find authentically new and safe paths in which to continue our struggle for racial justice and reconciliation, then all of our institutions must eventually go through this transformation.

Thus, as we explore these last two stages, we are journeying to places in the undoing of white institutional racism where no one has yet traveled. Whenever we do get there, our work will require a great deal of inventiveness. There are no pre-existing or generic models for creating an anti-racist church. The new anti-racist structures of the church must reflect the church's specific purpose, language, and values. Leaders of the restructuring process will need to develop a planning, implementation, and evaluative process, with a clear timeline. All levels of the church must be included in the commitment to change and in the process of bringing these changes about. Many bumps in the road that are not even imagined have yet to emerge.

At the same time, this kind of institutional transformation is not without precedent in the church and society in areas other than racism. Many prior experiences of organizational restructuring for other purposes can offer insight and guidance into this experience. In order to learn from the experience of others, we also need to study other areas of institutional and societal life where it has been done before. One set of examples has already been mentioned: we need to learn from the history of establishing of laws and cultural changes in favor of handicapped people and from the institutionalizing of restrictions on smoking. It is also very important that we identify with allies in other areas of social justice work—those who struggle for change within the issues of class, gender, sexual orientation, and peace—who are engaged in the pioneering work of making similar changes with regard to their issues and who are working toward institutionalizing other areas of systemic transformation.

As we move forward we also need to deal with the inevitable fear of entering into strange and difficult territories; we need to support each other, seeking the strength of collective action. Like pioneers in every other walk of life, we are making new paths where they have never before existed, but we are also walking with the certainty that it can be done. We need to maintain our conviction that institutionalized racism can be eliminated. Structures of equity can be built.

Above all, as we continue counting the costs and the benefits in continuing our path on the continuum, it is most important to maintain awareness that we are led on this path of reclaiming our common humanity by the one who has already reclaimed us. God is breaking down the dividing walls of hostility and making it possible for us to tackle the walls that are still standing before us.

Moving into Stage Five

In some ways it is deceptive to portray stages five and six as consecutive, with stage six being dealt with only after stage five has been completed. The *Continuum on Becoming an Anti-Racist Multicultural Church* is a linear chart, and does not show all the interrelationships between the different stages. In reality, many of the items in these two stages will be dealt with simultaneously, and thus they might best be seen parallel to each other. Nevertheless, in our examination of these two stages, it is easier to discuss them consecutively. Readers will need to make adjustments in their own minds in order to address the reality of their specific situations.

Stage Five: Structural Change—A Transforming Church

The following is the list of actions copied from stage five of the continuum. Although we will address each of them one by one, it will be helpful if readers maintain a picture of them as they are listed as a whole. Only when they are all completed will it be possible to say that a church or other institution has holistically addressed structural change.

Step One: Commitment to Institutionalizing. The church commits to the new stage of redesigning, restructuring, and institutionalizing an anti-racist identity.

Step Two: Full Power Sharing. Restructuring ensures full participation of people of color in decision making and other forms of power sharing on all levels of the church's life and work.

Step Three: Assured Cultural Inclusion. Inclusion of worldviews, cultures, and lifestyles of people of color is ensured in all aspects of church life.

Step Four: Mutual Accountability. Authentic and mutually accountable anti-racist relationships are structured between people of color and white people within the church.

Step Five: Multiplying Inclusion. There are similar institutional changes toward other socially oppressed groups, including women, gays and lesbians, Third World citizens, and others.

Step Six: Restored Community. There is within the church a sense of restored community and mutual caring.

Keeping in mind the complete picture of all six steps, let us now proceed to address these structural changes one at a time. Some of these items will be discussed briefly. Others require more extensive comments. Where possible, I will provide notes for extended resources that readers might pursue for further information.

Step One: Commitment to Institutionalizing

In this first step, the church commits to the new stage of redesigning, restructuring, and institutionalizing an anti-racist identity.

Reflect for a moment on the following quote from Ezra Earl Jones: "The system is designed for the results it is getting. If you want different results, you will have to redesign the system."[1] Any system or institution—including the church—will produce what it is designed to produce. Therefore, any institution—including the church—that is designed to produce racism will produce racism. If the church is designed to produce white power and privilege, it will produce white power and privilege. And if the church is designed to subordinate people of color, it will subordinate people of color.

> *The system is designed for the results it is getting. If you want different results, you will have to redesign the system.*

The church's institutional systems are designed for the results we are getting. If we want different results, we will have to redesign the church. By the end of stage five, an anti-racist identity has become official and institutional transformation—the changing of the church's design and structure—has become a mandate.

We are now about the task of institutionalizing anti-racism. As discussed earlier, when something is "institutionalized" it will be self-perpetuating without requiring additional thought or input. It is not enough to make superficial changes in institutional policies and practices in the church that can be changed back with ease by simple decision of institutional leaders. By institutionalizing anti-racism, it will be made a part of the church at its deepest foundational levels.

Step Two: Full Power Sharing

In step two, restructuring ensures the full participation of people of color in decision making and other forms of power sharing on all levels of the church's life and work.

The central feature of an anti-racist church is the redefinition and restructuring of how power is exercised—changing who makes decisions, how decisions are made, how decisions are implemented, and the accountability arrangement that evaluates how power has been used. A new understanding and use of power must be institutionalized within the church's organizational structure, demonstrated by new leadership and new relationships, expressed in programs and services, and implemented by all personnel.

This means that for the first time there will be *full* participation of communities of color in decision making and other forms of power sharing on all levels of the institution's life and work. Restructuring and institutionalizing the right use of power means far more than pledges and personal commitments to do things differently. While good will and good intentions are necessary ingredients for reaching this stage of the continuum, they are not the primary marks of institutional change. Here we are talking about people of color and white people working together to create structures and defining clear standards and criteria by which the institution will function differently and in measurable ways at all levels of organizational life.

Remember our first presupposition about power: although it may be misused, power is a gift of God and it is good. In the analysis of racism that forms the foundation for this book, it is crucial to have this understanding of power. Ending racism does not mean ending power, but transforming the misuse of power into the good and proper use of power. Ending racism means joining together of all people to share power as an anti-racist people in an anti-racist church. Through the power of God's liberation, ending racism means reclaiming and redeeming power to use it as God intends.

Changing the way we understand and use power begins with the realization that democratic means of decision making in the past have been used to produce inequality. Likewise, our normal democratic decision-making processes have not worked in recent efforts to include people of color in existing systems. We have made token representational changes, and we have tried to be caring about people of color, but we have not changed our "normal" assumption that the majority rules. When the white majority makes the decisions, white power and privilege continues to perpetuate a white church with a white culture, administered by a white majority and its effectiveness measured by a white accountability process.

What kind of decision-making process will create an effective, equitable, and anti-racist power sharing process? Should people of color have greater representation than their proportionate numbers? Should they have weighted votes so that they carry more power? Should people of color have veto power on decisions that directly affect them? The answer to these questions will evolve from a people working to transform systems from an anti-racist perspective.

One bold but short-lived effort to answer these questions took place in the 1970s, when the National Council of Churches—which at that time had an organizational structure of four commissions—added a "fifth commission," composed of people of color, that was given the power to veto race-related decisions made by the other four commissions. On the one hand, this was a creative and courageous new effort to deal with the imbalance of power and accountability in an institution structured to favor white people. On the other hand, as might be expected, this experiment produced fear, mistrust, anger and hostility everywhere, and was ended soon after it was started. From the stand point of the analysis presented in this book, the reasons for its failure are obvious: there was no strategic preparation for these sudden structural changes; the action was not based on a common understanding of racism; and there were no common anti-racist goals or objectives instilled throughout the organization.[2]

What is the alternative? It will make a great difference in answering this question when those working for change—white people and people of color alike—have a shared anti-racist analysis and identity with a common commitment to institutionalizing anti-racism. The goal that must be clearly accepted by everyone is to end white power and privilege through the right use of shared power by everyone. The answers will not come easily nor all at once. It will be years before the transformation nears completion, when every program, every curriculum resource, every policy, protocol, and practice, and every cultural occasion and special event have been addressed and subjected to rigorous examination, redesign, and evaluation. But those who have adopted a new anti-racist identity and a new decision-making process will gladly participate in making and following a long-term plan, committed to its implementation.

Step Three: Assured Cultural Inclusion

The third step ensures the inclusion of worldviews, cultures, and lifestyles of people of color in all aspects of church life.

It is now possible to achieve authentic multicultural diversity within the church. Racist multicultural diversity is replaced by anti-racist multicultural diversity. We have described racist multicultural diversity as making white-controlled institutions appear more colorful while still being dominated by white culture, lifestyle, and worldview. By contrast, anti-racist multicultural diversity means that people of color will have the *power* to ensure the inclusion of worldviews, cultures, and lifestyles of communities of color in all aspects of institutional life. Moreover, the institutionalization of anti-racist multicultural diversity means it will be self-perpetuating and not need to be an occasional reality as a result of resentfully received reminders from a persistent minority.

There is no end to the list of aspects of institutional life that will be affected by the rich and full presence of people of color's culture and worldview: the style and content of worship, addition of new rites and holidays, artistic expression, theological perspectives and perceptions, transformation of educational curriculum, measurement of time and motion, interpersonal relationships, and a myriad of other changes. The emphasis will no longer be on fear of loss and struggle to dominate. Each group's cultural expression will be valued and shared, and the resulting collage will enrich everyone.

Step Four: Mutual Accountability

This fourth step makes sure that authentic and mutually accountable anti-racist relationships are structured between people of color and white people within the church.

Although redefining accountability is an extension of refining power structures and decision making, the subject requires separate and careful attention. We have discussed thoroughly the necessity of white people learning to be authentically accountable to communities of color. In stage four of the continuum, we saw that one of the major criteria of achieving a white anti-racist identity is learning to listen to, believe, trust, and follow the leadership of people of color. Without white people being answerable to communities of color, accountability continues to be completely one-sided. It takes time, practice, honesty, willingness to be vulnerable, and new institutionalized practices for white people to move beyond internalized superiority and its insistence on always being in charge.

Now, however, the discussion must go beyond white accountability to communities of color, to a discussion of authentic and mutual accountability that must be structured between people of color and white people within an anti-racist church. True accountability can never be one-sided. All of us must learn to be responsible to each other in an anti-racist way and in a way that is based upon a shared analysis of racism.

Mutuality in accountability begins at the communion table, where all the family of God expresses accountability to God and receives from God new power to build community. In the new anti-racist community, mutual accountability moves from the communion table and is consciously and intentionally infused and practiced in all aspects of the life of the church.

Step Five: Multiplying Inclusion

The fifth step deals with the inclusion of similar institutional changes toward other socially oppressed groups, including women, gays and lesbians, Third World citizens, and others who are marginalized.

In the introduction to this book, the interrelationship of all forms of oppression was affirmed. In the church, as well as in all parts of society, there cannot be changes in one form of oppression without the willingness to bring about changes in all forms of oppression. Although this book has focused only on transformation of racist oppression in the church, an anti-racist church will be clear about the interrelationship and interdependency of liberation from all forms of oppression. Authentic anti-racism requires also authentic anti-sexism, antiheterosexism, anti-classism, anti-nationalism, and so forth. An institution that has reached this stage of the continuum must be also working on similar institutional changes toward other socially oppressed groups.

Step Six: Restored Community

At the sixth and final step, there is within the church a sense of restored community and mutual caring.

The conclusion of stage five of the continuum will not be signaled by the end of struggle and the completion of change, but by the presence of a new sense of well-being while continuing to implement change. In fact, there is no timetable for concluding this stage. Rather, it is an ongoing, living, transformative process that should never end.

Entering into and completing this and the next stage of anti-racist transformation is a calling from God and a vision not only for the churches but also for all humanity. Its product, not only in its completion but also in the process of going through these stages of change, is a sense of restored community and mutual caring within the family of God.

Looking to the Future: Institutionalized Anti-Racism in Your Church.

What is your vision of your denomination, congregation, or religious institution as a restructured anti-racist church? Even while maintaining the discipline of not actually going there until a critical mass has claimed an anti-racist identity, it's not too soon to dream, visualize, and plan for the day when anti-racism will not simply be a transitory desire of a few, but the defined structure and design throughout the institution. What will your church look like with full power sharing, ensured cultural inclusion, mutual accountability, diversity without disparity, and a sense of self-perpetuating restored community?

Moving into the Final Stage of the Continuum

Working for change inside the church is only one part of anti-racism transformation. The church is also a part of the larger society, and its primary reason for existence is to implement a mission to that society: a mission of good news, a mission to restore the family of God, a mission of love and justice. Therefore, there must be a conscious and intentional linking of the anti-racism transformation process within the church in order to shape an anti-racist mission to the larger community. Stage six of the *Continuum on Becoming an Anti-Racist Multicultural Church* outlines the steps that are needed in order to fulfill this part of the church's anti-racism work.

As already mentioned, stage six of the continuum is not accurately described as a sequential stage that follows the completion of stage five, but rather a parallel stage that is being implemented simultaneously with the implementation of stage five. The intention of linking change in the church to change in society must be clearly present throughout the second half of the continuum. Nevertheless, it is important to describe this stage in terms of a separate organizing process, with a distinct strategy of planning and implementation.

Stage Six: A Changing Church in a Changing Society

Printed below are the steps associated with stage six. Please take a moment to read them together as a whole to develop a picture of the interrelatedness of every step. While each of these items will be discussed briefly in the following pages, I will

> *Step One: An Anti-Racist Church in Society.* The church commits to participation in the struggle to dismantle racism throughout society, and rebuilds and redefines all relationships and activities between the church and the wider community on the basis of anti-racist commitments.
>
> *Step Two: An Accountable Anti-Racist Church.* Clear lines of mutual accountability are built between the church and racially oppressed people in the larger society.
>
> *Step Three: An Ecumenical Anti-Racist Church.* The church builds anti-racist relationships with other churches, particularly with churches of color, with emphasis on mutual accountability, reconciliation, and reparations.
>
> *Step Four: A Globally Interdependent Anti-Racist Church.* Alliances with allies in church and society ensure links to all aspects of social justice, particularly to issues of global interdependence and international structures of justice and equality.

provide an extended discussion on step three, the building of anti-racist ecumenical relations with other churches, particularly with churches of color.

Step One: An Anti-Racist Church in Society

The church commits to participation in the struggle to dismantle racism throughout society, and rebuilds and redefines all relationships and activities between the church and the wider community on the basis of anti-racist commitments.

The ultimate vision that drives the process of institutional change is a future in which both the church and the wider community overcome systemic racism. Thus, working toward shaping an anti-racist multicultural church must include an intentional commitment and process by which the church reshapes its relationships with the larger society in working to end racism. The goal is a partnership of mutual support and common work in dismantling racism. An anti-racism partnership will eventually include all other societal systems, such as social services, criminal justice and law enforcement, education, government, the corporate world, and other groups in the wider community.

Those working to shape and structure anti-racism in a particular institution need friends and allies outside the institution. There are other individuals and organizations in the larger community with a commitment to dismantle racism. It is important for those working for change in the church to be in contact with and to build relationships between the church and these other groups. Moreover, it is by working with these other groups that the church can begin to participate in the struggle to dismantle racism in the wider community.

There are historically formal and informal relationships that already exist between the church and the larger society of which it is a part. However, given the nature of racism, these relationships have always been and still are defined in terms of the perpetuation of white power and privilege. Therefore, each of these relationships must now be redefined and rebuilt from an anti-racist perspective. Of course, this will often entail extremely difficult work, since it cannot be assumed that the larger society shares the same anti-racist commitments of the church. Thus, in these and in other ways the task is not simply redefining and rebuilding relationships; it must also include the work of challenging and transforming the larger society.

Step Two: An Accountable Anti-Racist Church

Clear lines of mutual accountability are built between the church and racially oppressed people in the larger society.

Just as we have stressed the importance of building mutually accountable relationships inside the church between white people and people of color, so also clear lines of mutual accountability need to be built between the churches and racially oppressed people in the larger society. Once again, mutual accountability begins with predominantly white churches learning for the first time to be accountable to racially oppressed communities of color. This accountability relationship must be defined and structured in measurable ways and not simply stated with good intentions.

Step Three: An Ecumenical Anti-Racist Church

The church builds anti-racist relationships with other churches, particularly with churches of color, with emphasis on mutual accountability, reconciliation, and reparations.

An anti-racist identity will dramatically affect ecumenical relationships among Christian churches, whether between predominantly white mainline Protestant and Roman Catholic denominations, or between white denominations and denominations of color. For more than a century, the ecumenical movement has placed a high priority on dealing with differences and divisions, seeking unity among Christian denominations that have been separated by theology, history, language, culture, and worship styles. Now more than ever, as denominations engage in the mission of anti-racism and explore what it means to become anti-racist churches, the ecumenical movement needs to redefine ecumenical cooperation and collaboration from an anti-racist perspective.

More particularly, relations between denominations of color and predominantly white denominations need to be reconsidered and redefined. For the most part, since the earliest days ecumenical relationships between white churches and African American churches have been either non-existent or extremely tenuous. The same reality exists with separated, racially defined denominations among Hispanic/Latino, Native American, Asian American, and Arab American people. Ever since the 1960s, efforts to construct ecumenical relationships between white churches and churches of color—both within and between denominations—for the most part have been avoided or largely unsuccessful when they have been tried.

There is a long list of issues that needs to be faced in order to overcome racially defined denominational divisions, including history, culture, theology, language, national origin, and much more. All of these issues are directly or indirectly related to the continued presence of racism, and all of them will be profoundly affected when approached from an anti-racist perspective.

Let's take a brief look at four specific signs of transformation of relationships and reconciliation between white denominations and denominations of color. All four of these have been highly controversial and divisive in the past. However, when seen through the lens of an anti-racist identity, each of them takes on a completely new light and is approachable from an entirely new and life-giving perspective. These four items can be remembered as "the four R's" of cross-racial denominational reconciliation: Remembering, Repenting, Repairing, and Reunifying.

1. Remembering—One of the many positive results of anti-racism is the overcoming of amnesia. The history section of this book recalls that which is too easily forgotten: our churches' participation in our nation's tragic and ugly history of racism toward African Americans, Native Americans, Hispanic/Latinos, Asian Americans, and Arab Americans. With the end of amnesia we can also recall the positive history that we have seldom have realized or taken into account: the resistance to racism that was led by churches of color, the remembrance of the stirring story of one part of the church being faithful to the gospel's call to justice.

An anti-racist church recovering from amnesia will place a high priority on remembering and telling the truth to its members. Like the German people and their commitment to never forgetting the reality of the holocaust, so our constant remembering of the history of our racism is a fundamental requirement in ensuring that it will not be repeated. It is not for purposes of maintaining a "guilt trip" that these memories must be preserved, but rather to maintain a mark of how far forward we are moving. The churches need to develop solemn "rites of remembering" that regularly recall the horrors of the past and also give expression to the new anti-racist relationships of the present and future with great celebration.[3]

2. *Repenting*—In recent decades, some of our churches have made public apologies for the racism of the past. As important as these events have been, they have also been filled with great limitations. One of the limitations of these apologies is that they usually point only to the past, as though the reality of racism does not continue in the present. Another issue is that these apologies are often done without a firm anti-racist commitment to rebuilding in the future and almost never approach the subject of repairing the damage that has been done. Public apologies emphasize that repentance is a very important adjunct to remembering. However, neither remembering nor repenting is complete without addressing the subject of reparations.

3. *Repairing*—The other word—the very controversial word—for repairing the damage caused by racism is *reparations*. In chapter 5, I mentioned the impact of the "Black Manifesto" as an illustration of how conversations about reparations almost always spark serious discord and often increase rather than decrease the anger and lack of trust between white churches and churches of color. Despite the fiery context and confrontation that surrounded the publication of the "Black Manifesto," it needs to be recognized as one of the earliest attempts to address the central issues involved in correcting the ravages of racism, and a great deal can be learned from it.[4]

When approached from an anti-racist perspective, the terms of the conversation about reparations significantly change. No longer is this an issue defined simply by anger on one side and guilt on the other side, with both of these elements in a conversation being the inevitable cause of breakdown in the search for reconciliation. An honest appraisal of the damage done by racism reveals that all sides have been damaged and nearly destroyed by this profound evil. The effect of reparations will inevitably be healing for both sides. When white people and people of color sit down at a common table, facing squarely the destructive results of our history of racism from an anti-racist perspective, it will be clear that repayment of people of color by white society and by white churches will be the basis for restoring health and wholeness to all concerned. The terms and conditions of reparations of course need to be negotiated. Rebuilding relationships and communities will be painstaking and demanding. But the process is essential and the results will be restorative to white people and people of color alike.

4. *Reunification*—In terms of ecumenical relations among the churches, another very difficult question around reconciliation is whether, when, and how to build formal relationships or even unity or union between white churches and

denominations of color. Many churches of color that share a historic denominational identity with white counterparts have either lived with the results of forced separation from white churches since their inception, or are separated by language, culture, or national origin.

There are multiple issues that make ecumenical relationships between white churches and churches of color difficult to tackle. At the center of these issues is the reality of racism and racial separation. These issues have been long avoided in the ecumenical movement, and desperately need to be initiated. They also need to be conducted in ways that do not perpetuate the disempowerment of churches of color. The basis for these conversations must be the willingness of mainline Protestant and Roman Catholic churches to begin a process of learning to listen to, trust and follow, and be accountable to the leadership of churches of color.

The primary realization must be that we—all the Christian churches of our society—are the interconnected body of Christ. No matter how profound and painful the damage and destruction that racism has done to our denominational identities, it has not and cannot eradicate our common identity as the family of God. But only a process of willingly re-approaching each other, of truth telling and of grace-filled re-acceptance as an anti-racist people of God will make our family membership visible once again, both to ourselves and to the world.

Step Four: A Globally Interdependent Anti-Racist Church

Alliances with others in church and society ensure links to all aspects of social justice, particularly to issues of global interdependence and international structures of justice and equality.

Anti-racism is an international and global issue. The ever-expanding concentric circles of change must lead ultimately to global issues of poverty, racism, and related forms of injustice. As indicated throughout this book, the continued presence of white power and privilege within our churches and society is a product of centuries-long colonialism and racism that has left similar expressions of oppression throughout the world. Both the World Council of Churches and the United Nations have long histories of promoting global programs against racism. Anti-racist churches in the United States must become part of the global movement for change.

Another Look into the Future: Your Church Constructing an Anti-Racist World.

What is your vision of your denomination, congregation, or religious institution redefining its relation to the world from an anti-racist perspective? How will it express mutual accountability to the poor, to communities of color, and to other oppressed peoples? How will it live out ecumenical relations with denominations of color? How will it interrelate with anti-racist movements globally?

End Word: The Death of Racism

*Sometimes I feel discouraged and think my work's in vain;
But then the Holy Spirit revives my soul again.*
—*African American Spiritual*

"We had to let mom go." The voice on the phone was that of a friend. He called to let me know that he and his family had made the decision to take his mother off of life-support and allow her natural passing from life to death. For months, his mother had been kept alive artificially. Long after it was obvious that her death was near, her children were not prepared to let it happen. "We finally came to the realization that we were keeping her alive for our sake," my friend said. "Still, we weren't ready to accept her death, to consent to her dying."

Racism is dying, but it is being kept alive on institutional life-support systems. We are helping to keep it alive because we think we need it to survive; we are not ready to accept its death, to consent to its dying. We are still stuck somewhere in the stages of grief: in denial, guilt, anger, depression, or bargaining. We need to move to the stage of accepting the death of racism. We have to let it go, to consent to its passing.

As Christians, we are called to assist in bringing about the death of racism. God calls us to this task, and we are borne on the shoulders of a host of witnesses who surround us and join us in carrying out this task. We need to reclaim an anti-racist gospel and work together to shape an anti-racist church. With the death of racism, new life is possible and the whole family of God can discover new freedom.

It is long past time to let racism go. It is time to accept, consent to, struggle for, and celebrate its dying. We don't need it anymore. We never did.

NOTES

Introduction

1. Written by C. Herbert Woolston (1856–1927). Public domain.

2. Joseph Barndt, *Understanding and Dismantling Racism: The Twenty-First Century Challenge to White America* (Minneapolis: Fortress Press, 2007).

3. One example: Prior to the Civil War, the Presbyterian Church separated in 1861 into "northern" and "southern" branches. The churches began in the 1960s to work toward merger and were reunited in 1983 in the Presbyterian Church (USA). Another example: The "Southern Methodist Church," which divided in 1844, was reunited with the mainstream of Methodism in 1939 to form The Methodist Church. It became the United Methodist Church in 1968.

Chapter One

1. My emphasis here is our human family, but it is important to note the broader concept of God's family, stressed particularly in Native American religious understanding, which goes beyond humans to include all "two-legged and four-legged" living things. See George Tinker, *Encyclopedia of North American Indians* (Houghton Mifflin: December 2007).

2. For more information, see the books on liberation theology in Additional Resources on page 207.

3. For documentation and statistics on the distribution of wealth and poverty, see: Friends Committee on National Legislation (FCNL), http://www.fcnl.org/index.htm; EurekAlert! Advancing Science, Serving Society (AASSS), http://www.eurekalert.org; The Hunger Site, http://www.thehungersite.com (all accessed September 30, 2010).

Part One

1. Johnny Ray Youngblood, pastor of St. Paul Community Baptist Church, Brooklyn, New York, in "Ma'afa," Religion & Ethics Newsweekly (September 29, 2000), http://www.pbs.org/wnet/religionandethics/week405/cover.html.

2. The term "MAAFA" was first used by African American scholar Dr. Marimba Ani in reference to Middle Passage, the forcible journey of slaves from Africa to the Americas as part of the Atlantic slave trade. See Marimba Ani, *Let The Circle Be Unbroken: The Implications of Afrikan Spirituality in the Diaspora* (New York: Nkonimfo, 1988). For more information about the MAAFA observance see http://www.themaafa.com (accessed redirected site September 30, 2010).

3. For more information, see "*Traces of the Trade: A Story from the Deep North.* http://www.tracesofthetrade.org (accessed September 30, 2010).

4. George Santayana, *Reason in Common Sense, The Life of Reason*, vol.1 (New York: Dover Publications, 1980).

5. See chapters 1 and 2 in Joseph Barndt, *Understanding and Dismantling Racism: The Twenty-First Century Challenge to White America* (Minneapolis: Fortress Press, 2007).

Chapter Two

1. Among many excellent writings on the theology of the cross, my favorite is the classic book by Douglas John Hall, *Lighten Our Darkness: Towards an Indigenous Theology of the Cross*, Revised Edition (Lima, Ohio: Academic Renewal, 2001).

2. For example, in an article on ecumenism by Dr. John Pobee of Ghana: "Baptismal Recognition and African Instituted Churches," in Michael Root and Risto Saarinen, eds., *Baptism and the Unity of the Church* (Grand Rapids: Eerdmans, 1998), 164–82.

3. My focus in this brief overview is on the western church; I have not taken into account the split in the Christian Church in 1054, which resulted in the Eastern Orthodox and Roman Catholic Churches. Although the Orthodox Church avoided much of the western churches' direct alignment with the state, this did not necessarily produce a theology of the cross or identification with the poor and oppressed.

4. Charles Villa-Vicencio, "Right Wing Religion: Have the Chickens Come Home to Roost?" in *Journal of Theology for Southern Africa* (December 1989): 7–16.

5. For a listing of papal bulls related to colonialism and slavery, see http://en.wikipedia.org/wiki/List_of_papal_bulls (accessed September 30, 2010).

6. See the article by Ontario Consultants on Religious Tolerance, "Christian Attitudes towards Slavery: 5th to late 17th Century C.E.," http://www.religioustolerance.org/chr_slav4.htm (accessed September 30, 2010).

7. Villa-Vicencio, "Right Wing Religion," 10–11.

Chapter Three

1. Bishop Steven Charleston, "Facing Up to Colonialism and Its Consequences," *The Witness Magazine* (January/February 2001). Bishop Charleston, of the Choctaw Nation of Oklahoma, is President and Dean of Episcopal Divinity School in Cambridge, Mass., and the former Bishop of Alaska.

2. The Southern Argument for Slavery; *U.S. History Online Textbook,* http://ushistory.org/us/27f.asp.

3. For a very helpful article summarizing legal enactments in the colonies to prevent using baptism and Christian conversion as justification for emancipation, see Marcus W. Jernegan, "Slavery and Conversion in the American Colonies," in *American Historical Review* 21 (April 1916):504–27. Available online at http://www.negroartist.com/writings/Slavery%20and%20Conversion%20in%20the%20American%20Colonies.htm (accessed September 30, 2010).

4. Larry E. Tise, *Proslavery: A History of the Defense of Slavery in America, 1701—1840* (Athens: University of Georgia Press, 1987), xvii.

5. Emphasis added; find a transcript of the Declaration of Independence at http://archives.gov/exhibits/charters/declaration_transcript.html (accessed December 14, 2010).

6. United States naturalization laws (1790, 1795); United States Congress, "An act to establish a uniform Rule of Naturalization" (March 26, 1790); TEXT SOURCE: 1 Stat. 103–4. Edited version: Linda Grant De Pauw et al., eds., *Documentary History of the First Federal Congress of the United States of America, March 4, 1789–March 3, 1791* (Baltimore: Johns Hopkins University Press, 2004), 6:1516–1522.

7. Stephen Douglas, The Lincoln-Douglas Debates of 1858; Fifth Debate: Galesburg, Illinois, October 7, 1858. http://www.teachingamericanhistory.org/library/index.asp?documents=102.

8. Tise, *Proslavery*, 189.

9. Helpful resources on this topic include: Andrea Smith (Cherokee), "Soul Wound: The Legacy of Native American Schools," *Amnesty Magazine* (Summer 2003), http://www.amnestyusa.org/amnestynow/soulwound.html (accessed December 14, 2010), and Charles E. Hendry, *Beyond Traplines: Does the Church Really Care?* (Toronto: Anglican Book Centre, 1998).

10. Senator H. V. Johnson, quoted by Howard Zinn, in *A People's History of the United States* (New York: Harper Perennial Modern Classics, 2005), 155.

Chapter Four

1. "As they go through the valley of Baca they make it a place of springs," NRSV.

2. From "Lift Every Voice and Sing," a poem written by James Weldon Johnson in 1900 and put to music by his brother John Rosamond Johnson. Public domain.

3. Two helpful articles on this topic include: "Who Were the Anabaptists?" http://www.anabaptistnetwork.com/pdf/ and "Anabaptists," an article from the *Encyclopedia Britannica*: www.britannica.com/EBchecked/topic/22160 (accessed December 14, 2010).

4. John R. McKivigan, "A Brief History of the American Abolitionist Movement," http://americanabolitionist.liberalarts.iupui.edu/brief.htm (accessed September 30, 2010).

5. Quotation from Charles William Heathcote, *The Lutheran Church and the Civil War* (Burlington, Iowa: Lutheran Literary Board, 1919), 54–55. For more information on the Frankean Synod, see Richard M. Chapman, "Just Enough? Lutherans, Slavery, and the Struggle for Racial Justice," *The Cresset* 71 (Trinity 2008), and The Wittenberg Archives, http://listserv.cuis.edu/cgi-bin/wa?A1=ind9805&L=WITTENBERG (accessed September 30, 2010).

6. Dr. Martin Luther King, "I Have a Dream," Address at March on Washington, August 28, 1963, http://www.mlkonline.net/dream.html (accessed October 15, 2010). Dr. King quotes from "Free at Last," a spiritual by J. W. Work. The actual lyrics are "Free at last, free at last/I thank God I'm free at last."

7. Dr. Martin Luther King Jr., ed. James M. Washington, "Facing the Challenge of a New Age" (Montgomery, Ala., December 1956), quoted in *A Testament of Hope: The Essential Writings and Speeches of Martin Luther King, Jr.* (San Francisco: HarperCollins, 1986), 141.

8. Leslie Takahashi Morris, Chip Roush, and Leon Spencer, eds., *The Arc of the Universe Is Long: Unitarian Universalists, Anti-Racism and the Journey from Calgary* (Boston: Skinner House, 2009), 1, 5–7,16.

9. Daniel G. Reid et al., *Dictionary of Christianity in America* (Downers Grove, Ill.: InterVarsity, 1990).

10. See "Liberty Lost; Lessons in Loyalty," a re-enactment by the Japanese American Citizens League of the evacuation and internment of all Japanese and Japanese American (Nikkei) residents from the Pájaro Valley in California during WWII, and a tribute to Pájaro Valley citizens who supported and protected them, http://www.watsonvillesantacruzjacl.org/reenactment/index.htm (accessed September 30, 2010).

Chapter Five

1. For documentation and statistics on racial disparity see Margaret Simms, Karina Fortuny, and Everett Henderson, "Racial and Ethnic Disparities among Low-Income Families," Urban Institute (August 7, 2009), http://www.urban.org/publications/411936.html, and

Friends Committee on National Legislation (FCNL), http://www.fcnl.org/index.htm (both accessed September 30, 2010).

2. Elisabeth Kübler-Ross, *On Death and Dying* (New York: MacMillan, 1970).

3. Vine Deloria, *God Is Red* (Golden, Colo.: Fulcrum, 1994), 47–48.

Part Two

1. Joseph Barndt, *Understanding and Dismantling Racism: The Twenty-First Century Challenge to White America* (Minneapolis: Fortress Press, 2007).

Chapter Six

1. Rev. Dr. Safiyah Fosua, "Ash Wednesday Reflections: The Acknowledgement of Sin," *The United Methodist Book of Worship,* adapted from The Revised Common Lectionary, Consultation on Common Texts (Abingdon, 1992), copyright © by the Consultation on Common Texts (CCT), PO Box 340003, Room 381, Nashville, TN 37203-0003.

2. Hans Brandt, ed., *Outside the Camp: A Collection of Writings by Wolfram Kistner* (Johannesburg: South African Council of Churches, 1988), 8.

Chapter Seven

1. C. Eric Lincoln, *Race and Religion and the Continuing American Dilemma* (Toronto: Collins, 1986), 3.

2. Ibid., 111–42.

3. I have benefitted greatly from the insights of Marcus Borg and his tracing of three "macro-stories" in the Bible and in the message of Jesus: the exodus story, the story of exile and return, and the priestly story. The problem, according to Borg, is when one of these (in our case, the priestly story) becomes primary and the others submerged and nearly lost. In liberation theology, the exodus story and the story of exile and return regain equal status with the priestly story. See especially Marcus Borg, *Meeting Jesus Again for the First Time* (San Francisco: Harper San Francisco, 1994).

4. There are very few compilations of apologies to people of color, but one such book is Melissa Nobles, *The Politics of Official Apologies* (New York: Cambridge University Press, 2008).

5. "But when he saw many Pharisees and Sadducees coming for baptism, he said to them, 'You brood of vipers! Who warned you to flee from the wrath to come? Bear fruit worthy of repentance'" (Matthew 3:7-8).

Chapter Eight

1. For a more in-depth consideration of institutionalized racism, see chapter 5 of *Understanding and Dismantling Racism: The Twenty-First Century Challenge to White America* (Minneapolis: Fortress Press, 2007), as well as other resources listed on pages 207–8.

2. Institutional Levels Chart, © Crossroads Ministry, modified by Joseph Barndt to apply particularly to the church. Adapted and used by permission.

Chapter Nine

1. Hopefully, you find familiarity and agreement with the summary of these five concepts related to culture and cultural racism, but it may be helpful to explore culture and cultural racism in greater depth by referring to chapter 5 of *Understanding and Dismantling Racism: The Twenty-First Century Challenge to White America* (Minneapolis: Fortress Press, 2007).

2. Crossroads definition for cultural racism, modified by Joseph Barndt. Adapted and used by permission.

3. Marjorie Bowens-Wheatley, "Cornrows, Kwanzaa and Confusion: The Dilemma of Cultural Racism and Misappropriation," http://www.uua.org/leaders/idbm/multiculturalism/misappropriation/37852.shtml (accessed September 30, 2010).

Part Three

1. *Continuum on Becoming an Anti-Racist Multicultural Church* © Crossroads Ministry, adapted by Joseph Barndt. Adapted and used by permission.

Chapter Ten

1. If this brief review of the assumptions behind the idea of an anti-racist identity is insufficient, see chapter 7 in *Understanding and Dismantling Racism: The Twenty-First Century Challenge to White America* (Minneapolis: Fortress Press, 2007) for a more in-depth review.

2. See Robert Terry, "The Negative Impact on White Values," in Benjamin P. Bowser and Raymond Hunt, eds., *Impacts of Racism on White Americans* (Newbury Park, Calif.: Sage, 1981), 120.

3. Crossroads and the People's Institute for Survival and Beyond, as well as a number of other anti-racism training organizations have developed materials to guide the process of organizing and facilitating caucuses. See Additional Resources on pages 207–8 for contact information.

4. See Malcolm Gladwell, *The Tipping Point: How Little Things Can Make a Big Difference* (Boston: Little, Brown, 2000).

Chapter Eleven

1. Pamela Warrick-Smith, "Work, Fight, and Pray," Greenhays Recordings #90721. To listen to a sample, go to http://www.jeanritchiehome.com/folklife/recordings.htm.

2. Faith-based community organizing networks are another resource for organizer training that is readily available to many churches. The most well known of these are Industrial Areas Foundation (IAF), Gamaliel Foundation, Pacific Institute for Community Organization (PICO), and Direct Action and Research Training Center (DART). There is, however, a significant shortcoming within these organizations with regard to anti-racism work. Although these faith-based organizing networks already have a relationship with many denominations and have the ability to teach the skills needed for organizing, their limitation is that none of them have thus far demonstrated the willingness or the ability to specifically address the task of organizing to understand and eliminate racism.

Chapter Twelve

1. Ezra Earl Jones, *Quest for Quality in the Church* (Nashville: Discipleship Resources, 1993), vi.

2. The formal name of this fifth commission was the Commission on Justice, Liberation and Human Fulfillment. Very little has been written to document or evaluate the work of this commission. Two specific sources of information are in the archives of the Institute of the Church in an Urban Industrial Society at the University of Illinois as Chicago (ICUIS, Box 37, file 584, "National Council of Churches of Christ USA-Commission on Justice, Liberation and Human Fulfillment, 1973-1983"; and in the General Commission on Archives and History (GCAH) of the Women's Division of the United Methodist Church, http://archives.gcah.org/eadweb/gcah3622.htm (accessed December 14, 2010).

3. In the Introduction to part 2, I referred to the MAAFA as one model of a rite of remembering. Perhaps you are aware of other models or may be prepared to create your own.

4. See Amy Kedron, "Freedom, Reparations and the Black Manifesto" (CURE, Caucasians United for Reparations and Emancipation), http://reparationsthecure.org (accessed September 30, 2010).

ADDITIONAL RESOURCES

The following select list of resources may be helpful to readers who wish to pursue further anti-racism work in the church. For a more complete general bibliography on race and racism, see *Understanding and Dismantling Racism*.

Allen, Robert. *Reluctant Reformers: Racism and Social Reform Movements in the United States.* Washington, D.C.: Howard University Press, 1983.

Alvis, Joel L. *Religion and Race: Southern Presbyterians, 1946 to 1983.* Tuscaloosa and London: University of Alabama Press, 1994.

Barndt, Joseph. *Understanding and Dismantling Racism: The Twenty-First Century Challenge to White America.* Minneapolis: Fortress Press, 2007.

Braxton, Brad R. *No Longer Slaves: Galatians and African American Experience.* Collegeville, Minn.: Liturgical, 2002.

Campolo, Tony, and Michael Battle. *The Church Enslaved: A Spirituality of Racial Reconciliation.* Minneapolis: Fortress Press, 2005.

Chisom, Ronald, and Michael Washington. *Undoing Racism: A Philosophy of International Social Change.* New Orleans: People's Institute Press, 1997. (Out of Print)

Cone, James H. *God of the Oppressed.* Maryknoll, N.Y.: Orbis, 1997.

Davies, Susan E., and Paul Teresa Hennessee. *Ending Racism in the Church.* Cleveland: United Church Press, 1998.

Deloria, Vine. *God Is Red: A Native View of Religion.* Golden, Colo.: Fulcrum, 1994.

Emerson, Michael O., and Christian Smith. *Divided by Faith: Evangelical Religion and the Problem of Race in America.* New York: Oxford University Press, 2000.

Felder, Cain Hope. *Race, Racism, and the Biblical Narratives.* Minneapolis: Fortress Press, 2002.

Findlay, James F., Jr. *Church People in the Struggle: The National Council of Churches and the Black Freedom Movement, 1950–1970.* New York: Oxford University Press, 1989.

Gilbreath, Edward. *Reconciliation Blues: A Black Evangelical's Inside View of White Christianity*. Downers Grove, Ill.: InterVarsity, 2006.

Hobgood, William Chris. *Born Apart, Becoming One: Disciples Defeating Racism*. St. Louis: Chalice, 2009.

Jewett, Robert. *Mission and Menace: Four Centuries of American Religious Zeal*. Minneapolis: Fortress Press, 2008.

Jha, Sandhya Rani. *Room at the Table: Struggle for Unity and Equality in Disciples History*. St. Louis: Chalice, 2009.

Kistner, Wolfram. *Justice and Righteousness Like a Never Ending Stream*. Johannesburg: South African Council of Churches, 2008.

Kistner, Wolfram. Hans Brandt, ed. *Outside the Camp: A Collection of Writings by Wolfram Kistner*. Johannesburg: South African Council of Churches, 1988.

Lincoln, C. Eric. *Race, Religion, and the Continuing American Dilemma*. New York: Hill and Wang, 1984.

Lincoln, C. Eric, ed. *The Black Experience in Religion*. Garden City, N.Y.: Anchor/Doubleday, 1974.

McKenzie, Seven L. *All God's Children: A Biblical Critique of Racism*. Louisville: Westminster John Knox, 1997.

Morris, Leslie Takahashi, Chip Roush, and Leon Spencer, eds., *The Arc of the Universe Is Long: Unitarian Universalists, Anti-Racism, and the Journey from Calgary*. Boston: Skinner House, 2009.

Murray, Peter C. *Methodists and the Crucible of Race, 1930–1975*. Columbia and London: University of Missouri Press, 2004.

Newman, Mark. *Getting Right with God: Southern Baptists and Desegregation, 1945–1995*. Tuscaloosa and London: University of Alabama Press, 2001.

Nothwehr, Dawn M. *That They May Be One: Catholic Social Teaching on Racism, Tribalism, and Xenophobia*. Maryknoll, N.Y.: Orbis, 2008.

Shattuck, Gardiner H., Jr. *Episcopalians and Race: Civil War to Civil Rights*. Lexington: University Press of Kentucky, 2000.

Tinker, George E. *Spirit and Resistance: Political Theology and American Indian Liberation*. Minneapolis: Fortress Press, 2004.

Tise, Larry E. *Proslavery: A History of the Defense of Slavery in America, 1701–1840*. Athens: University of Georgia Press, 1987.

Wink, Walter. *Naming the Powers: The Language of Power in the New Testament*. Philadelphia: Fortress Press, 1984.

Yang, Fenggang. *Asian American Religions: The Making and Remaking of Borders and Boundaries*. New York: New York University Press, 2004.

Young, Josiah Ulysses, III. *No Difference in the Fare: Dietrich Bonhoeffer and the Problem of Racism*. Grand Rapids: Eerdmans, 1998.

Zinn, Howard. *A People's History of the United States: 1492 to Present*. New York: HarperCollins, 2003.

CONTACTS

Many denominations and religious organizations are engaged in active anti-racism work. The following list provides information readers may find helpful in researching the work of particular denominations and organizations. Contact names and information tend to change. However, national denominational headquarters can usually supply updated information.

Christian Church (Disciples of Christ)

Many of the thirty-three Regions of the Christian Church (Disciples of Christ) are engaged in anti-racism work. Links to these regional offices can be found at the website below.

Program: Reconciliation Ministry of the Christian Church (Disciples of Christ)
Contact: Minister of Reconciliation
Address: 130 E. Washington, Indianapolis, IN 46204-3645
Telephone: (317) 713-2587
Email: ajohnson@ogmp.disciples.org
Website: www.reconciliationministry.org

Episcopal Church

Most of the dioceses of the Episcopal Church are engaged in anti-racism work. Links to these diocesan programs can be found at the Episcopal Church website.

Contact: The Episcopal Church Center, Intercultural Ministries
Address: 815 2nd Av., New York, NY 10017
Telephone: (646) 875-2430
Email: akronenmetter@episcopalchurch.org

Lutheran Church
Evangelical Lutheran Church in America (ELCA)

Many of the sixty-five synods of the ELCA are engaged in anti-racism work. Links to these synodical programs can be found at the ELCA website below.

Program: Racial Justice Ministries/Anti-Racism Program
Contact: Director for Racial Justice Ministries
Address: 8765 West Higgins Road, Chicago IL 60631
Telephone: (773) 380-2835
Website: www.elca.org/Growing-In-Faith/Ministry/Multicultural-Ministries/
    Racial-Justice-Ministries.aspx

Lutheran Church Missouri Synod

Program: Northern Illinois District Anti-Racism Team—"One Lord One Faith"
Contact: Northern Illinois District, LCMS
Address: 2301 S. Wolf Road, Hillside, IL 60162
Telephone: (708) 449-3020
Email: nidpres@aol.com
Website: www.ni.lcms.org

Mennonite Church

An important segment of Mennonite Anti-Racism work, the "Damascus Road Anti-Racism Process" is an Anabaptist anti-racism training and skill development program. A further description of this training program and of resources can be accessed via the website below.

Program: Anti-Racism Program of the Mennonite Central Committee US
Contact: Anti-Racism Director
Address: 21 South 12th Street, Box 500, Akron, PA 17501-0500
Telephone: (717) 859-1151
Email: Antiracism@mcc.org
Website: http://antiracism.mcc.org/

Methodist Church
United Methodist Church

The purpose of the General Commission on Religion and Race of the United Methodist Church is to challenge and equip United Methodists at every level of the denomination to effectively eradicate racism and its causes.

Program: General Commission on Religion and Race of the United Methodist
    Church
Contact: General Secretary
Address: 100 Maryland Ave., NE, Suite 400, Washington, DC 20002
Telephone: (202) 547-2271
Email: info@gcorr.org
Website: www.gcorr.org

National Council of Churches (NCC)

The NCC's Racial Justice Program seeks to advance policies that will help confront systemic racial inequalities, and dismantle structural barriers to people of color.

Program: Program for Racial Justice
Contact: Washington Policy Advocacy Officer for Racial Justice and Human
    Rights
Address: 110 Maryland Ave. NE, Washington, DC 20002
Telephone: (202) 544-2352

Email: nsylver@ncccusa.org
Website: http://bruno.ncccusa.org/exchweb/bin/redir.asp?URL=http://www
.ncccusa.org

Presbyterian Church (USA)
Program: Facing Racism: A Vision of the Beloved Community
Contact: Racial Justice Office
Address: Presbyterian Church (USA), 100 Witherspoon St., Louisville, KY
40202
Telephone: (502) 569-5490; Toll Free (800) 728-7228 ext. 5490
Email: nancy.young@pcusa.org
Website: www.pcusa.org/racialjustice

Reformed Churches
Christian Reformed Church (CRC)

Three Grand Rapids congregations of the Christian Reformed Church provide anti-racism training and leadership development.

Program (regional): Congregations Organizing for Racial Reconciliation
(CORR)
Contact: CORR Leadership Team
Address: 3835 Burton St. SE, Grand Rapids, MI 49546
Telephone: (616) 956-7611
Email: office@churchoftheservantcrc.org
Website: http://www.churchoftheservantcrc.org/ministries/anti-racism

Reformed Church in America (RCA)

RCA seeks to transition into a denomination that is truly multiracial and freed from racism by promoting system change, multicultural ministry, and anti-racist multicultural training.

Program: Office of Multiracial Initiatives and Social Justice
Contact: Coordinator of Multiracial Initiatives and Social Justice
Address: Reformed Church in America, 475 Riverside Dr., 18th Fl., New York,
NY 10115
Telephone: (212) 870-3254
Website: www.rca.org (click on *Multiracial Future* menu on the homepage)
Email: ejames@rca.org

New Brunswick Theological Seminary

One of the very few seminaries with serious commitment to anti-racism principles and action.

Program: New Brunswick Theological Seminary Anti-Racism Team
Contact: ART Leadership Team
Address: 17 Seminary Place, New Brunswick, NJ 08901
Telephone: (800) 445-NBTS (6287)
Email: artleadership@nbts.edu
Website: www.nbts.edu/newsite/art.cfm

Roman Catholic Church
Diocesan Work

Program: Office for Racial Justice, Archdiocese of Chicago
Contact: Sister Anita Baird, DHM, Director
Address: Archdiocese of Chicago Office for Racial Justice, P.O. Box 1979, Chicago, IL 60690
Telephone: (312) 534-8336
Email: abaird@archdiocese-chgo.org
Website: http://www.archchicago.org/departments/racial_justice/racial_justice.shtm

Religious Orders
Sisters of Providence

Program: Sisters of Providence Anti-Racism Team
Contact: Chairperson
Address: Sisters of Providence, Owens Hall, St. Mary-of-the-Woods, IN 47876
Telephone: (812) 535-2897
Email: jhoward@spsmw.org
Website: www.sistersofprovidence.org

Dominican Sisters of Sinsinawa

Program: Anti-Racism Transformational Team
Contact: Office of Promoter of Peace and Justice
Address: 585 County Road Z, Sinsinawa, WI 53824
Telephone: (608) 748-4411, Ext. 164
Email: opjustice@aol.com
Website: www.sinsinawa.org

Springfield Dominican Sisters

The Springfield Dominican Anti-Racism Team consists of sister members and also lay partners of color. In working on developing an anti-racist identity for the congregation, the team also connects with the health care and education institutions sponsored by the congregation.

Program: Springfield Dominican Anti-Racism Team (SDART)
Contact: Sr. Marcelline Koch, OP / Leroy Jordan
Address: 1237 W. Monroe
Telephone: (217) 787-0481
Email: smkoch@spdom.org
Website: www.springfieldop.org

Pax Christi (Roman Catholic Peace Movement)

Pax Christi USA is committed to transforming itself into an anti-racist multicultural Catholic movement for peace with justice. Resources can be found at the Pax Christi website under "Programs & Campaigns."

Program: Brothers and Sisters All—The Anti-Racism Team of Pax Christi
Address: Pax Christi USA 532 West 8th Street, Erie, PA 16502
Telephone: (814) 453-4955
Email: info@paxchristiusa.org
Website: www.paxchristiusa.org

Unitarian Universalist Association of Congregations (UUA)
The UUA has produced excellent resources for anti-racism organizing and training, which can be found on their website.

Program: Journey toward Wholeness
Contact: Office of Racial and Ethnic Concerns
Address: 25 Beacon Street, Boston, MA 02108
Telephone: (617) 742-2100
Email: idbm@uua.org
Website: http://www.uua.org/members/justicediversity/racialand/index.shtml

United Church of Christ
Program: Sacred Conversations on Race
Contact: Minister for Racial Justice, Justice and Witness Ministries
Address: United Church of Christ, 700 Prospect Ave., Cleveland, OH 44115
Telephone: (216) 736-3719
Email: thompsonk@ucc.org
Website: http://www.ucc.org/justice/issues.html; http://www.ucc.org/sacred
-conversation

INDEX